Revelation

THE UNVEILING OF GOD'S LOVE

AN OVERVIEW BY

Cathy Dickinson

PAINTINGS BY SHARON MAYFIELD

REVELATION
The Unveiling of God's Love

Translational emendations, amplifications, and paraphrases are by the author.

To order copies of this book or to contact Cathy Dickinson, please visit www.CathyDickinson.com.

ISBN: 978-1-5323-4974-4

Printed in the United States of America

Acknowledgments

This is a book about Jesus. If it were not for Him, I would have nothing to write. The more He unveils His attributes to me, the more I fall in love with Him, the more I trust Him, and the more I want to live for Him. I thank God for the inspiration of the Holy Spirit. He amazes me.

This book was a labor of love for many who came alongside and tirelessly edited my messages, striving to retain my personality and be faithful to the truths of God's Word. Their prayers, encouragement, and professionalism have astounded me.

I thank my wonderful husband, Dale, who countless times reminded me to "press on." I thank Amy and Ponzio Oliverio for their love, hours of work, and attention to detail. I thank Darla Grisez for not only proofing the text of this book, but for partnering with me for twenty-one years of proofing Bible studies. We are a good team. I thank Cathy Rich for taking what we have provided to her and putting it all together, along with Toni Scott for formatting and cover design. And thank you, Miriam Rogers, for proofing it.

The book in your hands is the product of much labor from these precious people.

To God be the glory. May your reading and studying of this book invoke you to proclaim, along with the apostle John, "Come, Lord Jesus!"

The grace of our Lord Jesus Christ be with you all.

Table of Contents

Introduction

IT'S ALL ABOUT HIM

For I testify to everyone who hears the words of the prophecy of this book: If anyone adds to these things, God will add to him the plagues that are written in this book; and if anyone takes away from the words of the book of this prophecy, God shall take away his part from the Book of Life, from the holy city, and from the things which are written in this book. Revelation 22:18-19

I have great fear and trembling as I begin this study of the book of Revelation. Maybe that's why so many people shy away from teaching it. Yet at the same time there are many who do not seem to fear the Lord in their willingness to tweak His Word and teach their personal interpretation of what it means.

So if I faithfully present to you this book of Revelation, I have the promise of a blessing. If I present it to you unfaithfully, I'll be cursed. And take heed, this warning is also to those who hear it. So why take the chance?

All God is asking us to do is honor what the apostle John has written. I love the blessings of God and I want them for both of us. But then there's also the misconception that the book of Revelation cannot be understood. I think that's Satan's lie to keep us from the blessing of understanding Jesus in a deeper way. Satan hates when that happens. This is why I'm writing this: I want you to know Jesus in a deeper way.

IT'S ALL ABOUT HIM

I don't know what your summer was like, but mine went really, really quick. Although it was packed with a lot of great things, I think the key word just might be "packed." If you asked me to write a paper about it, I could write from two different viewpoints: what I did or what I learned. In a nutshell, I went to Hawaii with friends, camped at the beach with family, I perfected my cleaning and painting skills on the buildings at our church, and taught a few conferences—two of which allowed Dale and I to travel to Upstate New York and West Virginia. If I parked on what I did this summer, I doubt if it would challenge your life. So, I'll tell you what I learned.

I had been sick for a week or so and hadn't been able to do much studying. I found myself feeling unable to concentrate, but I had to. I remember praying, *Lord, I can't do this!* Moses basically said the same thing. "Lord, I'm not the man. I don't speak well." But the Lord told Moses, as He has conveyed to His servants over and over again throughout the millennia, "It's not about you. I AM." And that's what I've been learning. It's not about me. It's about Him.

IT BELONGS TO HIM

It reminded me of when I was in Hawaii with friends, and we were reading our morning devotions together. One day we read the story of the Moabites and the Ammonites coming against King Jehoshaphat and the people of Israel in battle.

> The Lord said this to King Jehoshaphat: "Listen, all you of Judah and you inhabitants of Jerusalem, and you, King Jehoshaphat! Thus says the Lord to you: 'Do not be afraid nor dismayed because of this great multitude, for the battle is not yours, but God's.'" (2 Chronicles 20:15)

It hit each one of us all at once. Yes, God fights our battles. But that's not the best perspective. God wants us to know that the battle is His. It's about Him and it's for Him. Think about that and how it would change things if we would only remember it is not our battle. It is His battle and if He wants us to be a part of the fight, He will let us know. Our part is to let Him be God and let Him fight the battle. If we have done nothing wrong, then the battle is really against Him, isn't it?

SHOW THE WORLD JESUS

That was the beginning. Then as summer came to a close, Dale and I taught at a couples' retreat. I have heard his message many, many times, but each time the Lord shows me something new.

In Ephesians, Paul spoke of a mystery revealed: "This is a great mystery, but I speak concerning Christ and the church" (Ephesians 5:32). This new entity is comprised of both male and female, slave and free, Greek and Jew, for the purpose of revealing what God is like through Jesus to the world. Then Paul went on to write, "Nevertheless, let each one of you in particular so love his own wife as himself, and let the wife see that she respects her husband" (Ephesians 5:33). This mystery of marriage represents Christ and the church. This displays the oneness that Jesus prayed in John 17 so that the world might know Him.

> That they all may be one, as You, Father, are in Me, and I in You; that they also may be one in Us, that the world may believe that You sent Me. (John 17:21)

> I in them, and You in Me; that they may be made perfect in one, and that the world may know that You have sent Me, and have loved them as You have loved Me. (John 17:23)

Again, even in marriage, it's not about you and it's not about me—it's about Jesus. It's about showing the world what Jesus is like. Do you really think your purposes are better? Are you really happy when you are about you and not about Him? Somehow, being about Him gives us more of a sense of value—not less.

So the battles are about the Lord. The church is to be about the Lord, and our marriages are to be about the Lord. We can live our lives ignoring that fact, but when we do, we fall short and miss out on His purposes. That's why the book of Revelation is best titled the "Revelation of Jesus Christ."

As we study chapter one, we'll see what Jesus revealed to John, but we'll also see Jesus being revealed to John as never before! We will see our Lord Jesus, who came in the flesh to suffer and die for our sins, revealed as the conquering King.

But before we dig in to chapter one, I want to give an overview of Revelation, serving as kind of a "flyover" since I highlight some points of interest about each of the chapters. As we study, we want to focus on what is obvious in the book of Revelation, rather than taking wild guesses or forcing something to fit our own thinking. It will be academic, as well as seeking the Lord's personal application. I believe just looking at what the Bible says will amaze you. So as we fly over, don't get disappointed because you want to zoom in on something. We will be zooming in for the next twenty-two chapters.

THE FOCUS OF REVELATION

As we begin our study, keep in mind four things:

1. Out of the 404 verses in Revelation, 278 refer to Old Testament verses; therefore, much of our understanding will come from within the Bible itself.
2. The teaching of Jesus in Matthew 24-25 (the Olivet Discourse) is also evident.
3. Many of the things that are unclear, God explains by telling us what they represent.
4. The first five words of this book give us our focus, "The Revelation of Jesus Christ."

This is so important. God's intent is to reveal Jesus to us in a way He has not been revealed before. When you come to places of possible confusion, pause and ask yourself, "What am I seeing about Jesus here?" You'll be amazed at how that clears up your confusion and refocuses your priorities as you study. Remember, this is the unveiling of Jesus Christ. If all you do is get answers and fill in timelines, you will simply be feeding your mind, and your soul will be left virtually untouched—and unblessed.

USING THE BIBLE AS OUR COMMENTARY

We will use the Bible to interpret the Bible. When I taught this study of Revelation to the women at our church, I was often asked for suggestions of commentaries or translations that are easier to understand than the New King James Version. I encourage you not to use commentaries for interpretation for two reasons:

1. They tend to make us lazy, enabling us to quickly look to man to help us understand.

2. I want you to experience the joy of the Holy Spirit personally showing you truths.

Having said that, commentaries do have their place—mainly as a check. If I see something no one else has seen, it prompts me to double-check and triple-check my thinking. We want to approach this by studying first on our own, then studying words and their context by cross-referencing (finding other portions of Scripture that relate or give further understanding); and then as a last resort, we'll consult the commentaries.

LET'S DIVE IN

And now, as we dive into the book of Revelation, remember this is all about Jesus. It is about how He is going to wage the biggest battle ever against those who have rejected Him with the culmination of making all things new—for you and for me and for all who have believed Him.

Overview

THE FLYOVER

There is no book like Revelation. No other book in the Bible reveals the glory of God and Jesus in more splendor than this one. Yet it has been the most misunderstood, misinterpreted, and neglected, partly because we've heard so many different descriptions from other people, throwing us off and causing us to miss the real message.

I'm here to tell you that this is a book for present believers, as well as believers who will be living while the prophecies in this book are unfolding. For instance, when we read about the locusts mentioned in Revelation 9, I am sure those believers living at the time will be able to identify what those creatures really are. Presently, we cannot.

Looking at time frames, we will be examining people who lived during the time before Christ, the time of Christ on earth, and the time of the Holy Spirit moving through the church. And finally, we will be looking at the time God wraps everything up so we can live in the time that is without time, eternity with Jesus.

> And he said to me, "Do not seal the words of the prophecy of this book, for the time is at hand." Revelation 22:10

Do not seal it, John. John, don't put it away. I want people to know these things. The time is at hand—this is what will happen next.

The apostle John wrote the book of Revelation. He loved to describe himself as "the disciple whom Jesus loved," although in Mark's gospel, Jesus described John and his brother James as "sons of thunder." John wrote Revelation about AD 95, during the reign of the Roman emperor Titus Flavius Domitian who demanded that he be worshiped as "Lord and God." The refusal of Christians to obey his edict led to severe persecution. Tradition says that Domitian tried to boil John in oil, but he survived. He then sentenced John to the Isle of Patmos, a Roman penal colony off the coast of Asia Minor. He survived to experience the greatest revelation of Jesus that anyone has ever experienced—and he was told to write down what he saw—so you and I could get a glimpse of Jesus' majesty too.

THE BLESSING

The Revelation of Jesus Christ begins and ends with a blessing:

> Blessed is he who reads and those who hear the words of this prophecy, and keep those things which are written in it; for the time is near. Revelation 1:3

> Behold, I am coming quickly! Blessed is he who keeps the words of the prophecy of this book. Revelation 22:7

Revelation is the only book that begins and ends with a promise of blessing to those who read it. But notice the blessing is for those who not only read it, but hear it, and who keep those things that are written (with the intention of doing something about it). So, it's not just a story about the future. It has things within it for you and me to apply in our lives today—and when we do so, we are blessed.

THE UNVEILING OF JESUS

The key to the book of Revelation is found in the very first verse.

> The Revelation of Jesus Christ, which God gave Him to show His servants—things which must shortly take place. And He sent and signified it by His angel to His servant John. Revelation 1:1

The Revelation of Jesus Christ—that's what the book of Revelation is about. It's the unveiling or uncovering of things about Jesus that had not been known prior to this writing. We are going to learn things about Jesus that we could not know if we didn't study this book. I want to know all I can about Him, don't you?

Yes, this book reveals Jesus as a Judge who will take vengeance, but we will also see it reveals His majesty, His strength, His grace, His love for all people, and His plans for our eternal home. Verse 1 says, "the things which must shortly take place." This is a glimpse of the future as reported by His designated angel.

THE FLIGHT PLAN

So for this chapter, I'm going to take you on a flyover, and then, in a sense, turn over the wheel to the angel who will dive down deeper into the scenes of the future in the other chapters. As the angel revealed things to John, he wrote what he saw.

Revelation 1:2, speaking of John, says, " … who bore witness to the word of God, and to the testimony of Jesus Christ, to all things that he saw."

John just wrote what he saw. He didn't analyze; he didn't interpret. He just wrote what he saw. It was a revelation of Jesus unlike anything John had ever seen, except for the time when he saw Jesus shining in His glory on the Mount of Transfiguration. Maybe that preview helped John to be really sure it was Jesus who was standing before Him on that Lord's Day on the island of Patmos.

If you have studied even just a few of the New Testament letters, you know that most of them start with a greeting of some sort. Look at verses 4 and 5.

> John, to the seven churches which are in Asia: "Grace to you and peace from Him who is and who was and who is to come, and from the seven Spirits who are before His throne, and from Jesus Christ." Revelation 1:4-5a

When we zoom in on chapter 1, I'll go into a further explanation of the "seven Spirits who are before His throne," but for our flyover, it is generally accepted that this refers to the Holy Spirit. So having said that, this letter is presented with great authority—that of each member of the Holy Trinity.

So, what was John to write? Revelation 1:19 gives us a pretty good outline.

> "Write the things which you have seen, and the things which are, and the things which will take place after this."

Let's begin with "the things which you have seen." This is referring to John's vision of Jesus as revealed in chapter 1.

Secondly, we have "the things which are." These are the things that Jesus was seeing right then—in John's time. But as we will see, if we fail to personally apply these things to our lives now, we would be foolish. Maybe a better way to look at "the things which are" would be to look at "the things which refer to the church age," the time between the coming of the Holy Spirit in Acts 2 and the rapture of the church in Revelation 2 and 3.

Finally, we'll look at "the things which will take place after this." This encompasses the events that begin in Revelation 4 and continue through chapter 22.

CHAPTER 1

The book of Revelation begins with a message for the seven churches in Asia. They were seven literal churches that were in seven different conditions—not unlike the churches today—or the people in churches today—not unlike you and me. But before Jesus told John what to write to the churches, John got to see Jesus. His reaction? John fell at His feet like a dead man. I love chapter 1! It tells us some really, really wonderful things about Jesus. When He walked this earth, He seemed reluctant to reveal His divinity—but no more—not in Revelation. You can't read this book and not know Jesus is God.

CHAPTERS 2 AND 3

Jesus delivers the messages to the seven churches and lets them know that He is walking among them and He sees everything that is going on. He points out the good and the bad. He gives warnings and He gives promises to overcomers. Who is an overcomer? This is important to know since the overcomers are the ones who receive the blessings.

Some churches get no praise, some get no warnings, but all get a promise. Is Jesus promising blessings to you too? That's part of the blessing of reading Revelation!

CHAPTER 4

In this chapter John finds himself in heaven before the throne of God. One of the first things John noticed in heaven was worship. It's here that "the things which will take place after this" begin to be revealed.

CHAPTER 5

The angel zooms in a little closer for John and he saw something in the right hand of the One who was on the throne. It was a scroll with seven seals. A strong angel cried out, "Who is worthy to open the scroll and loose its seals?" When John heard this, he wept because no one was found. Then John saw a Lamb—but the elders called Him the Lion. Next—more worship. This time John knew they were worshiping the Lamb.

CHAPTER 6

The Lamb begins opening the seven seals, one at a time, revealing only six of the seals. In each of the first four seals, John saw a horse with a specific power.

Seal 1: a white horse representing conquering power.

Seal 2: a red horse representing war and bloodshed.

Seal 3: a black horse representing famine.

Seal 4: a pale horse representing pestilence and death.

In the next two seals, two different responses—that of the souls of the martyrs and that of the unsaved.

Seal 5 reveals the souls of martyrs slain for the Word of God, who cry out, "How long?" How long until you do something about this, Lord?

Seal 6 unleashes cosmic disturbances on the unsaved. There is a great earthquake, the sun darkens, the moon becomes like blood, stars fall, the sky recedes like a scroll, and every mountain and island is moved out of its place. In Hebrews chapter 1, we are told that Jesus holds all things together. Here though, in Revelation 6, it's like He's starting to let go.

The response of the unsaved? They hide themselves in caves and rocks and cry out for protection from the wrath of the Lamb.

CHAPTER 7

We read the words, "After these things." Four angels are told not to harm the earth until the servants of God are sealed for protection. Twelve thousand from each of the twelve tribes of Israel are sealed, 144,000 in all. But salvation is not just for the Jews. It is also for the people from every nation. This chapter wraps up with John's vision of those who are saved during the great tribulation.

CHAPTERS 8 AND 9

The seventh seal is opened. "There was silence in heaven for about half an hour." No worship. No sound at all. "And the seven angels who stand before God were given seven trumpets." From the seventh seal came seven trumpets.

Trumpet 1 sounded and hail and fire mingled with blood was thrown down to the earth, resulting in a third of the trees burning, and all the grass was burned.

Trumpet 2 sounded and a burning mountain was thrown into the sea causing a third of the sea to turn to blood, killing a third of the creatures and destroying a third of the ships.

Trumpet 3 sounded and a star named Wormwood fell from heaven making a third of the waters bitter.

Trumpet 4 sounded and the sun, moon, and stars darkened a third of its light. An angel cried, "Woe, woe, woe to the inhabitants of the earth." In other words, it's been bad, but now it's about to get really, really bad for those who live on earth.

Trumpet 5 sounds and a plague of locusts are given power to torment, but not kill, those who did not have the seal of God on their foreheads. One woe is past.

Trumpet 6 sounds and releases four angels of the Euphrates River and 200,000,000 horsemen that kill a third of mankind. But the rest of the people on the earth do not repent.

CHAPTER 10

John eats a little book; sweet to taste, but bitter to the stomach. And John prophesies again.

CHAPTER 11

Two witnesses appear on the scene. For three-and-a-half years they have power to kill anyone who tries to harm them, power to stop the rain, power to turn water into blood, and power to strike the earth with plagues.

Then the beast ascends out of the bottomless pit and kills them. Their bodies lie in the street for three-and-a-half days as the whole world watches and celebrates (that would have been hard to believe before television). After three-and-a-half days, God restores them to life for all to see and then takes them up into heaven. A great fear falls on the people, and in the same hour there is a massive earthquake, killing 7,000 people. The second woe is past.

Trumpet 7 sounds and heaven proclaims God's kingdom.

CHAPTER 12

Satan is cast to the earth and persecutes the Jews. They flee to the wilderness where Satan releases a flood of water—sounds scary—but God just opens up the earth and it swallows the water. Satan is foiled again. God is in charge.

CHAPTER 13

The Antichrist is introduced during the last half of the seven-year tribulation—awful guy, awful things. He blasphemes God, and Satan gives him tremendous power. He demands people take a mark or they cannot buy or sell anything. There is a lot of speculation about that mark, but what we do know is that somehow people can't transact business without it. In this day of technology, it's pretty easy to authorize or deny purchases.

CHAPTER 14

We see the 144,000 sealed Jews in heaven praising the Lord. Our God is such an amazing God. It says they have their Father's mark on their forehead showing that they belong to God, our heavenly Father. The followers of Satan and the beast may have a mark on their hand or forehead, but it's only an imitation.

Before the last woe, three angels are sent to preach the gospel to all the people on the earth. God still doesn't give up on them—warning that judgment is just around the corner. We certainly can see the wrath of God in these chapters; it is important to see His longsuffering as well.

Then John says that he looked and saw "One like the Son of man sitting on a white cloud, with a golden crown on His head, holding a sharp sickle in His hand." Then He thrust the sickle to the earth.

CHAPTERS 15 AND 16

Seven angels are given seven golden bowls full of the wrath of God. The last of the three woes has begun.

Bowl 1 pours out boils upon those with the mark of the beast who worship his image.

Bowl 2 is poured out and the sea is turned to blood and every sea creature dies.

Bowl 3 is poured out and rivers are turned to blood.

Bowl 4 is poured out on the sun and men are scorched with great fire.

Bowl 5 pours out darkness and pain.

Bowl 6 pours out causing the Euphrates River to dry up, making way for the kings of the east to prepare for the final battle, Armageddon.

Bowl 7 is poured out, and an angel cries out, "It is done!" Thunderings, lightnings, great hail, and the greatest earthquake the earth has ever known struck the earth and all the nations fell. And still—still—men blasphemed God.

CHAPTERS 17 AND 18

These chapters tell us about "the harlot," false religions that people will follow during the tribulation. God's judgment is revealed against the religious, political, and economic systems. It all falls. It is all crushed and the world mourns her fall.

CHAPTER 19

Begins with the words, "After these things." After these things, John heard a voice in heaven saying, "Alleluia! Salvation and glory and honor and power belong to the Lord our God! For true and righteous are His judgments." Then John heard another voice saying, "Praise our God, all you His servants and those who fear Him, both small and great!"

And then the voice of a great multitude—will it be you? Will it be me?—saying "Alleluia! For the Lord God Omnipotent reigns! Let us be glad and rejoice and give Him glory, for the marriage of the Lamb has come, and His wife has made herself ready."

Overwhelmed, John fell down and worshiped—the angel! The angel said, "I am your fellow servant. Worship God!" Even John messed up. I can't wait until I get my perfect body, heart, and mind and I never, ever mess up again.

Then John saw heaven opened and Jesus sitting on a white horse going forth with the armies of heaven. I love what H.A. Ironside says this chapter reveals about Jesus: "He rises. He returns. He reigns."[1]

Finally, the beast, the kings of the earth, and their armies gathered together to make war against Jesus and His army. They lose. The beast and his False Prophet are thrown into the lake of fire.

CHAPTER 20

Satan is bound for a thousand years.

Those believers alive at the end of the tribulation move into a period of time we call the millennium, a time when Jesus and His saints reign with a rod of iron. A lot of believers don't tend to care much about this time—they just want to be in heaven. But the Lord has spent a lot of time telling us about this time of reigning in the Old Testament. If He looks forward to it, certainly we should too. You and I, as believers, will reign with Jesus.

When the one thousand years have passed, Satan is released again. Amazingly, he deceives many and gathers them to battle. Satan is so very powerful, but he is just absolutely a wimp against the Lord. Verse 9 simply tells us: "And fire came down from God out of heaven and devoured them." Finally, Satan will join the beast and his prophet in the lake of fire.

After Satan is cast into the lake of fire, the unbelieving dead will stand before the Lord to be judged. "And anyone not found written in the Book of Life was cast into the lake of fire (hell)."

CHAPTER 21

John wrote, "I saw a new heaven and a new earth ... and I heard a loud voice from heaven saying, 'Behold, the tabernacle of God is with men, and He will dwell with them, and they shall be His people. God Himself will be with them and be their God.'" There will be no tears, no death, no sorrow, no crying, and no pain for the former things have passed away. Then He who sits on the throne will declare, "Behold, I make all things new."

CHAPTER 22

The book of Revelation wraps up with "Behold I am coming quickly!" (v. 7) He says this again in verse 12, "Behold! I am coming quickly and My reward is with Me, to give to every one according to his work." But before verse 12, it reads, "And he said to me, 'Do not seal the words of the prophecy of this book, for the time is at hand.'"

Although there is a blessing to the believer for reading this book, there can be a blessing to the unbeliever (if heeded). Look at the stark warning in verse 11, "He who is unjust, let him be unjust still; he who is filthy, let him be filthy still; he who is righteous, let him be righteous still; he who is holy, let him be holy still." I think that's one reason God does not want the book sealed up, but rather wants it exposed.

After this final invitation, there will be no more. Whatever condition you are in when God rolls up the scroll and wraps up this earth, or wraps up your life, that is your condition for all eternity.

> For those who belong to Jesus, they respond to the fact of His coming. "And the Spirit and the bride say, 'Come!' And let him who hears say, 'Come!' And let him who thirsts come. Whoever desires, let him take the water of life freely." Revelation 22:17

And then, in verse 20, John penned his agreement, "Even so, come, Lord Jesus!"

COMING IN FOR A LANDING

I found it difficult sometimes to figure out what verb tense to use as I reviewed Revelation. It's the future—it hasn't happened yet. But John saw it as if it already had happened because as Revelation says, "These things are true and faithful." John saw reality.

God wants us to know this: Jesus is coming back in His way and in His timing. Before He does, He wants us to know that there are things in this life that please Him and things that do not, things He will reward, and things for which we will suffer consequences. So, that's the flyover, even though you may have felt like you flew in a Concorde jet.

CLOSING THOUGHTS

In the room that Dale and I stayed in at the couple's retreat, it had a lot of old classic books. One was a book by Amy Carmichael titled, *God's Missionary*, a short little book, yet powerful. This one phrase captured my attention, "A kind word pleases God."[2] Park on that for a while. He is not only walking among the churches, He is walking among the rooms in your house. Although one day God will roll up this earth like a scroll, what happens on it matters to Him. How you and I live matters to Him, and He wants us to know that He sees—and He responds to what He sees.

We get some glimpses of heaven in the book of Revelation. Heaven is a lot about worship and it's a lot about being with the Lord. It's not about the ways and pains of this life.

When we were camping this past summer, one of my grandsons told me he wasn't sure he wanted to go to heaven. His cousin reminded him of the alternative, but still, he wasn't sure. He thought that everything in heaven would be perfect and boring. When you read the last couple chapters of Revelation, you pick up on God's excitement about all He has made new. He made the earth and called it good, before the fall. How much better do you think He has made heaven? It won't be boring!

In between Jesus' message to the churches and the description of heaven is a time when God deals with all that is bad—all who have refused His touch. But even in judgment, we see His grace, we see His longsuffering, we see that He truly does love all those in the world. But He will not—He cannot—tolerate the final rejection of His Son.

In the coming chapters, we will look at the judgments. They are there for a reason. But mainly we will look at Jesus, as Revelation 1:5 says, "Him who loved us and washed us from our sins in His own blood." This Jesus wants you and I to read, hear, and heed the words of this book of the Revelation of Jesus Christ—and the One who is faithful and true promises to bless us if we do.

Chapter One

THE REVELATION OF JESUS CHRIST: REVELATION 1

> The Revelation of Jesus Christ, which God gave Him to show His servants—things which must shortly take place. 1:1a

The word *revelation* is translated from the familiar Greek word "apocalypse." Our exposure to that word outside of church has been associated with the coming of the end, and a very bad thing by those of the world—because it is very bad to those who are worldly. But the word *apocalypse* literally means "an unveiling, an uncovering, a disclosure, bringing light or understanding to something previously unknown or unseen."

Think of a statue in the middle of a town square covered with a huge tarp. You can imagine the band playing and a great anticipation. Then *shortly* (keep that word in mind), the tarp is removed and the statue is unveiled. This is what *revelation* means: "the uncovering, the unveiling, or the disclosure of Jesus as we have not yet seen Him." God's intention is to give this revelation to John and for him to write it down for God's servants—not to confuse us, but to bless us.

The word *servants,* as used here, is often translated as "bondservants." A bondservant of Jesus is one who wants to follow and obey Him—that's the level of commitment necessary to hear and to heed, isn't it?

Remember I said to keep in mind the word *shortly*. In Revelation 1:1 the idea of this word is "suddenly" or "quickly." John wasn't being told that these things would happen soon. When these things will take place remains the secret of the ages—the secret that keeps us living in anticipation and hopefully living our lives close to Jesus. Once it starts happening, it's going to happen fast. *Shortly* means "suddenly or quickly."

It reminds me of our national security. It's amazing how quickly our military can intercept an incoming missile and shoot it down. For a very long time the United States lived with the assurance that the enemy couldn't get us—until 9/11. We found out differently that day as we watched on television the Twin Towers collapse suddenly. Our nation was *suddenly* and *quickly* changed. So too God wants His servants to understand that when things start happening, they are going to happen suddenly.

Notice the word *must* in verse 1, "things which must shortly take place." This means there is absolutely nothing that will prevent it. It will happen.

> And He sent and signified it by His angel to His servant John, who bore witness to the word of God and to the testimony of Jesus Christ, to all things that he saw. 1:1b-2

John is telling us that he wrote what he saw, and what he saw was from God.

> Blessed is he who reads and those who hear the words of this prophecy, and keep those things which are written in it; for the time is near. 1:3

This is the first of seven promises of blessing recorded in the book of Revelation (Revelation 1:3, 14:13, 16:15, 19:9, 20:6, 22:7, 22:14). I love that a blessing comes right at the beginning of the book, don't you? Put yourself in the place of the first-century congregants hearing this book read for the first time, maybe sizing up the width of the scroll and thinking, *Oh! This is going to take a while* but then you hear the promise of a blessing. Right away you're going to pay attention.

After the time John wrote this, not everyone had a Bible nor did they have a copy of this book. So, it properly states "he who reads" and "those who hear" the words of this prophecy. The messenger read, the congregation heard, all were to obey. And still today we are to listen and read with the intent of finding blessing with spiritual ears ready to respond.

Pause for a moment and think about what God's blessing means to you. It's a challenge to us. I thought about the promise of blessing in the Beatitudes: the kingdom of heaven, comfort, being filled with righteousness, mercy, seeing God, being called the sons and daughters of God. Are those kinds of blessings important to you? I believe those are the kinds of blessings that God is promising. That's why this book is written to His servants—because only His servants would recognize them.

In the gospel of John, the people asked Jesus, "What sign will You perform then, that we may see it and believe You? What work will You do? Our fathers ate the manna in the desert; as it is written, 'He gave them bread from heaven to eat.'"

> "Then Jesus said to them, 'Most assuredly, I say to you, Moses did not give you the bread from heaven, but My Father gives you the true bread from heaven. For the bread of God is He who comes down from heaven and gives life to the world.'
>
> "Then they said to Him, 'Lord, give us this bread always.'
>
> "And Jesus said to them, 'I am the bread of life. He who comes to Me shall never hunger, and he who believes in Me shall never thirst. But I said to you that you have seen Me and yet do not believe.'" (John 6:32-36)

When the people sincerely asked Jesus to show them that He was God, He offered them the bread of life, but they wanted daily, physical bread. Jesus challenged the people but they weren't interested in what He had to offer so they walked away. But Jesus' disciples knew that He alone had the words of life and they wanted what He had to give, so they stayed. May that be the case for each one of us.

John, to the seven churches which are in Asia: 1:4a

John wrote what he saw to the seven churches in Asia. This is not the Asia as we know it today, but Asia Minor or modern-day Turkey. The seven churches are identified in verse 11: [3]

Why these seven churches? Anything I say would just be a guess. However, when you look on a map, they kind of form a circle and we are told later in this chapter that Jesus stood in the middle of them. They were postal regions where information could have been sent out from these cities.

Significantly, "seven" represents the number of God's completeness. So you will probably agree as we study them that they represent all churches, but we don't have a definitive answer as to why these particular seven churches.

Grace to you and peace from Him who is and who was and who is to come, and from the seven Spirits who are before His throne and from Jesus Christ, 1:4b-1:5a

John begins the letter to the churches with a greeting, "Grace to you and peace." And notice grace always comes before we can experience peace. Secondly, this greeting would be pretty insignificant if it came from just anybody, but look where this grace and peace comes from. It comes from:

1. Him who is and who was and who is to come
2. The seven Spirits who are before His throne
3. Jesus Christ

JESUS IS, JESUS WAS, AND JESUS IS TO COME

"Him who is and who was and who is to come" could easily identify Jesus, but since it says "and from Jesus Christ," it can't be referring to Jesus here. Therefore, since there is simply One other that has always been (and who was), it could only be the Father.

THE SEVEN SPIRITS BEFORE HIS THRONE

Bible translations that capitalize all references to God have "Spirit" capitalized in this verse indicating that this refers to the Holy Spirit. Similarly, Isaiah 11:2 reads, "The Spirit of the LORD shall rest upon Him (Jesus), the Spirit of wisdom and understanding, the Spirit of counsel and might, the Spirit of knowledge and of the fear of the LORD."

Here we find the sevenfold role of the Holy Spirit; this is not referring to an essence. Again, notice the capitalization of *Spirit*. In the New Testament, actually, the phrase, "Spirit of the Lord" is used to describe the Holy Spirit; such as in Acts 8:39, "the Spirit of the Lord caught Philip away." So here, and throughout our study, we are going to use Scripture to validate and to give us understanding of what John saw in Revelation.

Also, as an afterthought, if the seven spirits are anything or anyone else, this puts them or him on an equal basis with the Father and Son.

JESUS CHRIST

Lastly, this greeting of grace and peace is from Jesus Christ. He is identified by titles Jesus alone has proven Himself to be.

> the faithful witness, the firstborn from the dead, and the ruler over the kings of the earth. To Him who loved us and washed us from our sins in His own blood, 1:5

Jesus is:

1. The faithful witness
2. The firstborn from the dead
3. The ruler over the kings of the earth
4. Him who loved us and washed us from our sins in His own blood

JESUS IS THE FAITHFUL WITNESS

He is the true and accurate witness of the Father. Remember what Jesus said to the disciples in the upper room: "He who has seen Me has seen the Father" (John 14:9). The fact that He is the "faithful witness" of the Father is supported further by Scripture: "Do you not believe that I am in the Father, and the Father in Me? The words that I speak to you I do not speak on My own authority; but the Father who dwells in Me does the works" (John 14:10). Isaiah, speaking of the Messiah, wrote, "Indeed I have given him as a witness to the people" (Isaiah 55:4).

JESUS IS THE FIRSTBORN FROM THE DEAD

There were others who had been raised from the dead, but Jesus raised Himself. *Firstborn* here speaks of priority. At the time of this writing, the firstborn son had priorities and privileges that the other siblings did not. Jesus is supreme and, as we will see in verse 18, has authority over death.

JESUS IS THE RULER OVER KINGS OF THE EARTH

Psalm 72:11 confirms, "Yes, all kings shall fall down before Him; all nations shall serve Him."

That puts Him at a great distance from you and me. Still, John makes quite a jump with the next two descriptions of Jesus.

JESUS LOVED US

The verb tense here is interesting. Scholars argue quite a bit as to whether it's past tense or present tense, whether it speaks of Him proving His love to us in the past through the cross, or whether it speaks of His continual love for us. Since He is the same yesterday, today and forever —He has always loved us—so both work. The point is, this awesome Son of God, this awesome member of the Trinity loves me and He loves you. Do you believe the first three things on the list about Him? Then you must—you must—believe this one—He loves you! So much so that He died for you.

> "But God demonstrates His own love toward us, in that while we were still sinners, Christ died for us." (Romans 5:8)

JESUS' OWN BLOOD WASHED US

Jesus washed us with His own blood because the stain of scarlet sins just couldn't be removed by anything man could come up with. There is only one sin stain remover and that's the blood of Jesus Christ. He bled so He could wash us with "His own blood"—no other sacrifice will do. And you know what He does after He has applied His cleansing blood to our sin-stained lives? He declares us clean, whiter than snow.

> "Come now, and let us reason together," says the LORD, "Though your sins are like scarlet, they shall be as white as snow; though they are red like crimson, they shall be as wool." (Isaiah 1:18)

> "Purge me with hyssop, and I shall be clean; wash me, and I shall be whiter than snow." (Psalm 51:7)

> and has made us kings and priests to His God and Father, to Him be glory and dominion forever and ever. Amen. 1:6

The order of these things is worth noting: He first loved us, washed us, then He made us kings and priests to His God. Most translators say this is better translated as "kingdom of priests." Certainly not worth quibbling over. We will one day reign with Him.

> "And you shall be to Me a kingdom of priests and a holy nation." (Exodus 19:6)

> "You also, as living stones, are being built up a spiritual house, a holy priesthood, to offer up spiritual sacrifices acceptable to God through Jesus Christ." (1 Peter 2:5)

JESUS' TWOFOLD ROLE OF PRIEST

What was the role of the priest?

1. The priest was to represent God to the people
2. The priest was to represent the people to God (by praying for them)

In order to do those two things, they had to have access to God. And for us, the veil has been torn giving us access to Him at all times. He who loves you did that for you.

The acknowledgment of this revelation brought John to worship and adoration—the same place it should bring us: "to Him be glory and dominion forever and ever. Amen"

> Behold, He is coming with clouds, and every eye will see Him, even they who pierced Him. And all the tribes of the earth will mourn because of Him. Even so, Amen. 1:7

JESUS IS COMING WITH CLOUDS

Verse 7 begins with a *Now pay attention*, "Behold," and ends with an "Amen." When we say amen, we often are declaring *so be it*. But it also means, as it does in this case, *so be it* or *so it is*. This is trustworthy. He is coming.

In Acts 1:9 when Jesus ascended into heaven, the angel told His disciples that Jesus would return just as He left—being caught up in a cloud. When the rapture occurs, those who are believers will be caught up together with Him. Every eye will not see Him when the rapture occurs, but in His second coming, we are promised that "every eye will see Him." No one alive on earth at that time will miss it.

You see, the fact that He has made us a kingdom of priests is not the end. We've got to include, "He's coming again." John doesn't see that as a thing to dread, even though there are two groups of people that will react differently. John wrote, "Amen" which should have been especially important to the seven churches of Asia reading this book.

But these other two groups of people, "those who pierced Him" (the Jews), and "all the tribes of the earth" (the unbelieving Gentiles at the time), "will mourn" when they see Him. *Mourn* is "to wail, to beat and strike one's body."

> "I am the Alpha and the Omega, the Beginning and the End," says the Lord, "who is and who was and who is to come, the Almighty." 1:8

Who is speaking? The Old Testament gives these titles to the Father (many, many times). Here are just two Scriptures:

> "Listen to Me, O Jacob, and Israel, My called: I am He, I am the First, I am also the Last." (Isaiah 48:12)

> "Also God said to him: 'I am God Almighty.'" (Genesis 35:11)

When we read Revelation 1:4, the Father identified Himself as "He who was and is and is to come." Hold that thought for a moment while we look at verses 9 and 10.

> I, John, both your brother and companion in the tribulation and kingdom and patience of Jesus Christ, was on the island that is called Patmos for the word of God and for the testimony of Jesus Christ. 1:9

JOHN, YOUR BROTHER AND COMPANION

John identifies himself, not as an apostle, not as a church leader, but as a brother and companion. A companion: "one who is traveling with," "walking in the same paths," "a partaker of common experiences as followers of Christ." Don't miss what John and these servants had in common: tribulation, kingdom living, the benefits of knowing Jesus, and patience and perseverance in the hard times.

As we progress in our study, Jesus takes notice whether we hang in there in Him or we bail and run to someone else, or something else, for comfort and relief.

THE ISLAND OF PATMOS

John was imprisoned on the island of Patmos for the Word of God and the testimony of Jesus Christ about AD 94-95, a time when the emperor of Rome, Titus Flavius Domitian, had demanded that he be worshiped as lord and god. The refusal of the Christians to obey his edict led to severe persecution. Tradition says that it was Domitian who sent John to the Isle of Patmos, a Roman penal colony off the coast of Asia Minor, to do hard labor in his very old age.

John was banished. Have you ever been banished? Or at least felt like it? Most of us have, but few of us for doing the right thing.

> I was in the Spirit on the Lord's Day, and I heard behind me a loud voice, as of a trumpet, 1:10

IN THE SPIRIT

Can you imagine being in that banished state, feeling so forsaken, and suddenly the Lord appearing? He often appears to us when we feel banished—if we are in the Spirit—not in our flesh. Not to say that the Lord can't or doesn't speak to us when we are in the flesh. Paul on the road to Damascus certainly is an example of that. But John "was in the Spirit." John was in that place where he was more attentive to the Holy Spirit than he was to his flesh.

Not long ago when I was doing my devotions, the only sound I was aware of was the noise of our refrigerator running, but then the noise of the refrigerator stopped and there was the still, small voice of the clock, "tick tock, tick tock." I hadn't heard it while the refrigerator was running. In the same way, we need to tune out other noises to hear God speak to us. It was when John was in the Spirit that Jesus revealed Himself to him.

ON THE LORD'S DAY

Although many people today refer to Sunday as the Lord's Day, the phrase is used in no other place in the Bible. Sunday was the day when the church began to meet and it was referred to as the first day of the week. So, it was probable that John was referring to Sunday here. Some say it refers to the Day of the Lord, the time of God's judgment—but that seems like a stretch. We know, for certain, it was a day that John separated from others and called it "the Lord's Day."

I really love what Max Lucado says about this verse.

> "We don't know who first called this day the Lord's Day, but we know why. It was and is a day. It belongs to Him. He left His imprint on hell itself that morning. Friday's trial became Sunday's trumpet. This is the Lord's Day. This is also John's spiritual birthday.
>
> "Decades earlier on the first Lord's Day, John was shaken from his sorrow and sleep by the announcement, 'They have taken the Lord out of the tomb and we don't know where they have put Him' (John 20:2). On legs much younger and stronger, John sprinted to the empty tomb and the fulfilled promise. Seeing for himself, he later confided, the other follower, who had reached the tomb first, also went in 'he saw and believed' (John 20:8).
>
> "On this Sunday, he had no friend to take to the tomb. He is exiled, banished from his friends. Alone on Patmos, cut off with the stroke of a magistrate's pen he was sentenced to pass his days with no companion, with no church.
>
> "What Rome intended as isolation, heaven ordained as revelation. Rome placed John on Patmos for punishment. Heaven placed John on Patmos for privilege. The same apostle who saw the open grave of Christ was to glimpse the open door of heaven.

"It was the Lord's Day, you see. Nothing Rome could do could change that fact. It was the Lord's Day in Rome and in Jerusalem. It was the Lord's Day in Egypt and Ethiopia and even along the barren stretches of Patmos. It was the Lord's Day. Though he was cut off from man, he was in the very presence of God. Though he was far from friends, he was face to face with his Friend. He was praying.

"And as he prayed he again was met by an angel. He again saw what no man had ever seen. The same eyes that saw the resurrected Lord now saw heaven open." [4]

A LOUD VOICE AS A TRUMPET

John said, "I heard behind me a loud voice, as of a trumpet." Trumpets are mentioned over 100 times in the Bible. They were primarily used as calls to meet together for a significant event. Men blew them to get others' attention. Here, God's voice was compared to it. What did the voice say?

> "'I am the Alpha and the Omega, the First and the Last', and, 'What you see, write in a book and send it to the seven churches which are in Asia:'" 1:11

JESUS IS ALPHA AND OMEGA

The voice was claiming to be "the Alpha and the Omega," "the First and the Last." We've seen those titles before in verse 8. He calls Himself "the First and the Last" again in verse 17. Verse 12 tells us that John said he saw "one like the Son of Man"—that's Jesus. In verse 18, He identifies Himself as "He who lives, was dead and is alive forevermore." That can't be the Father—that can only be Jesus.

Why is this so important? Because it helps us identify who is speaking back in verse 8, here, and in verses 12 and 18. In identifying who is speaking, we separate Christianity from all other religions.

One day two Jehovah's Witnesses came to our door. I wanted to use this verse to prove to them that Jesus is God. I didn't have my Bible so I asked if I could use theirs and I turned to Revelation 1:8. Their Bible says this: "'I am the Alpha and the Omega,' says Jehovah God, 'the One who is and who was and who is coming, the Almighty.'" [5]

They added, "says Jehovah God!" They said it wasn't Jesus. I was in dismay and, with as much excitement as my personality allows, I said to them, "You changed it! Why did you change it?!" This one who is speaking is undoubtedly Jesus. We will see it even more clearly as we continue to study this book.

> Then I turned to see the voice that spoke with me. And having turned I saw seven golden lampstands, 1:12

SEVEN LAMPSTANDS

John saw seven golden lampstands. We are told in verse 20 that these lampstands represent the seven churches that Jesus will be addressing.

We have a menorah on the communion table at our church. When the menorah is lit, it symbolizes the holy place as one unit, representing Israel as a nation. But here we see the churches, although meant to function in unity, they are depicted as seven individual lights.

> and in the midst of the seven lampstands One like the Son of Man, clothed with a garment down to the feet and girded about the chest with a golden band. 1:13

JESUS IS THE SON OF MAN

In the midst of the lampstands John saw "One like the Son of Man"—Jesus. He was "clothed with a garment down to the feet and girded about the chest with a golden band." That was the garb of the priests, except their band had golden threads, while Jesus' had pure gold.

> "I lifted my eyes and looked, and behold, a certain man clothed in linen, whose waist *was* girded with gold of Uphaz!" (Daniel 10:5)

> His head and hair were white like wool, as white as snow and His eyes like a flame of fire. His feet were like fine brass, as if refined in a furnace, and His voice as the sound of many waters. 1:14-15

Surely, John had read about what he was now seeing before him.

JESUS' PURITY

> "I watched till thrones were put in place, and the Ancient of Days was seated; His garment was white as snow, and the hair of His head was like pure wool." (Daniel 7:9)

JESUS' BODY

> "His body was like beryl, His face like the appearance of lightning, His eyes like torches of fire, His arms and feet like burnished bronze in color, and the sound of His words like the voice of a multitude." (Daniel 10:6)

The white was not just white, but blazing white. His eyes were penetrating, burning through dross and seeing it all. His feet were like brass.

JESUS' VOICE

> "And behold, the glory of the God of Israel came from the way of the east. His voice was like the sound of many waters; and the earth shone with His glory." (Ezekiel 43:2)

"His voice as the sound of many waters." We were at Niagara Falls this summer and the sound of those waters rushing over the cliffs was astounding and exemplified the power of God in nature.

> He had in His right hand seven stars, out of His mouth went a sharp two-edged sword, and His countenance was like the sun shining in its strength. 1:16

JESUS' SWORD

Hebrews 4:12 refers to the Word of God being like a two-edged sword. The sword in Hebrews describes a short sword, used in close combat. This sword that John saw was a very large sword, up to five feet in length. Those who could wield a sword like that could cause tremendous devastation. Jesus' words will bring tremendous devastation to those upon whom He will unleash His wrath. Here's a couple of examples of that devastation.

> "Now out of His mouth goes a sharp sword, that with it He should strike the nations. And He Himself will rule them with a rod of iron. He Himself treads the winepress of the fierceness and wrath of Almighty God." (Revelation 19:15)

> "And the rest were killed with the sword which proceeded from the mouth of Him who sat on the horse. And all the birds were filled with their flesh." (Revelation 19:21)

JESUS' COUNTENANCE

"His countenance was like the sun shining in its strength." That's bright. Our natural eyes can't even look at the sun when it's shining like that, but one day, with our new sight, we will behold Him and worship Him and, I think, find it very hard to take our eyes off of Him.

I tried to find some artists' renderings of this description of Jesus but I didn't like any of them. It's how they drew His face that I didn't like. How do you picture a powerful shepherd, a judging, merciful God? How do you picture grace and wrath?

As I wrote that, I don't know what John saw, but you know what, I will never have His face of judgment directed towards me. That is a glorious thought.

> And when I saw Him, I fell at His feet as dead. But He laid His right hand on me, saying to me, "Do not be afraid; I am the First and the Last." 1:17

DO NOT BE AFRAID

What a glorious contrast! When John saw Him he "fell at His feet as dead. But He laid His right hand on me." John had felt that hand upon him many times. John knew the physical touch of Jesus. He even wrote about it in First John that he had personally handled the Word of Life. That touch was familiar.

Then Jesus said to John, "Do not be afraid." He had heard Jesus say those words before. When Jesus walked out on the sea and the disciples thought He was a ghost, He told them, "It is I. Do not be afraid." When Peter, James and John saw Jesus in His glory on the Mount of Transfiguration, they fell on their faces and Jesus said, "Arise, do not be afraid." And John heard those words again when Jesus appeared to the disciples after His resurrection and they worshiped Him.

Here John finds himself on his face and Jesus' words to him are the same, "Do not be afraid." You know when a person speaks to you after a long time, and their voice sounds so familiar? Can you just imagine John, after feeling Jesus' touch and hearing His familiar words again, what that must have been like?

> "I am He who lives, and was dead, and behold, I am alive forevermore. Amen. And I have the keys of Hades and of Death." 1:18

JESUS IS ALIVE FOREVERMORE

Only Jesus has always been, has died, and yet will always be. He is alive forevermore and He will always be who He proclaims to be.

JESUS HAS THE KEYS TO HADES AND DEATH

Keys are symbols of authority. If you want to get into a room at the church, you would probably look for someone with authority. They have the keys. But there is only One who has the authority over Hades and Death—and it's not Satan; it's Jesus. He's in control. Aren't you glad He has opened the way to heaven for all who have come to Him?

> "Write the things which you have seen, and the things which are, and the things which will take place after this." 1:19

The chapter closes with Jesus telling John to write:

1. The things which you have seen (Chapter 1: This vision)
2. The things which are (Chapters 2 and 3)
3. The things which will take place after this (Chapters 4-22)

> The mystery of the seven stars which you saw in My right hand, and the seven golden lampstands: The seven stars are the angels of the seven churches, and the seven lampstands which you saw are the seven churches. 1:20

Revelation 1:16 says that Jesus "had in His right hand seven stars," which He identifies here as the angels of the seven churches. In chapters 2-3 when Jesus addresses each letter, he addresses them as "the angel of the church." Does this trigger a question for you? It does for me. Does each church have an angel watching over it or in charge of it? If the letter is to be read, what part does an angel have in that?

This Greek word translated *angel* is a word that is also translated "messenger" in other parts of the Bible. John the Baptist was called this same word, translated as "messenger" (see Matt. 11:10). His followers were called *messengers* of John (see Luke 7:24). Jesus sent *messengers* to Samaria (see Luke 9:52). So what determines the correct translation? Using the Bible to interpret the Bible, we look at the context (the surrounding text) and the precedent (looking at other incidences of the word in the Bible). When we look at the precedent, we see that angels didn't read messages; they delivered them. God didn't write messages to angels; He spoke to them Himself. He didn't give a message to a man (in this case, John) and then tell the man to write the message down and give it to angels. Therefore, I think we can safely say that the *angels* are likely messengers akin to those Jesus sent to Samaria.

CLOSING THOUGHTS

These are the things that John saw revealed to him. Hopefully, you have been blessed as we considered and studied the vision of Jesus. Over the next several chapters, we will be slowing down and looking at *the things which are*, to study what Jesus had to say to each individual church.

REFLECTION QUESTIONS

(For more extensive study questions visit CathyDickinson.com)

1. Write the focus of this book stated in the first five words of Revelation 1:1. Thoughtfully write it here. The Revelation of Jesus Christ is the focus of this book.

2. What is the meaning of the word *shortly* as it is used to describe the events that will take place in Revelation? (1:1a) The word shortly means suddenly or quickly.

3. What is promised to those who read, hear, and keep the words of Revelation? (1:3)
Those who read, hear and keep the words of Revelation are promised a blessing.

4. What six things are revealed about Jesus in verses 5 and 6?

a. Jesus is a faithful witness.

b. He is the firstborn from the dead

c. He is the ruler over the kings of the earth

d. Jesus loves us and washes us from our sins with His blood.

e. Jesus is the priest who represents God to the people.

f. Jesus represents the people to God by praying for them.

5. In verse 11, John was told to write what he saw in a book. After writing the book, what was he told to do with it? He is to send the book to the seven churches which are in Asia.

6. Define the sound of Jesus' voice as revealed in verses 10 and 15.

Jesus has a loud voice as of a trumpet. (v 10)
He also has a voice like many waters. (v 15)

7. In verses 13-16, John describes Jesus. Next to the descriptions, write what they signify.

a. White like wool represents purity.

b. Jesus body is like beryl

c. His face is like lightning and his eyes are like torches - they penetrate and burn through dross

d. His voice is like many waters - loud and powerful

e. He wears a gold band like a perfect priest
He is called the Son of Man

f. He has seven stars in his right hand

g. A sword comes out of His mouth

8. Verse 17 tells us that when John saw Jesus, he fell at His feet as dead. Write Jesus' four words of comfort to John. Do not be afraid. I am The First and the Last.

9. What were the three things John was to write? (1:19)

a. Things which you have seen

b. Things which are.

c. Things which will take place after this

10. Who are the seven stars that Jesus holds in his right hand? (1:20)

The seven stars are the angels of the seven churches.

Chapter Two

REMEMBER, REPENT, RETURN: REVELATION 2:1-7

The next seven chapters of our study will look at Jesus' messages to the seven churches. Since the intent of this New Testament book is to reveal Jesus, it's valuable to study what He said to these seven churches. Jesus' message to each church gives us good insight as to what our Lord is like and what is important to Him. If you are primarily interested in what you can get from God, you may find nothing in His messages. But if your goal is to know Him and to please Him, you will learn a tremendous amount from these passages.

JESUS' MESSAGES HAVE A PATTERN

As we study Jesus' messages to the churches, we will see a similar pattern:

1. Jesus identifies the church.
2. Jesus introduces Himself (using a description from Revelation 1).
3. Jesus tells them what pleases Him.
4. Jesus tells them what displeases Him.
5. Jesus gives the remedy.
6. Jesus warns them.
7. Jesus reminds them of His promise.

It is just as important to spend time on the things Jesus saw that pleased Him as it is on the things that displeased Him, so we will not just be do-ers, but *don't-ers* as well.

To the angel of the church of Ephesus write, 2:1

EPHESUS

Although Scripture is inspired by the Holy Spirit, nowhere are we told that chapter titles are inspired. They were added afterwards. Some Bible translations title this message identifying the church in Ephesus as "The Loveless Church." I'm not so sure Jesus would have given it that title. He had a lot of good things to say about them—more good than bad. Unlike our Lord, man seems prone to dwell on the negative and thus identified the church in Ephesus for what it did wrong.

THE CITY OF EPHESUS

This first message was specifically for the church in Ephesus. Referring to the map, it was the city closest to the island of Patmos. The letters appear to be delivered in the order of proximity to Patmos. (See map on page 23.)

Ephesus was a harbor city, a port town. It was on the main trade route from Asia Minor to Rome and had a population of about 200,000. It was a large and very prominent city. It was also the home of many gods and goddesses. Paul established a great church foundation in Ephesus about 53 AD and stayed approximately three years. We find the account of its establishment in Acts chapters 19 and 20.

Why is this so important? Jesus tells them to remedy their situation by remembering from where they had fallen; repent and do the first works. We actually have a description of what they had fallen from and what their first works were like in Acts 19 and 20. We'll get back to this in a little while. (Side note: I feel like the Lord just personally showed me this—I didn't get it from a commentary. I want that for you, too.)

THE EPHESUS PASTOR

Sometime after Paul left Ephesus, Timothy took over and later John pastored the church. Then in about 63 AD, Paul wrote the epistle to the Ephesians from a Roman prison. As I skimmed the letter, I was reminded of how Paul compared the church of Ephesus to a marriage relationship, teaching us what a love relationship with Jesus should be like.

It is believed that when the Roman emperor, Titus Flavius Domitian, was assassinated in 96 AD, probably not too long after John wrote Revelation, that the new emperor released John who then went back to Ephesus and remained there until his death. Tradition tells us that because of his old age, the believers would carry John to church, and his simple message to them was, "Beloved … love one another" (1 John 4:7, 11). Now, that's all tradition, although I found some of it to be confirmed in secular history books.

I love to try to get into the author's head or heart when I study a book. I couldn't help but wonder what John thought as he wrote about what Jesus saw in the church that was once his. Then I thought about how, knowing what Jesus saw, John's final messages to his congregants were about love.

Consider your own household. If Jesus were to say to you, "This is what I see in your children…." Even though you know that you gave birth to sinners, just like your mother did, you wouldn't be able to help but wonder where you failed; and sadly, take pride in what they did right. If the Lord told me that some of the women within my church needed correction, I would take it a little personally since I hadn't taught them correctly. It's just human nature. And then, if I had the opportunity, I certainly would reiterate what Jesus showed me. How do you view His correction? As warnings or criticisms?

The first church Jesus exposed was John's own church. It was a church that had been the recipient of the best teaching. The church at Ephesus experienced not only the teaching of Paul and John, but also of Apollos, who was known for his eloquence, as well as being ministered to by Aquila and Priscilla.

> These things says He who holds the seven stars in His right hand, who walks in the midst of the seven golden lampstands: 2:1

THE WALKING STAR HOLDER

Jesus introduces Himself. In each of the seven messages to the churches, including Ephesus, Jesus identifies Himself as, "He who holds the seven stars (the messengers of the churches) in His right hand" (Revelation 1:16). This word *holds* has the sense of not only "has a grip on," but "has power over." We know that God is not a dictator and He does not force His will on anyone. And we know there have been far too many *messengers* who have not rightly represented the Lord. As I consider myself to be the *messenger* of this Bible study, I think of how this might be a reminder to me. Although I can make my own choices, God is in charge; He sees and will still be the ultimate authority. It's also a reminder to the people that God has the ultimate authority, power, and control over the messenger.

We already established that the stars are seven churches. A star is a light. If Jesus is holding the light in His hand and it's doing what it's supposed to do, it will shine for Him and show Him better. Does that mean this is only for these churches? As we study, we will see that the church throughout the centuries has been, at one time or another, like these churches, and you and I personally could be described by a lot of the things Jesus saw. Some have divided the seven messages to describe the church at different periods of time throughout history. That's an interesting thought, but it seems to me like trying to jam a puzzle piece in a space where it really doesn't fit. To dwell on that would not help you or me in our walks with the Lord at all—and that's what Jesus is interested in—our relationship with Him.

I love that Jesus says He "walks in the midst." Jesus isn't sitting on His heavenly throne casually observing. When the sound tech tests the sound on Sunday morning, he doesn't just listen from the soundboard. He walks throughout the sanctuary and occasionally stops to pay attention to what he hears in each area. Jesus walks among us. He stops and pays attention to what He sees and hears; and always remember, Jesus does something. In the case of these churches, He gives them a message.

> I know your works, your labor, your patience, and that you cannot bear those who are evil. And you have tested those who say they are apostles and are not, and have found them liars and you have persevered and have patience, and have labored for My name's sake and have not become weary. 2:2-3

This is what pleased Jesus. Not only does Jesus see, but He also knows. He is aware of what they are doing in a way no one else does. In the church of Ephesus, here is what He sees that pleases Him. He knows their …

WORKS

It's just as it seems. The "works" are the deeds they did. Jesus knew the Pharisees' works were only done to be seen by men, just as He knew the church at Ephesus was about doing good works for the right reasons. Jesus did not rebuke them for the heart behind their works. Before we move on, keep in mind that Jesus is speaking to believers here. Unbelievers can never be commended for their works, no matter how good, because none are done for His name's sake. Jesus does not ask the world to do good works.

LABOR

This labor works to the point of weariness; that feeling when you get home and crawl into bed because of utter exhaustion. This is the kind of labor that doesn't quit because you're tired or because you don't want to do it or something better has come up. In verse 3 Jesus commends the Ephesians that they "have not become weary." It is comforting to know He notices.

Hebrews 6:10 supports this: "For God is not unjust to forget your work and labor of love which you have shown toward His name, in that you have ministered to the saints, and do minister." This indicates there is a kind of weariness the Lord commends and a kind of weariness He does not. Dwight L. Moody once said, "I grow weary in the work but not of the work." Paul expressed a weariness that pleases the Lord in 2 Corinthians 12:15 when he said, "And I will very gladly spend and be spent for your souls."

God definitely sees things man does not. He sees us when we go home. He sees us flop into bed after a day of seemingly tirelessly serving Him.

In her song, "The Warrior Is a Child," Twila Paris describes it this way:

> "They don't know that I go running home when I fall down
> They don't know who picks me up when no one is around
> I drop my sword and look up for a smile
> 'cause deep inside this armor, the warrior is a child." [6]

There is a satisfaction in this kind of weariness that only you and He know.

PATIENCE

This kind of patience is to "bear under something," "a steadfast endurance," "hanging in there when you want to quit." God likes that. It's such a denial of the flesh and of choosing Him, isn't it? Patience is not only a choice, but it is a choice we cannot make without the enabling of the Holy Spirit. Patience is a fruit—or the result of the Holy Spirit's work in our lives. How many times are we exhorted in God's Word to be steadfast, to be patient? Don't quit. Patience is ultimately proof of our surrender to the Lord. Patience, or lack of it, is a good indication of who is presently ruling in our lives.

CANNOT BEAR EVIL

The church of Ephesus couldn't bear evildoers. They couldn't support, tolerate, or put up with evil in the church. Dr. Spiros Zodhiates, a Greek-American Bible scholar, defines this evil as "one who is evil in himself and thus gets others in trouble."[7] Remember, the Corinthian church prided themselves in their tolerance of evil and Paul rebuked them for that.

APOSTLE TESTERS

The Ephesians tested those who said they were apostles and found them to be liars. This seemed to be a predominate problem in the early churches.

Second Corinthians 11:12-15 says: "But what I do, I will also continue to do, that I may cut off the opportunity from those who desire an opportunity to be regarded just as we are in the things of which they boast. For such are false apostles, deceitful workers, transforming themselves into apostles of Christ. And no wonder! For Satan himself transforms himself into an angel of light. Therefore it is no great thing if his ministers also transform themselves into ministers of righteousness, whose end will be according to their works."

Today, people do not claim to be apostles, since one of the qualifications for apostleship is to have seen Jesus. However, men still come into churches and claim authority God has not given to them.

Here is the warning Paul gave to the Ephesian elders in Acts 20:28-31: "Therefore take heed to yourselves and to all the flock, among which the Holy Spirit has made you overseers, to shepherd the church of God which He purchased with His own blood. For I know this, that after my departure savage wolves will come in among you, not sparing the flock. Also from among yourselves men will rise up, speaking perverse things, to draw away the disciples after themselves. Therefore watch, and remember that for three years I did not cease to warn everyone night and day with tears."

Apparently, the Ephesian church continued to be faithful to heed Paul's warning. Most churches fail because of problems within. We must be watchful of those within the church who have agendas other than the Lord's.

PERSEVERERS

Revelation 2:3 reveals the Ephesians' reaction to those who are evil and claim to be apostles but are not. They "persevered." In the Greek text, *persevered* is the same word as "bear" in verse 2. They could not handle evil, but they persevered through it; they bore the brunt of it. They handled persecution.

So notice the contrast here. They did not bear that which was against Jesus (those who were evil), but they did bear that which was for Him (persecution). This adds to our understanding of how they labored.

They did it for Jesus' name sake. They did it for Him and were about Him. Jesus knew their works. He knew the motive behind their works. If it's not done for His name's sake, it's just wood, hay, and stubble. And they had not become weary—another contrast—they were weary in the work, but not of the work.

Nevertheless I have this against you, that you have left your first love. 2:4

LEFT THEIR FIRST LOVE

This displeased Jesus. Jesus saw a lot of good but Jesus also sees something else—something that probably was not apparent outwardly. You see, their works were still reflecting right motivations. They worked for His name's sake. They did what they did because of Jesus. That's a good thing, right? Nevertheless, they left their first love.

I sat at my desk and pondered this for a while. First Corinthians 13 tells us if we have not love, we have become a clanging cymbal to the Lord. I'm sure that's a pretty obnoxious sound in heaven. But if Jesus is pleased with their works and even their motives, than how can that be?

Well, here's what I think—and I couldn't find a commentary to support this—I think their works were motivated out of old love. You who are married might relate. It's that place a marriage can get to where you do what you do out of commitment and routine, a love you haven't really renewed in a while. Your marriage looks good on the outside. You're doing the right things and your motivation is still good, but the first love part is gone. You've left your first love.

We often have married couples come in for counseling claiming they no longer love each other. But Dale and I both know what they really mean is that they have just left their first love; not lost it. And we ask a simple question like, "What was it like when it was good?" or "What was it about him or her that attracted you?" As much as couples don't always listen to each other, when that question is asked, the other person is all ears. And if we can get them back to remembering when it was good, they both realize they want that.

Notice, Jesus didn't say they had *lost* their first love; He said they had *left* it. That's a big difference. When you lose something, you don't know where it is. When you have left something, you know right where it is.

Sometimes when I give my granddaughter Janae a snack, she takes it to another room and then wanders back into the kitchen to get more. Why does she leave her snack? Because she's lost interest or something else caught her attention. The next day when I find Janae's snack, it's all shriveled up and dry. This could be a picture of what happens to our love for Jesus when we leave it.

Remember therefore from where you have fallen; repent and do the first works, 2:5a

This is the remedy. Jesus, always being the wonderful Lord that He is, does not point out our failures without giving us a remedy. Our love relationship with Jesus is restorable. He is all about fixing us, not judging us. What is the remedy for leaving our first love? Three things.

1. REMEMBER

"Remember therefore from where you have fallen." When we look at the beginning of the church in Ephesus, we find men possessed by the devil, many practiced magic, and the city was the center of worship of gods and goddesses, since one of the main sources of income was the manufacturing of idols—little figurines of the gods Diana and Zeus. But then something happened.

> "… fear fell on them all, and the name of the Lord Jesus was magnified. And many who had believed came confessing and telling their deeds. Also, many of those who had practiced magic brought their books together and burned them in the sight of all. And they counted up the value of them, and it totaled fifty thousand pieces of silver. So the word of the Lord grew mightily and prevailed." (Acts 19:17-20)

Have you lost the zeal to remove anything from your life that doesn't magnify your love for Him?

I was listening to a song by Keith and Kristyn Getty, and one of the lines was "Don't let me lose my wonder." [8] That's good advice. One way we keep our wonder is to slow down and meditate on God; who He is, His creation, what He has done, and specific things He's done in our lives. Determine to praise our Lord for different things about Him, not just the same things all the time. He inhabits the praises of His people. He is drawn to you and me when we acknowledge Him. You know, when someone is saying nice things about you, you could sit with them for a very long time. He is attracted to your praise. And right there we have a love relationship blooming.

What have you forgotten about the Lord—in the sense that you haven't thought about it in a while?

Maybe as you read some of this, you realize you've never really had a love relationship with the Lord. You can begin right now by meditating on the wonderful things about Jesus.

2. REPENT

Since the word *repent* is mentioned twelve times in Revelation, it's important. *Repent* means "to turn around." It's a change in direction. You see, these believers in Ephesus were doing good things, but they were headed in the wrong direction. They had placed their love for God second, and put good works first. Jesus said repent. Their love for Jesus was of utmost importance—and they had left it for good works.

If leaving our first love requires repentance, then God sees it as sin. Repent has the attitude, "if God hates it, I'm going to hate it too." We need to see it as God sees it. That's often what prohibits us from really changing. We don't get it. We don't think what we're doing is that bad or dangerous. We are either moving toward God's love or we are leaving it.

> "Keep yourselves in the love of God, looking for the mercy of our Lord Jesus Christ unto eternal life. Now unto him that is able to keep you from falling." (Jude 21, 24)

This is a life verse for me because like everyone else in ministry, I am tempted to settle for the works as evidence of my love relationship with the Lord. If we stay in love with Him, He will keep us from falling. Jesus holds us in His grip. When we leave His love, we leave His grip—and we begin to lack. We try to fill that lack with something or someone else. That's a message to the church, as well as to the messengers/pastors of the church.

Jesus knew that would eventually happen if the church did not repent and return to their love relationship with Him. Works will never ever mean more to God than our love relationship. Our works are a result of our love relationship with Him. They must not ever come first.

3. RETURN

They were to go back and "do the first works." Again, marriage is such a good example. When Paul taught the Ephesians, he compared the marriage relationship to the relationship of Christ and the church.

A wife will often take those verses in Ephesians 5 to remind her husband how he should love her as Christ loved the church. But it should also be a reminder of how we should love Christ.

Wives, remember how you used to meet your husband at the door when he came home? You were so excited to see him. Remember how you tried to do things that pleased him and the sweet looks you used to give him? If you're reading this and the Lord is using it to convict you that you have left your first love in your marriage, take these three remedies to heart. Remember. Repent. And return. Go back to the things you did when you first fell in love.

> Or else I will come to you quickly and remove your lampstand from its place—unless you repent. 2:5b

OR ELSE

This is the warning. Did you notice the phrase in the middle of verse 5? Oh parents, how many times have you said "or else" to your children? Do this—or else. Don't do that—or else. They are usually hollow threats. "Stop crying or I'll give you something to cry about." "If you keep making that face, it's going to freeze that way."

But Jesus means what He says. He said, "I will come to you quickly and remove your lampstand from its place." The word *quickly* has the same meaning as "shortly take place" in Revelation 1:1, when Jesus spoke of the things which must take place. They will happen fast—all of a sudden.

Because the Lord is so very patient, He often holds off consequences. Samson is a good example. Though Samson sinned, the Lord anointed him; Samson sinned again, and again the Lord anointed him. But one day, the Scripture says, "But he did not know that the Lord had departed from him" (Judges 16:20).

In the same sense, the Lord warns the church of Ephesus, "Remember, repent and return … or else I will depart." If they kept doing works without loving God first, He would put an end to their effectiveness.

Many times when we labor to the point of weariness, we get to see the results. But sometimes, only God sees, yet knowing He is pleased is so rewarding. I can't imagine doing the works they did, laboring to the point of weariness, and doing it all for nothing—it didn't even please the Lord. Maybe it means He'll take away the anointing. The effectiveness of what we do is always and only because of Him.

But this you have, that you hate the deeds of the Nicolaitans, which I also hate. 2:6

THE NICOLAITANS

Jesus pointed out one more thing that pleased Him: They hated "the deeds of the Nicolaitans." Who were the Nicolaitans? Are they still around? Do we need to be aware of them?

The word itself means "control over the laity." Many say it was those (and is those) who put a man in the place of God—who honor a man, instead of the Lord. That certainly would fit within this section since Jesus expresses His concern about their love.

There was also a man named Nicolas around that time who was a gnostic, a leader of a cult that was causing a whole lot of trouble back then and people were falling for their false teachings.

I don't think it's the word *Nicolaitans* that we need to be concerned with. It's the phrase at the end of verse 6, "which I also hate." He hates the deeds of the Nicolaitans, not the Nicolaitans themselves. Today, there are surely many other practices like the deeds of the Nicolaitans. Whatever it is, we should hate what Jesus hates.

> "I will set nothing wicked before my eyes; I hate the work of those who fall away; it shall not cling to me." (Psalm 101:3)

Jesus noticed and commended that they hated what He hated. The patience, the bearing He commended them for in verse 2, was never that of tolerance.

He who has an ear, let him hear what the Spirit says to the churches. 2:7a

THE HOLY SPIRIT SPEAKS

Hear what? "What the Spirit says to the churches." Jesus was giving this message, right, then why attribute this to the Holy Spirit? Think about this. Who has ears to hear? Believers. Spiritual things are spiritually discerned.

> "For what man knows the things of a man except the spirit of the man which is in him? Even so no one knows the things of God except the Spirit of God. Now we have received, not the spirit of the world, but the Spirit who is from God, that we might know the things that have been freely given to us by God." (1 Corinthians 2:11-12)

Although this is a message from Jesus, it is the Holy Spirit who speaks to us. So, the call is to "hear"—spiritually hear—what He is saying.

> To him who overcomes I will give to eat from the tree of life, which is in the midst of the Paradise of God. 2:7b

TO THE OVERCOMER

Finally, the promise—to the overcomer.

Who is an overcomer? John knew very well. "For whatever is born of God overcomes the world. And this is the victory that has overcome the world—our faith. Who is he who overcomes the world, but he who believes that Jesus is the Son of God?" (1 John 5:4-5).

The overcomers are we who believe that Jesus is the Son of God. In other words, if we believe that Jesus is the Son of God, we will *hear* Him.

THE TREE OF LIFE

Let's take a look at the tree of life that the overcomers will eat from in the midst of the garden. "And out of the ground the LORD God made every tree grow that is pleasant to the sight and good for food. The tree of life was also in the midst of the garden, and the tree of the knowledge of good and evil" (Genesis 2:9).

Then look at Genesis 3:24 as it describes a part of the consequence of sin:

> "So He drove out the man; and He placed cherubim at the east of the garden of Eden, and a flaming sword which turned every way, to guard the way to the tree of life."

After the tree of knowledge, the tree of life must have been the most dangerous tree in the garden, because if we ate of that tree in this life, we would live forever in our current state of sinfulness. That is a very dreadful thought. Instead, when we overcomers get to heaven, we will eat of it and will live forever in a totally blissful, wonderful state.

THE IMPORTANCE OF THE HOLY SPIRIT

As I complete this chapter, it's a pensive time for me. Pastor Chuck Smith went home to be with the Lord. A few days later, I attended the Calvary Chapel Pastors Wives' retreat with nearly 800 women. As one of the members of the planning board, each of us found ourselves reflecting on the beginning of the Calvary Chapel movement as the "good old days." I found myself thinking about what those days were like compared to what they are now.

I thought about our study of Revelation as Jesus walked among the churches, wondering what He sees as He walks amongst Calvary Chapels. A few weeks later I happened to be teaching at a Calvary Chapel Women's retreat and said, "As much as we grieve the loss of Pastor Chuck, we Calvary Chapels are facing an even greater loss. It is the loss of the working of the Holy Spirit in our midst." This wasn't in my notes! Then I encouraged them that we've got to get back to our roots. I think it hit me as strongly as it did those who were listening to me.

You see, in those early days, most of us would have said, "All I know is Jesus Christ and Him crucified for me." We so wanted to be a part of what God was doing that we rarely questioned His promptings. We just stepped out and obeyed Him.

Look at what Paul said to the Galatians, "Are you so foolish? After beginning by means of the Spirit, are you now trying to finish by means of the flesh?" (Galatians 3:3 NIV).

The New Living Translation says it like this: "How foolish can you be? After starting your Christian lives in the Spirit, why are you now trying to become perfect by your own human effort?"

Although I do not recommend using "The Message" as your Bible because it's more of a commentary, it paraphrases Galatians 3:3 this way: "Are you going to continue this craziness? For only crazy people would think they could complete by their own efforts what was begun by God. If you weren't smart enough or strong enough to begin it, how do you suppose you could perfect it?" [9]

> R.A. Torrey wrote, "The secret of effectual living is knowing the power of the Spirit through the Word. The secret of effectual service is using the Word in the power of the Spirit." [10]

My concern is that we know and cherish the power of the Word, but we are neglecting the dependency on the power of the Spirit. Many have lost the simplicity of Christianity, or maybe never knew it. It's a simple yet powerful way of living, as we learn what God has to say, and then we do what God says, depending on Him for the power to do it.

CLOSING THOUGHTS

Calvary Chapels are not part of a denomination; they aren't ruled by a governing body. They are simply a group of churches that believe in teaching through the Word of God, through the power of the Holy Spirit. But is it a group of people who go out and act upon the Word of God in the power of the Holy Spirit? Are we a people who respond to

His promptings? Or are we a people who have come to analyze those promptings—and then decide according to our own wisdom, or understanding, or fear of embarrassment, or of what people might think?

In this chapter we talked about Jesus' concern that we have a "first love" experience with Him all the time. Let's live in a "first love" relationship having the desire to both know what our God says to us and then respond to what He says—just because and only because of love. I long, for myself and for you, to live in love with Jesus. Let's not move on to the next chapter without heeding His desire that He expressed for Ephesus, because we won't have ears to hear His messages to the other six churches.

REFLECTION QUESTIONS

(For more extensive study questions visit CathyDickinson.com)

1. In the message to the church at Ephesus, Jesus established this pattern. Fill in the blanks.

He identifies the __church__.

He introduces Himself using a __description__ from Revelation 1.

He tells them what He __sees__ that __pleases__ Him.

He tells them what He sees that __displeases__ Him.

He __gives__ them as to the __remedy__.

He __warns__ them.

He __reminds__ them of His __promise__ to them.

2. What description did Jesus use to identify Himself to the church at Ephesus? (2:1)

Jesus is described as He who holds the seven stars in His right hand.

3. Jesus doesn't just observe from afar on His throne, but "walks in the midst" of the churches. What does this personally mean to you? He walks in the midst of my church and my life. Therefore He knows what hurts and troubles me. He also, however, knows what I do and he knows if it honors him.

4. What did Jesus see that pleased Him? (2:2-3)

1. The church worked tirelessly for Him.
2. They labored to a point of weariness.
3. They worked patiently – they continued without quitting.
4. They did not put up with evil in the church.
5. They tested the agendas of the leaders – they must serve Christ.
6. They persevered, put up with, persecution for Jesus -

5. Choose one or more of the things that pleased Jesus (from #4) and write an insight you gleaned. Do I work for Him? So many things can/are done - but does it bring Him glory? What is my motivation? Also, do I work to weariness - am I tired from my labors for Him? My work should be Kingdom worthy...

6. What did Jesus see that displeased Him? (2:4)

The church had left its first love. They had not "lost" it - they left it which means it can be found again.

7. Record what you learned from this message to the church at Ephesus about leaving their first love and how it applies to your own life. I can renew and return to my first love. Jesus waits, he stands in my midst - ready to receive my cry for forgiveness. He lets me return - read, worship, pray, fellowship.

8. List and describe the three-part remedy Jesus gives. (2:5)

- Remember who God is and what He has done - worship and renew your relationship.
- Repent - turn around and face Jesus - he is where we direct our lives and actions
- Return and seek the love relationship you have for the Lord - keep Him first.

9. If the remedy is not taken, Jesus warns "or else I will come to you quickly and remove your lampstand from its place" (Revelation 2:5). Describe what this means and how it applies personally to your life. I really worry about my motives and whether I do things to truly please Him. I worry about missed opportunities and not pleasing the Lord. Lord, please direct my path and establish my ways!

10. Who is an "overcomer" and what promise does Jesus make to those who overcome? (2.7) If you need more room to write, use the notes section on page 50.

One who believes in God is an overcomer. Our faith gives us victory. The overcomer, once in heaven, will eat from the tree of life - living forever with God in peace.

Notes

Chapter Three

HE KNOWS OUR SUFFERING: REVELATION 2:8-11

As we've already discovered, there is an outline to these messages. For the church of Smyrna it is:

1. Jesus identifies the church.
2. Jesus introduces Himself (using a description from Revelation 1).
3. Jesus tells them He saw their suffering.
4. Jesus warns them of more suffering.
5. Jesus gives the remedy.
6. Jesus gives two promises.

And to the angel of the church in Smyrna write, 2:8

SMYRNA

Smyrna was about thirty-five to forty miles north of Ephesus. Like Ephesus, it was a very prosperous harbor city. It is the only one of the seven churches that still exists today, now called the city of Izmir in Turkey. (See map on page 23.)

THE CITY OF SMYRNA

Because of Rome's great armies, the Smyrna rulers saw the benefit to align themselves with Rome. The Romans brought security keeping the seas and roads safe from the bad guys; therefore, the people loved the reign of Rome in their city, giving them a sense of peace and safety.

In Rome's attempt to unite the emperor with the city of Smyrna, they encouraged the people to worship Caesar. At first it was entirely voluntary, but when Domitian became emperor (or Caesar), worship became mandatory for the city of Smyrna, even including a temple dedicated to Caesar. Once a year, the citizens were required to burn incense on an altar to Caesar and declare him as lord. In so doing, they would receive a certificate of evidence to prove that they had performed their religious duty, an act of worship and loyalty toward Caesar. Even though the city of Smyrna worshiped their own gods and goddesses, Caesar wasn't jealous and he didn't seem to care; although he was insistent that he rank somewhere among their gods.

On the contrary, our God *is* a jealous God. Isaiah 45:18 tells us,

> "For thus says the LORD, who created the heavens, who is God, who formed the earth and made it, who has established it, who did not create it in vain, who formed it to be inhabited: 'I am the LORD and there is no other.'"

THE SMYRNA BELIEVERS

It would seem that the Smyrna believers were between a rock and a hard place, but not really. There was only one right thing for them to do. Our God expected them to bow their knee to Him only, so when they refused to bow their knee to Caesar, they were labeled as disloyal to the Roman Empire. I'm sure the unbelievers pressured them, "Why can't you just burn incense on Caesar's altar and declare him as lord? You'll get your little certificate and you can still go to church on Sunday and worship your God."

This is a kind of precursor to the tribulation. Without the mark of the beast, you won't be able to buy or sell. Without this certificate of evidence, believers found themselves in that same sort of predicament: automatic persecution and automatic rejection from others. At the time Jesus sent His message to the believers in Smyrna, the people in this prosperous city saw those of the church as poor and disloyal to Rome.

> These things says the First and the Last, who was dead, and came to life: 2:8

THE FIRST AND THE LAST

This is Jesus' description of Himself.

Imagine as the entire book of Revelation was being read to them, and they hear these words again. Jesus had already identified Himself as "the First and the Last"—twice, once in verse 11 and again in verse 17, adding the words, "Do not be afraid." So why did Jesus choose this description for the church of Smyrna?

They must have been scared, or maybe they questioned, "What's it gonna hurt to burn a little incense on an altar and mutter, 'Caesar is lord?'" Consider the parents at the church of Smyrna; bowing to Caesar would have prevented a whole lot of suffering for their children, wouldn't it? How about the teenagers at the church of Smyrna; worshiping Caesar would have made them feel accepted when they walked into town. After all, God knows their heart.

But Jesus reminded them, "I am the First and the Last." He is the First; He pre-existed. He is the Last; He will go on forever. I'm sure this triggered Isaiah 44:6 to their memory:

"Thus says the LORD, the King of Israel, and his Redeemer, the LORD of hosts: 'I am the First and I am the Last; *besides Me there is no God.*'"

DEAD AND CAME TO LIFE

Then Jesus says, "I was dead and came to life." He knows suffering unto death—as a result of persecution. But the story didn't end there. He passed through death and into life. He went through incredible suffering, but He survived it; it's past. He "came to life." Death wasn't the end for Jesus.

If you were in Smyrna, what would you have liked to hear from Jesus then? Well, if you're like me, you'd like to hear something more akin to, "I am He who will stop this horrible trial and take away the pain right now!"

For a moment, I thought about grabbing a concordance to try to find an instance where God had said that to someone, but I realized it was a waste of time. Even if God did, it's certainly not the norm. Certainly not what we should expect as Christians. But too often we find ourselves expecting relief from Him, don't we. And when it doesn't come, we accuse Him of not being faithful to us.

This is what Jesus wanted them to know about Him. "I am the First and the Last. I was dead and came to life." It is hard living in this world. It is really, really hard. He wants us to know that He was here before it all started and He will be here long after it's all over. And so will you.

> I know your works, tribulation, and poverty (but you are rich); and I know the blasphemy of those who say they are Jews and are not, but are a synagogue of Satan. 2:9

SUFFERING

First of all, Jesus let them know that He knew their works in the midst of suffering. Oh, how we long for someone to acknowledge that they see what we are going through, to understand. Jesus did. He knew how they were living in the midst of not just one, but three things that came against them:

1. TRIBULATION

Tribulation literally means crushed, pressed, compressed, squeezed, narrowness of room.

Notice, Jesus did not use the word *persecution* here. He used the word *tribulation*, which includes, but is not limited to, persecution. It refers to any trial that purposes to crush.

It is interesting that the name Smyrna comes from the word *myrrh*. Myrrh is a sweet-smelling herb used for embalming. The only way to release its fragrance is to crush it.

This word translated as *tribulation* was used to describe stepping on grapes in a vat until they were crushed and the juice came out. This word also described the process of forcing a criminal to confess by making him lie down on his back and placing a huge stone on his chest. When he exhaled, he wouldn't be able to draw air back in and ultimately died under the pressure.

For the church of Smyrna, much of their tribulation came from discrimination, since they couldn't buy or sell, but it also included an awful form of torture. Killing Christians was a spectator sport. People would throng to coliseums to watch Christians mauled and killed by dogs. They were crucified and set on fire. They were doused in oil and ignited to use as nighttime lamps.

Here's a sample of artwork found depicting the persecution many suffered. [11]

"I know your tribulation." Jesus knew pressure and He dreaded it too. Didn't He ask that the cup pass from Him? He wanted out, just like you and me. And you know what? His Father did not remove the cup. Jesus knows what it's like to want out of the suffering, even to ask for it to be removed, and it didn't happen. He knows pressing, crushing tribulation.

Are you experiencing crushing pressure right now? Jesus knows and He has something to say to you. But remember, it only profits those who have ears to "hear what the Spirit says."

2. POVERTY

They experienced poverty. In the Greek, *poverty* describes a person that only has what is necessary to survive—water, food, clothing, and not much else. There's another word that describes abject poverty; a person who has nothing at all. Jesus said—I know—you have nothing—but you are rich.

Jesus knew poverty. He said, "Foxes have holes and birds of the air have nests, but the Son of Man has nowhere to lay His head" (Matthew 8:20).

"For you know the grace of our Lord Jesus Christ, that though He was rich, yet for your sakes He became poor, that you through His poverty might become rich" (2 Corinthians 8:9). This word *poverty* is the same one used to describe the condition of the believers in Smyrna.

3. BLASPHEMY

They experienced blasphemy, slandering, speaking lies against another. They were being blasphemed by those "who say they are Jews and are not, but are a synagogue of Satan." Many groups throughout history, like the Nazis in the 40s, used to point to this verse to prove the Jews are of Satan. We see over and over again in the book of Acts how some would follow the apostles into other cities with the goal of destroying their ministries. They claimed to represent God, but they were guilty of rejecting Jesus and made every effort to prevent others from knowing Him too. These Jews claimed to be God's people, yet some Jews had this vendetta against Christians.

In one of His interactions with the Pharisees, Jesus said this to them: "You are of your father the devil, and the desires of your father you want to do" (John 8:44).

Attempts to destroy Christians and Christianity are the work of the devil. Jesus warned the Ephesus church about those who said they were apostles and were not. Now to the church in Smyrna, Jesus warned about those who said they were Jews but were not.

Now, you might have the question that I did. Weren't the Jews commanded to declare Caesar as lord too? Wouldn't they be subject to the same persecution as the Christians? Well, apparently not. Rome recognized the Jews' religion and they were exempt. The Christians were not. So, rather than help the Christians, some Jews chose to bring as many Christians as they could before the magistrates, forcing them to show certificates of proof that they had worshiped Caesar. With that accusation came slander and blasphemy, lies, and distorting Christian beliefs.

"I know," Jesus said to them. Not just, "I see," but "I know." Intellectually and experientially—not in the body of a god that was pain-free and free from agony—but in the body of a man who, from what we can understand, hated rejection as much as we do. He still does.

I read a statement that was made to someone who was suffering. I don't recommend repeating it, but indirectly stated, can be powerful. It's this: "Remember, they have not spit in your face yet." They did spit in Jesus' face. They smote Him, plucked the hair from His beard, beat and whipped Him until His flesh looked like hamburger, lied about Him, and they said slanderous statements that eventually led to His death. We are encouraged in Hebrews 12:3 to consider what Jesus endured. "For consider Him who endured such hostility from sinners against Himself, lest you become weary and discouraged in your souls."

Jesus knows; He knows tribulation, He knows poverty, and He knows blasphemy all to a much greater degree than you and I ever have or ever will.

> Do not fear any of those things which you are about to suffer. Indeed, the devil is about to throw some of you into prison, that you may be tested, and you will have tribulation ten days. Be faithful until death, 2:10a

TO TEST WHAT'S INSIDE

Jesus warns them of more suffering. He not only knows their present condition, but He knows their near future. It's bad now, but it's going to get worse. Look at the middle of verse 10: "the devil is about to throw some of you into prison." Certainly history has proven prison to be part of their suffering. So who is responsible? The devil. Remember, even some of the Jews were the devil's instruments. Why? "That you may be tested." Couldn't they just rebuke the devil and he would flee? Apparently not. God's purpose was to reveal what was in them when they were being crushed.

I had a bunch of grapes in the refrigerator; sometimes a bad grape is pretty evident. I don't need to bite into it to tell. Other grapes look great until you bite into one only to discover its true flavor. Some people are like that, aren't they? I love what Dale said a couple of weeks ago when he was talking about the parable of the sower. "The same sun that scorches the shallow-rooted one causes fruit in the deeply-rooted one. The difference is the condition of the soil." I doubt if the church of Smyrna had any shallow-rooted Christians. Shallow people don't hang around when persecution shows up. Crushing reveals what's inside—sweet or sour. It reveals the quality of the fruit. Just like myrrh, the only way to release its fragrance is to crush it.

We find insight as to what our response to crushing (persecution) should be in 2 Corinthians 2:14-16: "Now thanks be to God who always leads us in triumph in Christ, and through us diffuses the fragrance of His knowledge in every place. For we are to God the fragrance of Christ among those who are being saved and among those who are perishing. To the one we are the aroma of death leading to death, and to the other the aroma of life leading to life. And who is sufficient for these things?"

Notice the question, "Who is sufficient" not "Why me?" Our response to tribulation reveals our heart.

SATAN'S METHODOLOGY IS SUFFERING.

Satan has very few tricks in his bag. He doesn't need any more since he has been so effective over the ages. He knows that suffering can potentially sabotage our faith.

Remember Satan's strategy with Job? Satan said to the Lord, "Does Job fear God for nothing? Have You not made a hedge around him? You have blessed the work of his hands, and his possessions have increased in the land. But now stretch out Your hand and touch all that he has, and he will surely curse You to Your face!" (Job 1:9-11).

It didn't work with Job, but it did work with some saints that really loved the Lord. Believers, even strong believers, get shaken by hard times. Elijah knew God's power, but even Elijah lost his faith when he ran from Jezebel and hid in a cave (1 Kings 19).

John the Baptist was God's instrument to declare Jesus to the world. He saw the Holy Spirit fall upon Jesus and heard the words of the Father declaring Jesus to be His Son. But when John found himself in prison and sent his followers to ask Jesus a question, remember what it was? "Are You the Coming One, or do we look for another?" (Matthew 11:3). Why did John ask that? Jesus wasn't fitting John's expectations of the Messiah. Jesus' answer? "Go and tell John the things which you hear and see: The blind see and the lame walk; the lepers are cleansed and the deaf hear; the dead are raised up and the poor have the gospel preached to them. And blessed is he who is not offended because of Me" (Matthew 11:4-6). Jesus is not the Messiah because He does what we want Him to do, or even expect Him to do. He is the Messiah. He confirmed it by fulfilling all that was promised of Him. Look again at the last line of verse 6, "And blessed is he who is not offended (or stumbled) because of Me." Satan is out to stumble you and he so often does it by bringing suffering into your life.

GOD SETS THE TIME AND LIMIT

How long would Satan be able to keep the believers in Smyrna imprisoned? Ten days. Is this ten literal days or ten periods of time? The Greek could be translated as either. So, we don't really know. Since this was only for the believers in Smyrna, it really doesn't apply to you or me. They would know. What is important is that we understand that God is in control of our suffering, and it is God who sets its timing and its limits. They were about to suffer even more than they already have, but God had a purpose in it, and as always, a good one. Do you want more of an explanation than that? They probably did too, but that's what Jesus told them.

THE REMEDY

As a result of His knowledge, what does Jesus expect of them? What remedy does He give? Three things:

1. KNOW WHAT YOU HAVE

In verse 9 when Jesus said, "I know your works, tribulation, and poverty (but you are rich)," this word *rich* is the exact opposite of the word used to express their poverty, which meant they "had" nothing. *Rich* means they "lacked" nothing. I've heard the saying, "I've been rich and I've been poor. Rich is better." I think we would agree with that whether it be by experience or just theory. Lacking nothing materially is certainly better than lacking everything materially. But Jesus wasn't talking about material riches. He was talking about the riches that He alone gives.

We might imagine that material riches give us joy, peace, a sense of purpose, and well-being. But they don't. Those are things only God gives and the believers in Smyrna had them. These believers were living in a city among very materially prosperous people. Jesus reminded them, "You have what they want."

Hebrews 10:34 supports this: "For you had compassion on me in my chains, and joyfully accepted the plundering of your goods, knowing that you have a better and an enduring possession for yourselves in heaven."

2. STOP BEING AFRAID

Verse 10 literally translates as, "Do not fear any of those things." The King James Version says, "Fear none of those things." The verb tense seems to indicate that they were already afraid. I would be, wouldn't you? It's already scary bad and now Jesus is telling them it's going to get worse. Most of the time when He tells us not to be afraid, He also tells us that He is with us. He has already established that as He told them He walks among them.

As I think about it, I'm not so sure knowing that God is in charge and He has a purpose in it would be enough to keep me from that initial response of being afraid. Actually, He didn't say, "Don't be afraid," the translation means, "Stop being afraid." Fear is a natural reaction to a fearful situation. We really can't help that first reaction, but we can stop its process of causing us to be fear-driven, fear-motivated, or being a people gripped by fear. Jesus was telling them and tells us, "Stop being afraid." Don't let that happen.

But whether or not I remain afraid and operate out of that fear really comes down to what I know about God. If He says, "Don't be afraid of what is about to happen," that should be enough for us. Is it enough for you?

3. BE FAITHFUL TO GOD

Walk according to your faith. Walk trusting—even unto death. Don't let anything affect your faith. What would these words mean for you?

It's important to notice that Jesus' advice was contrary to the health and wealth doctrine, which says "*You* need to have more faith." Rather, Jesus encouraged them "to be faithful" to *Him*. The focus must be on Him, not on you or me!

In summary, Jesus' remedy for them was: (1) know what you have, (2) stop being afraid, and (3) walk according to what God has said; be faithful to Him—until death.

> and I will give you the crown of life. He who has an ear, let him hear what the Spirit says to the churches. He who overcomes shall not be hurt by the second death. 2:10b-11

TWO PROMISES

Jesus finishes His message with two promises that are future-focused. We don't like that, do we? We like promises that affect the here and now; however, if we would believe what we have in the future, our perspective of the here and now would be very different.

THE CROWN OF LIFE

This is not a king's crown, but a laurel wreath crown given to those who won the coliseum events. The people in Smyrna knew crowns; although, the saints in Smyrna probably viewed the coliseums very differently than the athletes. They weren't invited there to run in races with the possibility of the king crowning them with a laurel wreath acknowledging their strengths. No, the Smyrna saints faced the possibility of being dragged there to die.

Does everyone get the crown of life? I'm not so sure. It's not specifically promised to overcomers, but to those who are "faithful unto death." But lest you and I be discouraged, let's look at Jesus' promise in James 1:12. "Blessed is the man who endures temptation; for when he has been approved, he will receive the crown of life which the Lord has promised to those who love Him." The crown of life is promised to those who endure temptation and to those who love Him.

Answer these questions with me. Have you ever been tempted? Have you endured temptation? Then there is a crown of life awaiting you. Will there be a crown of life given for each temptation or trial you have endured? Maybe there will be jewels for each time and you can put them in your crown. Maybe you will decorate your crowns before you place them at Jesus' feet. I don't know, but I know this: Jesus knows and He knows every single time you have been faithful to Him in those hard times.

> "For God is not unjust to forget your work and labor of love which you have shown toward His name, in that you have ministered to the saints, and do minister." (Hebrews 6:10)

UNHURT BY THE SECOND DEATH

Verse 11 is a promise to all believers that we "shall not be hurt by the second death." What is the second death? Revelation 20:14-15 explains it for us, "Then Death and Hades were cast into the lake of fire. This is the second death. And anyone not found written in the Book of Life was cast into the lake of fire."

The first death is separation from the body. The second death is eternal separation from God.

Born once, die twice. Born twice (speaking of physical birth and then spiritual birth), die once.

You may, as did those in Smyrna, experience times of great pressing and crushing, but not like those who will experience the second death. This life on earth is as good as it will ever get for them. It's as bad as it will ever get for the believer.

You may experience poverty in this life, but remember the story of the rich man and Lazarus; the rich man in Hades craved just a drop of water to cool his tongue. You may experience slander, you may be lied about, you may be falsely accused, but you will never have to stand before God as an unbeliever and hear the truth about yourself.

CLOSING THOUGHTS

These are Jesus' words to His suffering church. May we remember our riches, may we stop being afraid, and may we be faithful, no matter what—even unto death.

> "And everyone who competes for the prize is temperate in all things. Now they do it to obtain a perishable crown, but we for an imperishable crown." (1 Corinthians 9:25)

REFLECTION QUESTIONS

(For more extensive study questions visit CathyDickinson.com)

1. In the message to the church at Smyrna, Jesus described Himself as "the First and the Last, who was dead, and came to life." List all of the things you learned about the significance of this title as it related to that church. ① Jesus, the only God, preexisted and goes on forever. Jesus suffered persecution and he survived it - He defeated death - He was here before all things started and he will be there after it is over.

2. What three things did Jesus see that were coming against the church at Smyrna? (2.9)
The three things coming against the church are tribulation, poverty and blasphemy.

3. Looking at verse 10, explain Jesus' purpose in allowing their suffering to intensify.
Suffering reveals a quality faith and a faith that endures.

4. Perhaps you are being "crushed" in some way now or have been in the past. Reflect on what the Lord revealed about you, to you, and through you, as a result of that crushing.

5. We can be certain about three things in our suffering. Fill in the blanks.

God is in ________________ of our suffering.

God sets the ________________ of our suffering.

God has a good ________________ in our suffering.

6. As a remedy in their suffering, Jesus told them to know "you are rich." Take some time to list the riches that you have in Christ.

7. Jesus told them, "Do not fear" as another remedy in their suffering. What is His comfort to us in our fear?

8. Jesus' final remedy in their suffering was "to be faithful." Describe what it means to be faithful or walk according to your faith. (*Take some time to ask the Lord to reveal to you anything that you may be allowing to affect your faith.*)

9. What two promises does Jesus make to the saints at Smyrna that also apply to those who are faithful unto death?

10. The message exhorts, "He who has an ear, let him hear what the Spirit says to the churches." As you read this message to the church at Smyrna, what is the Spirit saying to you personally? (If you need more room to write, use the notes section on page 62.)

Notes

Chapter Four

THE DANGER OF COMPROMISE: REVELATION 2:12-17

This is the outline for the church of Pergamos:

1. Jesus identifies the church.
2. Jesus introduces Himself.
3. Jesus tells them what pleases Him.
4. Jesus tells them what displeases Him.
5. Jesus warns them.
6. Jesus gives the remedy.
7. Jesus gives two promises.

And to the angel of the church in Pergamos write, 2:12

PERGAMOS

The city of Pergamos, or Pergamum, was not a harbor city, but it was a prosperous city. It was about forty miles north of Ephesus and about fifteen miles inland. (See map on page 23.)

Pergamos had some pretty high hills and mountains, so many of the temples were built on hilltops or mountain peaks. Pergamos was home to one of the wonders of the world, the Altar to Zeus. Zeus was known as the king of the gods. It looked like a huge throne that was built atop a high hill and was visible for fifty miles. In this reconstruction picture, it is the dominating structure of the city. [12]

Sometime in the early 1900s, the altar was excavated and brought to Germany. You may have seen films of Hitler's rallies in the Zeppelin field in Nuremburg, which was an open-air stadium used for parades. The arena had a large grandstand called the Zeppelintribüne, where the Führer emerged to hear the praise of the gathered masses. The Pergamon Altar was the model for the Zeppelintribüne. After the end of World War II, the Soviets took the Pergamon Altar to Leningrad, but it was returned to Germany in 1958. Here is a photo of the altar as it is in Germany today. [13]

Pergamos was also known for their worship of Asclepius, the god of healing. The emblem of Asclepius was a snake. [14]

At night, some of the people would go to the temple of Asclepius to be healed. In order to be cured, they had to go in and lie down as harmless snakes slithered all over the temple floor. As they slept, the snakes would crawl over their bodies and supposedly infuse them with Asclepius' healing power. The Hippocratic Oath, an oath taken by physicians to uphold specific ethical standards, originally began like this: "I swear by Apollo the Physician and by Asclepius ...." [15]

As we study Revelation, we will see many examples of Satan copying God. Asclepius is a copycat of God's work in Numbers 21 when there was a plague among the Israelites.

> "The LORD said to Moses, 'Make a fiery serpent, and set it on a pole; and it shall be that everyone who is bitten, when he looks at it, shall live.' So Moses made a bronze serpent and put it on a pole; and so it was, if a serpent had bitten anyone, when that person looked at the bronze serpent, he lived." (Numbers 21:8-9)

Jesus said this to the people: "And as Moses lifted up the serpent in the wilderness, even so must the Son of Man be lifted up, that whoever believes in Him should not perish but have eternal life" (John 3:14-15).

People, of course, still need healing. But the source of healing in the pagan minds of the people in Pergamos was not Jesus, but the snakes of the god called Asclepius. I think you can see that living in Pergamos, among a people who believed in worshiping such evil, would be rough for a believer.

> These things says He who has the sharp two-edged sword: 2:12

THE SHARP TWO-EDGED SWORD

Keep in mind, as Jesus identifies Himself to the churches, He is reminding them of something the church has lost sight of. For the church at Pergamos, He chose this description: He who has "a sharp two-edged sword" (from Revelation 1:16). This does not speak of the four- to five-inch sword used for close fighting referred to in Hebrews, "For the word of God is living and powerful, and sharper than any two-edged sword, piercing even to the division of soul and spirit, and of joints and marrow, and is a discerner of the thoughts and intents of the heart" (Hebrews 4:12).

This sword in Revelation 2 is thought to have been up to five feet long, designed to cause great damage. Speaking of the Messiah, Isaiah wrote this: "And He has made My mouth like a sharp sword" (Isaiah 49:2).

Under the Hebrew definition of this "sword" mentioned in Isaiah 49:2, Dr. Spiros Zodhiates wrote this: "The cutting action of a sword is likened to eating, and its edges are literally referred to as mouths. Similarly, the mouths of people are likened to swords." [16] Swords were often used to speak of God's judgment for the elimination of what was bad. Jesus reminds the church in Pergamos that He has this very big sword and He will use it if He must.

> I know your works, and where you dwell, where Satan's throne is. 2:13

PLEASING JESUS

Jesus referred to Pergamos as the place "where Satan's throne is" and "where Satan dwells." So it's safe to assume that Satan had a real hook in this city. Looking at the picture of the Pergamon Altar, certainly this could be the reason why Jesus titled it

"Satan's throne." Even the original Hippocratic Oath, an oath sworn by Asclepius, was certainly something we would call satanic.

Jesus knew what they were up against and He knows what you are up against—not just culturally—but what you are up against in your home, in your workplace, in your school, wherever you are. He knows. You may feel that Satan dwells in your place, and that may be so, but Jesus knows.

> And you hold fast to My name, 2:13

The saints at Pergamos held on to who Jesus is. They were not swayed. Could someone convince you that Jesus isn't the Savior, the Redeemer, the King of kings and Lord of lords, or anything else the Bible declares about Him? It is important to Jesus that we believe He is who He declares Himself to be and hold fast to His name.

> and did not deny My faith even in the days in which Antipas was My faithful martyr, who was killed among you, where Satan dwells. 2:13

Now we don't know a lot about Antipas—really, we know nothing for sure. Tradition tells us that John ordained Antipas as the bishop (or pastor) of Pergamos.

Some of the history books depict a hollow bronze bull with a door on one side. When a person was condemned, they were locked inside, and a fire was set under it, heating the metal until the person inside roasted to death. [17]

It is believed that Antipas died in this way. All we know for certain is that Jesus called Antipas His "faithful martyr." *Martyr* is translated as "witness" in other places in the Bible. The emphasis isn't so much that Antipas died faithfully, though it certainly seems like he did, but rather Jesus is pointing out that Antipas was a witness to others who *lived* faithfully—in the city where Satan dwelled.

The believers at Pergamos did not deny His faith. If someone asked them if they were Christians or if they were followers of Jesus, they had no problem in saying yes. Jesus liked that. He still does.

> But I have a few things against you, because you have there those who hold the doctrine of Balaam, who taught Balak to put a stumbling block before the children of Israel, to eat things sacrificed to idols, and to commit sexual immorality. 2:14

WHAT DISPLEASES JESUS

A little three-letter contrasting word starts verse 14, "But." Jesus had a few things against them. They were faithful to claim Him, but they were still a people of compromise. Jesus points out that there are those among them that are holding on to something else in addition—the doctrine of Balaam.

THE DOCTRINE OF BALAAM

When the children of Israel were trekking through the desert, they would have to travel through areas inhabited by other nations. They would ask nicely if they could pass through, promising no harm. But all too often, some of the nations didn't believe them and attacked Israel. Each time, these nations lost.

When the Israelites came to the land of Moab, Balak, the king of Moab, knew of their reputation and knew he would not be able to defeat them through standard military might. So Balak sent messengers to a prophet named Balaam. Now if you've studied this story at all, you probably have wondered why God would speak to a man like Balaam. You probably wouldn't rank him as one of God's godly men. Sometimes I think that the only reason God speaks to me is that I will be faithful to say what He has said. That seems to be the only godly thing Balaam had going for him. He said what God told him to say. He had high standards about that.

King Balak asked Balaam the prophet to curse Israel, but instead Balaam spoke God's words of blessing. He had warned Balak, "I can only say what God says." Even still, King Balak continued to ask Balaam to curse Israel, accompanied with offers of financial gain. So Balaam would take the wages and ask the Lord to curse Israel again, but without fail, the Lord would answer with blessings upon them.

Balaam the prophet is associated with loving the wages of unrighteousness and greed. "They have forsaken the right way and gone astray, following the way of Balaam the son of Beor, who loved the wages of unrighteousness" (2 Peter 2:15), and "Woe to them! For they have … run greedily in the error of Balaam for profit" (Jude 11).

What are wages of unrighteousness? Essentially it is the initial payoff of money or some other benefit—even fear—to compromise. You see, like the believers in Pergamos,

Balaam held on to the things of God. But because of his greed, he tried to find ways around what God had said. Balaam was a compromiser.

A STUMBLING BLOCK

So Balaam, knowing that King Balak could never defeat God's strength upon Israel, came up with an idea to weaken the nation of Israel. Balaam advised the king to send the Moabite women into Israel's camp to seduce the Israelites.

> "Now Israel remained in Acacia Grove, and the people began to commit harlotry with the women of Moab. They invited the people to the sacrifices of their gods, and the people ate and bowed down to their gods. So Israel was joined to Baal of Peor, and the anger of the Lord was aroused against Israel." (Numbers 25:1-3)

God is a holy God, a jealous God. When God saw the children of Israel committing harlotry and idolatry, He was forced in His righteousness to bring a judgment against them. King Balak did exactly as the prophet Balaam advised, and overnight God sent a plague that killed 24,000 (Numbers 25:9).

WHAT'S A STUMBLING BLOCK?

Look at Revelation 2:14 again. What did Balaam do? "Balaam taught Balak to put a stumbling block before the children of Israel." In this case it was sexual immorality and idolatry. Do you know what a stumbling block is? The Greek word is *skandalon.* It's where we get our English word *scandal. Skandalon* is "the trigger of a trap on which the bait is placed, and which, when touched by the animal, springs and causes it to close causing entrapment." *Skandalon* always denotes an enticement to conduct, which could ruin the person in question. [18] The Israelites didn't see the Moabite women as a trigger of a trap. They didn't know their idolatry was a trap that would lead to their ruin. Do you know what triggers are placed before you? Do you think you can handle them? Think again.

Interestingly, in the story of Balaam, as Balaam was riding his donkey to meet with King Balak, the Angel of the Lord appeared to him with a sword, and told Balaam that his way was perverse before God (Numbers 22:22-32). There is a very good chance that this Angel of the Lord with the sword was Jesus.

COMPROMISE IS A STUMBLING BLOCK

Just before Israel went into the Promised Land, God instructed them to kill those who dwelt in the land. Harsh instructions, you might think, but these people in the land were evil. God knew their immorality would cause His people to compromise. God so loves His people that He is intent on protecting us. Yet Israel allowed the people to live and many times allowed them to become their slaves. And it happened just as God said it would, the gods of the people became objects of worship to Israel—Israel even offered their children in sacrifices to idols. Do you think they would have done that if they hadn't been exposed to it? This is a good illustration of what a stumbling block looks like.

It is important to notice that Jesus' focus was not on those who held the doctrine of Balaam. He doesn't even address them. What Jesus had against the church in Pergamos was that they *had among them* "those who held the doctrine of Balaam." It's as if Jesus walked among the church in Pergamos and stopped to declare, "What are these people doing here? Why are you allowing this?" The church in Pergamos still held on to God's name and even His faith, but they compromised by allowing those who committed sexual immorality and idolatry.

HOW MUCH COMPROMISE?

How accepting are you of those who live according to the ways of the world—the ways of the world that God has specifically declared as sin? Now I'm not talking about those gray areas of opinion. I am talking about what God has clearly declared as sin.

Recently, our ten-year-old grandson was talking to me about Halloween. He said, "My mom said you didn't allow her to go trick-or-treating when she was little, is that right?" I admitted it. When Dylan asked why, I found myself explaining that moms and dads try to do the best they can at the time and that was something a lot of Christians believed. I told him that if I had it to do over again, I would let them dress up and go door to door in our neighborhood saying, "Trick or treat." I did clarify that I would not let them wear any type of evil costumes, as I believe that's making light of who the devil is and what he does. What I'm saying is, things like that are opinions and believers fall on both sides of the fence on that one.

But it's clear that Jesus has something against us if we accept sin, or those living a lifestyle of idolatry and sexual immorality in our churches. And certainly if they are not to be accepted in the church, they should not be accepted in our personal lives.

As an individual believer, are you like those in Pergamos who don't sway in what you say you believe, but allow in sexual immorality and idolatry through music, television, and movies? God will not turn His head. And do you think the church can handle it? Jesus doesn't. He knows that "a little leaven leavens (affects) the whole lump" (Galatians 5:9); it grows, it permeates. The church is called to love; the church is not called to accept sin. We the church, God's people, can bring judgment against ourselves if we allow sexual immorality and idolatry into our lives. In doing so, we will force God, because of His holy nature, to chastise us.

> Thus you also have those who hold the doctrine of the Nicolaitans, which thing I hate. 2:15

ALLOWING ERROR IN THE CHURCH

Now Jesus praised the church of Ephesus for *hating* the deeds of the Nicolaitans. The church of Pergamos *had* those who were of the doctrine of the Nicolaitans, which implies they allowed those in the church. The church in Ephesus *hated* them (their deeds); the church in Pergamos *had* them. Before we consider banning people who disagree to be part of the church, we need to remember that these people Jesus is referring to are negatively affecting others. They are not there seeking the truth, they are swaying others from it.

The word *Nicolaitans* comes from two words meaning "to conquer" and "the people." It has the sense of setting up the clergy over the congregation, telling the people what to do—not just what the Bible says, but in other areas of life. Many people are drawn to that because they love it when you make their decisions for them. Often it's just a form of spiritual laziness. "Tell me what to do, so I don't have to seek God."

It's not a slam on the Catholic Church; there have been Protestant cults guilty of what is called "shepherding the people." It is a form of setting up someone who dictates the decisions of the people's everyday lives.

Do you see why Jesus would hate that? It puts someone between Him and His own. It keeps His people from knowing the wonder of being personally led by Him. In a nutshell, it displeased Jesus that the church in Pergamos was allowing error in the church. And He told them to repent.

Repent, 2:16

CONFESS AND REPENT

Repent is mentioned twelve times in the book of Revelation. The first eight times are in the messages to the seven churches, though not every church was told to repent; only those Jesus had something against. The other four times are during the times of tribulation when, in spite of God's warnings and in spite of God pouring out His wrath, still people did not repent.

When we read of God's call to repentance, it seems to me that His concentration is not so much on the sin we've committed, but on what we do afterwards. God responds to repentance. But before repentance comes confession. The two must go together. Confession is agreeing with God before you can repent, before you can change direction. This is the remedy.

Jesus was calling these believers in Pergamos to agree with Him. He hated what Balaam did. He hated the deeds of the Nicolaitans. The believers in Pergamos didn't. Rather, they allowed what God hated to be right there in their midst while they were worshiping Him, giving an impression of acceptance that God doesn't give.

So in the case of Pergamos, what would confession entail? It would entail agreeing with God that it's not right to compromise by showing acceptance to things that He hates. What would that confession entail for us? For you?

WHAT GOD HATES

Here is a list of things the LORD hates from Proverbs 6:16-19: "These six things the LORD hates, yes, seven are an abomination to Him:

1. A proud look
2. A lying tongue
3. Hands that shed innocent blood
4. A heart that devises wicked plans
5. Feet that are swift in running to evil
6. A false witness who speaks lies, and
7. One who sows discord among brethren."

What about you personally? What are you tolerating or excusing in your own life? Jesus calls you to confess—agree and see the sin as He does. If you don't, you won't repent. You won't change. If you doubt that you can see your sin as God sees it, ask Him every day to show you what He sees about your sin that you don't see.

After confessing your sin, you are to repent—turn around. Go back toward the things of God and away from the things designed to trap you, ruin you, or pull you in the wrong direction. Repentance is: If I had it to do over again, I would choose otherwise—no matter what. The message is if you tolerate sin in or around your life, sin will eventually get you.

> or else I will come to you quickly and will fight against them with the sword of My mouth. 2:16

JESUS MEANS IT!

Following the word *repent* are the words *or else*. That's a threat, isn't it? But it's not an empty threat. Jesus means it and He is more than able to carry it out.

Jesus warns them and us to repent or else He will come quickly and will fight against them with the sword of His mouth. Judge them, deal with them, or Jesus will.

In James 4:4, Jesus called those who seek avenues of pleasure other than Himself adulterers and adulteresses. Then He says to them, "Do you not know that friendship with the world is enmity with God?" These are strong words.

We are encouraged again to deal with sin in 1 Peter 4:17. "For the time has come for judgment to begin at the house of God; and if it begins with us first, what will be the end of those who do not obey the gospel of God?"

Have you ever had someone say to you, "Take care of it or I will and you don't want me to step in here"? As Jesus challenged the church in Pergamos regarding those they allowed among them, the One with the sharp two-edged sword reminded them that He is the ultimate Judge.

> He who has an ear, let him hear what the Spirit says to the churches. 2:17

As we look at what Jesus has to say to the Pergamos saints, we certainly can see that each of us is bombarded with the things of this world in one way or another.

You see, these messages, although they contain corrections, are for those who desire God's will in their lives. Isaiah 51 has phrases in it like, "Listen to Me, you who follow after righteousness, you who seek the LORD," "Listen to Me, My people; and give ear to Me, O My nation," and "Listen to Me, you who know righteousness" (vv. 1, 4, 7). This is very similar to what Jesus said to each of these churches in Revelation: "He who has an ear, let him hear what the Spirit says to the churches." Listen!

These letters are written to those who follow after righteousness, who seek the Lord, and who know righteousness. I loved basking in this. Even when our walk is good with the Lord, we still need reminding. We always will. We live in a world that relates to things much differently than the Lord would have us to, and we can't live lives totally exclusive of this world. Remember in the upper room when Jesus washed the disciples' feet? It was to get the daily grime off. If He doesn't wash us daily, you and I can look as dirty and grimy as the rest of the world, even though our sins have been forgiven. These letters were not written to terrible Christians. They were primarily written to Christians who really did want to do well.

His word in Isaiah 51 was a word of comfort. It was a word reminding the church in Pergamos to look up to Him. It was a word reminding His people that the things of this world and the thinking of this world are temporary, but the things of the Lord are forever. It was a word reminding them that He alone is the One who comforts them and not to be afraid.

The idea of personal Christianity is great when each of us comes to church, closes our eyes, worships the Lord, and hears the message for how it applies to us personally. And of course, all that is very good. But the challenge is, how many of us also have the sense of worshiping and receiving as a church, as a body of believers, as a family responsible to the Lord?

When leading worship, our son, Tim, would often have us sing "we" instead of "I." I have to admit that I think I tend to worship as "I" because I love to think it's just me and the Lord. And, as I said, that's good. But may we also have a sense of worshiping Him and learning of Him together. What the Spirit has to say in these letters is for "he who has ears to hear." Whoever "has ears to hear" is not only to apply the message to himself or herself, but also to keep in mind this message is to each church—each body of believers. Do you have a sense of "we"? Do you need to cultivate that more?

The value of body encouragement is priceless. It is so important that we realize we are not alone in our struggles, but we are to stand strong together and avoid compromises together. It is so much easier to avoid compromising when others are fighting it too, isn't it?

> To him who overcomes I will give some of the hidden manna to eat. And I will give him a white stone, and on the stone a new name written which no one knows except him who receives it. 2:17

The message concludes with two amazing promises. They both apply to this life on earth for the believer and our lives in heaven. If we stop compromising in this life, we will get to enjoy it now.

HIDDEN MANNA

Jesus said, "To him who overcomes I will give some of the hidden manna to eat." What is hidden manna? Looking at other references in the Bible, manna was like white coriander seed (cilantro is green coriander). Its taste was as "wafers made with honey." It was God's way of supplying the physical needs for Israel while they were traveling to the Promised Land. Moses was told to take some of it and keep it in the ark, to be kept for generations (Exodus 16:31-32).

Referring to the manna, Jesus challenged, "Most assuredly, I say to you, Moses did not give you the bread from heaven, but My Father gives you the true bread from heaven. For the bread of God is He who comes down from heaven and gives life to the world" (John 6:32-33). Jesus continued, "I am the bread of life. He who comes to Me shall never hunger, and he who believes in Me shall never thirst" (John 6:35).

In the Old Testament, manna was their physical food. In the new covenant, Jesus is our spiritual food. When manna was eaten, it became part of them and they physically benefited from its properties. When we belong to Jesus, He comes in and permeates our lives. An uncompromising life enjoys the spiritual benefits. All overcomers get this—because all overcomers are believers; those who overcome in this life get to experience Him. We miss out on this when we compromise, because we look to other things and other people to sustain and refresh us.

When the people heard Jesus declare that He was the "bread of life," many walked away; they didn't want Him. They wanted that which would fill them physically. What about you? What do you spend most of your efforts trying to fill? Your flesh or your soul? To the one who overcomes—Jesus will fill.

A WHITE STONE

Then we have the second promise: "I will give him a white stone, and on the stone a new name written which no one knows except him who receives it." There are a few guesses as to what Jesus meant here. It would have been clearer to the believers at the time.

When a victor won in the games, it was common for him to be given a white stone as part of his prize. It was his pass or his admission to the festival that was held following the games, kind of like a ticket. Their name would be written on the stone.

The other possibility applied to a courtroom. Each member of the jury would be given a black stone and a white stone. Depending on whether they believed the defendant to be guilty or innocent, they would vote by placing a black or a white stone in the bag. If the majority voted innocent, the judge would give the defendant a white stone. Either way, the white stone seems to represent acceptance and admission.

What is the name on your stone? I don't know. "No one knows except him or her who receives it." When you receive it, you will know. It will be so personal from the One who knows how we have lived as we journeyed through this life. I can't wait!

CLOSING THOUGHTS

Jesus has declared that all overcomers and all believers are innocent and free of punishment and welcomes them to His great feast in heaven. May you and I be like Jesus, the One who freely accepts all who come to Him and rejects those who do not, making it clear, any stumbling blocks will not be tolerated.

Is the Word of God your standard? Anything short of that is compromise.

REFLECTION QUESTIONS

(For more extensive study questions visit CathyDickinson.com)

1. Jesus identifies Himself to the church at Pergamos as "He who has the sharp two-edged sword." What does this title mean and how does it apply to the church and individual believers today? Jesus comes with a large sword, often used for judgment. The sword would be used to eliminate what is bad.

2. Jesus encouraged the church at Pergamos that He knows "where they dwell." What does it mean to you that Jesus knows where you dwell, He knows your life circumstances, and knows what you are up against? Jesus knows we live in the world, a place dominated by the enemy of the believer, satan. We must remain in Him at all cost. We must live faithful to Jesus.

3. Although Jesus saw that they "held fast to His name," it displeased Him that they compromised by having among them those who held "the doctrine of Balaam." Describe the compromise this represents. Not upholding God's word or standards - a greater desire for financial or worldly rewards. Since cursing the Israelites did not work, Balaam urged the king to send women to lead them into sexual sin and idolatry.

4. The Pergamos church was guilty of compromise. One way this comes about is as a result of exposure to the wrong things. Take a moment to ask the Lord to search you and shed His light on any area of compromise in your life—what are you tolerating or excusing? Now agree with Him by confessing it below. Lord I am lazy and not much of a prayer warrior. I can be gluttonous and waste time - please cause reformation. I also argue and I am ~~self seeking~~ - please strengthen me to correct my ways for you

5. In your own words, explain what the doctrine of the Nicolaitans is and why Jesus hated this. It is rules and rulers who tell the people what to do - sometimes not lining up with scripture. The ~~people~~ became lazy and did not seek God on their own.

6. What was Jesus' remedy for the church of Pergamos?
Confess and repent 5 Jesus declaration to the church of Pergamos.

7. Jesus warned them to deal with the compromise in the church "or else." What was the warning? He will come quickly and fight against them with the sword of His mouth

8. The message to the Pergamos saints concludes with two promises. The first is that He will give the overcomer "some of the hidden manna to eat." What does this represent to us as believers? The Lord's provision for His saints.- Jesus is our provision - an uncompromised life enjoys spiritual benefits - Jesus will fill us.

9. The second promise Jesus makes is that overcomers will receive "a white stone, and on the stone a new name" that only the receiver knows. What does this represent for the believer? The white stone represents acceptance, innocence and admission to Him. Only the Lord knows our new name.

10. "He who has an ear, let him hear what the Spirit says to the churches." Summarize what the Spirit is saying to you personally through this study of the message to the church in Pergamos. Focus, keep my eyes on Jesus. Live for Him and do NOT compromise. Use your time well - Live for Him.

Chapter Five

ALLOWING JEZEBELS: REVELATION 2:18-29

Although the city of Thyatira was probably the most insignificant of the cities addressed, Jesus' message to its church is the longest of the seven messages.

This is the outline for the church of Thyatira:

1. Jesus identifies the church.
2. Jesus introduces Himself.
3. Jesus tells them what pleases Him.
4. Jesus tells them what displeases Him.
5. Jesus rebukes them.
6. Jesus gives the remedy.
7. Jesus gives two promises.

To the angel of the church in Thyatira write, (2:18)

THYATIRA

Before we read Jesus' message to the church in Thyatira, it is important that we understand the thinking behind the overriding moral standards of this city.

Thyatira was famous for the manufacture of a purple dye. Acts 16 provides the account of Paul, who, in obedience to the vision calling him to go to Macedonia, met and shared the gospel with a woman named Lydia. Lydia was a "seller of purple from the city of Thyatira" (Acts 16:14). Many believe that it was Lydia who brought the gospel to Thyatira and thus began the church there, almost forty-five years prior to the writing of this letter. (See map on page 23.)

There are numerous secular references to the period of the trade guilds that manufactured cloth in Thyatira. Thyatira was dominated by guilds, or what we would call today unions, and possessed more trade guilds than any other town of its size in Asia. If not part of a guild, it would have been difficult to run a business or to be employed.

The trade guilds would gather to meet and worship pagan gods. This meeting consisted of a common meal that would begin with pouring out wine and ended the same way. The pouring of wine symbolized prayer. The meetings would begin and end in tribute to their gods and idols, degenerating into sexual immorality and debauchery.

THE CHURCH IN THYATIRA

The seeming dilemma to the believer was the need to survive financially, yet live in a way that did not compromise their commitment to God. Certainly this was the challenge the Thyatira believers faced: how much could they join in when it came to the ways of Thyatira and still be okay with God?

Those questions make this letter to the church of Thyatira pertinent to each of us. Although our dilemma is not that of serving idols, it is how do we live in a world with standards so diametrically opposed to the life of a Christian without being spotted or influenced by their behavior? The unbelieving world shouts to us the need for tolerance and compromise. Jesus refuses to use those words in His message.

One ancient Christian named Tertullian wrote about believers who made their living in trades connected to pagan idolatry. A painter might find work in pagan temples or a sculptor might be hired to make a statue of a pagan god, and then justify it by saying, "This is my living, and I must live." Tertullian replied, "*Vivere ergo habes?*" "Must you live?"

The challenge is not whether we should work in a pagan environment. The challenge is, when the reason for doing what we do becomes a justification that is contrary to God's will, we need to examine our choices.

> These things says the Son of God, who has eyes like a flame of fire, and His feet like fine brass: 2:18

Jesus introduces Himself with three descriptions, basically taken from Revelation 1:13-15, one detail from each verse.

SON OF GOD

Unlike the description given to all seven churches in Revelation 1, Jesus used the phrase "Son of God," not "Son of Man," in His message to the church in Thyatira. This is an important distinction. Although Jesus qualifies for both titles, "Son of God" is the one that the church in Thyatira needed to be mindful of as He was deliberately emphasizing His deity.

In Jewish thought, to be the son of something meant you had the nature of that thing. Isaiah 57:3 says, "But come here, you sons of the sorceress, you offspring of the adulterer and the harlot!" Those being addressed as "sons of the sorceress" were being labeled as having the nature of a sorcerer. Jesus referred to James and John in Mark 3:17 as "sons of thunder," indicating they had a nature like thunder.

Here in His message to Thyatira, Jesus wanted the church to understand that the One addressing them is the Son of God and therefore had all the attributes and powers of God; that it was God Himself who was concerned for their ways.

EYES LIKE A FLAME OF FIRE

Jesus' eyes observe with penetrating judgment. He misses nothing and He misinterprets nothing. We often get distracted. In our own lives, we can easily fall prey to placing too much emphasis on either the good we do or the bad, and let one override the other. Jesus doesn't do that. He sees it all and He sees the value or the destructiveness of an action exactly as it is.

To clarify, Jesus sees those who belong to Him as righteous. But His eyes are watching our actions and behaviors, judging them as good or destructive. Keep this in mind as you consider His message to each church. We, as believers, are His beloved bride. Our status before Him has been settled. It's our actions and behavior that He approves or condemns. It's our choices that determine the effectiveness of our lives on this earth and the blessings or rewards we will enjoy in heaven.

FEET LIKE FINE BRASS

Jesus chose this description of Himself to emphasize His purity. He is not mixed with any other influences. Having "feet like brass" denotes His steadfastness, His immovability. Oh, how the church in Thyatira needed to be reminded of the importance of steadfastness.

> "Therefore, my beloved brethren, be steadfast, immovable, always abounding in the work of the Lord, knowing that your labor is not in vain in the Lord." (1 Corinthians 15:58)

As we will see in a few verses, the church in Thyatira was known for its work "in the Lord," but their witness had been compromised by their choice to *allow* the influences of "Jezebel." They did not realize the vanity of some of their labor.

JESUS STANDS

The Son of God is not a mere idol. The One with feet like brass—stands! Stand the things of this world up against Jesus. The prophet Isaiah challenged Israel to compare God to idols:

> "To whom then will you liken God? Or what likeness will you compare to Him? The workman molds an image, the goldsmith overspreads it with gold, and the silversmith casts silver chains. Whoever is too impoverished for such a contribution chooses a tree that will not rot; he seeks for himself a skillful workman to prepare a carved image that will not totter." (Isaiah 40:18-20)

I love that word *totter*! The skillful workman labors to carve an image that will not totter—that won't fall over.

IDOLS FALL

After the Philistines captured the ark of God, they set it by the statute of Dagon, in the house of their god.

> "And when the people of Ashdod arose early in the morning, there was Dagon, fallen on its face to the earth before the ark of the LORD. So they took Dagon and set

> it in its place again. And when they arose early the next morning, there was Dagon, fallen on its face to the ground before the ark of the LORD. The head of Dagon and both the palms of its hands were broken off on the threshold; only Dagon's torso was left of it." (1 Samuel 5:3-4)

Whoever made that idol of Dagon couldn't seem to make it strong enough to prevent it from toppling before the ark of God.

Oh how we, sadly, need to be reminded that our God has feet of brass; that our God will not topple before any god. Therefore, neither should we. I mean, isn't that what happens to us? We allow some worldly compromise, thinking we can handle it, thinking we can stand, thinking that our walk or relationship with the Lord will survive; and suddenly, we find ourselves toppling over. We find ourselves influenced by that which we thought we could stand just a little bit of in our lives, and soon we are unable to stand at all.

As we shall soon discover, Jesus rebuked the church in Thyatira because He had so much better for them, because Jezebel-type thinking corrupts and it makes our witness fall apart.

> I know your works, love, service, faith, and your patience; and as for your works, the last are more than the first. Nevertheless 2:19-20

NEVERTHELESS

Jesus acknowledged that the church in Thyatira had five really good things going for them. They had love, service, faith, patience, and their works were getting better instead of worse. Those are all very good things. *Nevertheless* there was something going on in their midst that Jesus had against them.

As I consider my life, I think that most would have described me as a good person, maybe even a caring person. I knew the rules and I followed them. I obeyed my parents and those in authority. I earned good grades in school and was kind to my friends. But there was a *nevertheless* in my life. I was cruel to my younger sister. I mistakenly felt justified. But to Jesus, it was a *nevertheless.*

One time I hit my sister on her head, right where she had a barrette. The points of the barrette spiked into her scalp and caused an immense amount of blood. I panicked, not because of fear of what might happen to my sister, but fear of what might happen to me. My mother considered my good deeds and overlooked what I had done. But I knew it needed to be addressed, knowing my good deeds couldn't make my wrong right.

Jesus knows that too. He cannot ignore our wrong choices. It would not be love if He did. Our wrong choices detrimentally affect us and they affect others.

DISOBEDIENCE

In His message to the church in Thyatira, the Lord addressed the problem of disobedience in His children. Even if most areas of our Christian life are in line with His will, this doesn't mean He will overlook those that are not. The point at which we knowingly disobey God is exactly where our faith needs to be reexamined. Our Father is patient and understanding, yet He takes our unfaithfulness seriously. In the matter of spiritual growth, the issue is not just what I am doing right, but also what I am doing wrong. There is no amount of good works that can make up for impure living. Many say "the end justifies the means." Jesus doesn't. The reasons behind what we do for the Lord matter to Him. The things we allow in our churches and in our lives also matter.

Is there a *nevertheless* in your life? Is there something that, in spite of the good you are doing, is provoking the Son of God, who has eyes like a flame of fire and feet like fine brass, to say to you, "Nevertheless"?

> I have a few things against you, because you allow 2:20

YOU ALLOW

Jesus' words to Thyatira were, "because you allow." This displeased Him. Soak in this definition of *allow*: permit, do not restrain, give up to, leave alone, fail to hinder.

Speaking of being ready for His coming, Jesus warned,

> "But know this, that if the master of the house had known what hour the thief would come, he would have watched and not allowed his house to be broken into." (Matthew 24:43)

Have you allowed your house (your life) to be broken into, to be influenced by and subjected to ways that are not God's choice for you?

Interestingly, this word translated *allow* is used in 1 Corinthians 10:13.

> "No temptation has overtaken you except such as is common to man; but God is faithful, who will not allow you to be tempted beyond what you are able, but with the temptation will also make the way of escape, that you may be able to bear it."

God will not allow you or I to be tempted beyond what we are able. So when we allow other influences, we have done just that—we have allowed them into our lives. We are without excuse.

As we look at the specifics of what some in the church of Thyatira allowed, don't lose sight of this word *allow*.

> that woman Jezebel, who calls herself a prophetess, 2:20

JEZEBEL

Jezebel was the most evil woman written about in the Old Testament. We can find most of her story in 1 Kings 16-21. She was the daughter of the king of Sidon. She married Ahab, the king of Israel, bringing with her the worship of idols, especially the worship of the god Baal.

The practice of Baal worship first infiltrated Jewish religious life during the time of the Judges and became widespread in Israel during the reign of Ahab and Jezebel. Baal was a fertility god who was believed to enable the earth to produce crops and people to produce children. Baal worshipers viewed him as a highly adaptable god as the people vainly sought him for different benefits. At times, Baal worshipers believed that appeasing their god required human sacrifice, usually the firstborn of the one making the sacrifice. [19]

> "And it came to pass, as though it had been a trivial thing for him to walk in the sins of Jeroboam the son of Nebat, that he took as wife Jezebel the daughter of Ethbaal, king of the Sidonians; and he went and served Baal and worshiped him. Then he set up an altar for Baal in the temple of Baal, which he had built in Samaria. And Ahab made a wooden image. Ahab did more to provoke the LORD God of Israel to anger than all the kings of Israel who were before him." (1 Kings 16:31-33)

Ahab's sin? He sold himself to do wickedness.

> "But there was no one like Ahab who sold himself to do wickedness in the sight of the LORD, because Jezebel his wife stirred him up." (1 Kings 21:25)

This phrase *sold himself* has the sense of exchanging one thing for another.

In Proverbs 23:23 we are cautioned, "Buy the truth, and do not sell it, also wisdom and instruction and understanding." Don't sell out. Don't exchange the wisdom and instruction and understanding of God for anything!

Ahab sold out in his values; he sold out in his responsibility to God. Why? Because Jezebel stirred him up.

Stirred is a verb meaning to "incite, to entice, to mislead." It has the sense of stirring up persons with the intention to get them to deviate, to act with destructive, harmful purposes in mind; to incite people to be evil, and to lead them astray. What an incredibly accurate portrayal of Satan's intentions for us.

The sin of the church in Thyatira appears to be the same as Ahab's sin—allowing Jezebel to stir them to deviate from what God had commanded. Remember, the believers in Thyatira were in a tough place. They belonged to trade guilds that highly encouraged sexual immorality and idol worship. Furthermore, there was a prevalent doctrine by religious leaders at the time teaching that their body and their spirit were separate. What they did with their body had nothing to do with their spirit. Just do whatever to get by in this world. What a freeing message that must have been, or rather, an ear-tickling one.

Jesus warned His followers: "Beware of false prophets, who come to you in sheep's clothing, but inwardly they are ravenous wolves" (Matthew 7:15).

REBUKED

Jesus warned; forty-five years later He rebuked. He rebuked His people for allowing false prophets among them rather than being alert to their destruction.

> "For the time will come when they will not endure sound doctrine, but according to their own desires, because they have itching ears, they will heap up for themselves teachers; and they will turn their ears away from the truth, and be turned aside to fables." (2 Timothy 4:3-4)

Thus we have Jesus' rebuke to the church in Thyatira. They "allowed" the message that scratched their ears, the message that was "according to their own desires."

> to teach and seduce My servants to commit sexual immorality and eat things sacrificed to idols. 2:20

MY SERVANTS

Look at the two words that precede the words "to commit sexual immorality and eat things sacrificed to idols." See them? "My servants." These are possessive words. Jezebel was seducing the servants of Jesus. These were not unsaved people in the church. She was teaching Jesus' beloved ones to commit sin. And Jesus didn't like it. Nor did He like that His servants were allowing her the power to take them down. Yes, there was love, service, faith, patience, and increased good works. "Nevertheless," there was sin in the camp and Jesus let them know that He was not going to tolerate it. This is dangerous territory.

SEXUAL IMMORALITY

In the church in Corinth, "sexual immorality" had been reported among them, and Paul rebuked, "Your glorying is not good. Do you not know that a little leaven leavens the whole lump" (1 Corinthians 5:6)? They should have been mourning over such sin. In his loving protection of the church, Paul exhorted them to judge the sin, lest that sin permeate others.

Jezebel's teaching had permeated the church in Thyatira and they, like the believers in Corinth, were allowing her sin.

EATING THINGS OFFERED TO IDOLS

About the eating of things offered to idols, Paul wrote: "Therefore concerning the eating of things offered to idols, we know that an idol is nothing in the world, and that there is no other God but one" (1 Corinthians 8:4).

Consider a rabbit's foot. You know that it has no power. But if you carry one, your message to others says it does.

> "But beware lest somehow this liberty of yours become a stumbling block to those who are weak. For if anyone sees you who have knowledge eating in an idol's temple, will not the conscience of him who is weak be emboldened to eat those things offered to idols? And because of your knowledge shall the weak brother perish, for whom

> Christ died? But when you thus sin against the brethren, and wound their weak conscience, you sin against Christ. Therefore, if food makes my brother stumble, I will never again eat meat, lest I make my brother stumble." (1 Corinthians 8:9-13)

When the church participated in these trade guild meetings, eating meat sacrificed to idols was only the beginning of their debauchery in these pagan celebrations. Jesus clearly states that these practices were sin; thus, they were not to be allowed.

And I gave her time to repent of her sexual immorality, 2:21

Jesus, in His loving mercy, gave this Jezebel time to repent. I love that. He didn't immediately judge her. As evil and destructive as she was, Jesus gave her time to repent. This word *time* speaks of a measured period or space of time. He does the same for us. But take heed; you and I don't know how long that space of time will be. We don't know the day that God will say enough and judgment will come; chastisement will be at our door—no longer knocking but entering the premises of our lives.

and she did not repent. 2:21

More literally, "but she does not want to repent." That's the same reason we don't repent. We don't want to. We can make excuses and greatly justify, but the fact is, we do not repent because we do not want to. We may even think we've sinned beyond forgiveness or just gone too far or sinned too much, but the bottom line is, we don't want to change.

WANTING SOMETHING ELSE

Mark 5 recounts the time when Jesus went to the country of the Gadarenes. When He came out of the boat, a man with an unclean spirit met Him. No one could bind him, not even with chains. Neither could anyone tame him—except Jesus.

Jesus cast the demons, which had tormented this man, into about 2,000 swine who ran violently down the steep place into the sea and drowned. And what was the people's response to this miracle of Jesus: "Then they began to plead with Him to depart from their region" (Mark 5:17).

The people didn't want Jesus among them. Maybe it was the loss of income from the demise of the swine. We don't really know. But they didn't want Jesus. They wanted something else.

This Jezebel of Thyatira wanted something else. The people who were seduced by her wanted something else. The people that allowed her teaching wanted something else. It doesn't matter what that something was.

The question to us is, "What do you want?" Do you want Jesus? Do you fully and entirely want Jesus? Or do you want something else too—in addition to Jesus? Do you want something that Jesus has forbidden? That's the spirit of Jezebel. It's disbelieving God when He wants to make a change in our lives that it is always a good change.

The spirit of Jezebel does not want to change or repent. May the Lord touch the hearts of those who read this chapter and convict of stubbornness and rebellion to His will.

> Indeed I will cast her into a sickbed, and those who commit adultery with her into great tribulation, unless they repent of their deeds. I will kill her children with death, 2:22-23

JUDGMENT

Judgment came upon Jezebel not after her sin, but after her refusal to repent of her sin.

The word *indeed* has the meaning of "for sure." The Greek word used here for *bed* is also the word for a banqueting couch; and thus, we may understand Jesus to mean that He will strike her down as she sits at her forbidden feasts—along with those who follow her and who are spiritual offspring of her heresy and compromise.

One of the characteristics of the Jezebel of the Old Testament was that she was able to surround herself with followers who supported her and actually performed many of her wicked schemes for her. The Jezebel of the church of Thyatira was able to do the same. The Jezebel of the Old Testament was able to convince men that her ways were not evil, thus they allowed her godlessness. The parallels in Jesus' message to the church in Thyatira are surely notable.

Be sure to also note that God is still seeking repentance and not judgment. He always does. You and I need to remember that awesome truth when we fall prey to believing that His goal is to punish or reject us.

> and all the churches shall know that I am He who searches the minds and hearts. And I will give to each one of you according to your works. 2:23

JESUS SEARCHES OUR HEARTS

Throughout the Old Testament if the people did not repent, God warned them of impending judgment, and then concluded with these words, "and then they shall know that I am the Lord."

Here, Jesus followed His warning with the words, "and all the churches shall know that I am He who searches the minds and hearts. And I will give to each one of you according to your works." This message is not singularly for the church of Thyatira. It is for all churches that name the name of Jesus Christ as the Son of God.

As He began, so He again warns: His eyes like flaming fire search the minds and hearts. This warning to the church in Thyatira is a precursor to His promise in Revelation 22:12, "And behold, I am coming quickly, and My reward is with Me, to give to every one according to his work." God is searching our hearts and minds to reveal the motive behind our works. Compromise taints our works.

> Now to you I say, and to the rest in Thyatira, as many as do not have this doctrine, who have not known the depths of Satan, as they say, I will put on you no other burden. 2:24

JESUS' HEART FOR THYATIRA

There were those who had not compromised. There were those who did not have this doctrine, who had not been duped into thinking the sins of adultery (physical and spiritual) were in any way tolerable to God. There were those who had not known "the depths of Satan." The word translated *known* is the Greek word *gnosko*, which has the sense of knowing experientially. You and I may know about Satan intellectually, but we are not to know him experientially. In allowing the teaching and seduction of Jezebel, people in the church had known the works of Satan in their lives. That causes God to grieve.

NO OTHER BURDEN

On these who had stood fast, Jesus said that He would put on them "no other burden."

It's interesting to read the account of the Jerusalem council in Acts 15. As Gentiles were receiving the gospel, the question arose as to what Jewish laws they should be expected to follow that were contrary to Gentile laws. One of those laws was to abstain from sexual immorality.

In these times, which are filled with Jezebels within and without the church that proclaim this sin should be *allowed*, Jesus proclaims otherwise. Also, He has announced that those who join in promoting her tolerance and compromise will receive "great tribulation" (v. 22).

The leaders of the church closed their letter to the Gentile churches saying, "For it seemed good to the Holy Spirit, and to us, to lay upon you no greater burden than these necessary things: that you abstain from things offered to idols, from blood, from things strangled, and from sexual immorality. If you keep yourselves from these, you will do well. Farewell" (Acts 15:28-29).

This was Jesus' heart for the church in Thyatira.

> But hold fast what you have till I come. 2:25

HOLD FAST

The Jezebels and those who tolerate her teachings and seductions will be with us until Jesus comes. Our place as believers is to "hold fast." This is Jesus' remedy.

> "Therefore, brethren, stand fast and hold the traditions which you were taught, whether by word or our epistle." (2 Thessalonians 2:15)

> "Seeing then that we have a great High Priest who has passed through the heavens, Jesus the Son of God, let us hold fast our confession." (Hebrews 4:14)

We are to "hold fast." We are to take God's truths and hold on to them, opening our hands to nothing contrary. Jesus calls us to hold on. Jezebel calls us to let go. God has drawn lines for His people and He has commanded not to cross them. Jezebel has redrawn those lines. She has placed them farther away and placed sin within the confines of acceptability. Jesus does not recognize her lines.

How long does He call us to hold on? Until He comes. Then we can let go and simply bask in those truths as there will no longer be Jezebels tempting us to compromise and doubt what God has proclaimed.

> And he who overcomes, and keeps My works until the end, to him I will give power over the nations—He shall rule them with a rod of iron; they shall be dashed to pieces like the potter's vessels—as I also have received from My Father; 2:26-27

There is great benefit in *holding fast*. "And he who overcomes … I will give power over the nations." This is the first of two promises. The word *rule* has the sense of shepherding. God's rule is not harsh, but always loving and merciful. So shall we be when we rule with Him. All believers who come with Jesus at His second coming will rule the nations that live during the millennium.

> and I will give him the morning star. 2:28

Secondly, Jesus will give to the overcomer the *morning star*. Who is the morning star? Jesus Himself.

> "I, Jesus, have sent My angel to testify to you these things in the churches. I am the Root and the Offspring of David, the Bright and Morning Star." (Revelation 22:16)

All believers will be given Jesus. But we who hold fast to what He has given us, will rule to a greater extent and will enjoy the benefits of belonging to Jesus, our Morning Star, in this life in a deeper way, because we have not allowed the teachings and seductions of Jezebel to compromise our faith and obedience to God.

> He who has an ear, let him hear what the Spirit says to the churches. 2:29

Each of us has a bit of Jezebel in us, a tendency to tolerate or allow sin in our own lives or in the lives of others. A spirit that really wants what we want and is willing to compromise to get it. We each are prone to be self-willed and self-ruled. The world today praises the spirit of Jezebel. God abhors it. Oh, may we allow the Spirit of God to search us with flaming eyes of fire and reveal to us any *nevertheless* things in our lives. If there is a *nevertheless* in your life, God is giving you space, a period of time, to repent.

May it not be said of you, "but she did not want to repent."

REFLECTION QUESTIONS

(For more extensive study questions visit CathyDickinson.com)

1. What is the significance of Jesus using the title "Son of God"? Jesus is declaring that He has all the attributes and powers of God. Jesus is the very nature of God the Father.

2. Jesus referred to Himself as having "eyes like a flame of fire." Describe what this means?

3. Jesus reminded them that He has "feet like fine brass." What does this represent?

4. Jesus saw their love, service, faith, patience, and their increasing works. *Nevertheless*, He had a few things against them because they allowed influences that were not of Him. For every believer, this *nevertheless* is the point at which we knowingly disobey God despite the good we are doing. What could be a *nevertheless* in the church today, or in your own life?

5. We were encouraged to soak in the definition of *allow* as it was used in Revelation 2:20. Define *allow* and ask the Lord to reveal anything you may be allowing that displeases Him.

6. Jesus used a possessive term for His people in the church in Thyatira (v. 20) that also applies to us as believers. How does this challenge you?

7. Judgment came upon Jezebel, not because of her sin, but because though she was given time, she "did not repent," or literally, "she did not want to repent." Today, what do you see as the sins of Jezebel and how do they stir up the church?

8. Jesus says, "I am He who searches the minds and hearts. And I will give to each one of you according to your works" (v.23). Why is Jesus searching our hearts and minds?

9. Jesus gives the church of Thyatira (and us) a remedy to "hold fast what you have till I come" (v. 25). What do you have that you can "hold fast" until He comes?

10. To the "overcomer" the Lord promises the morning star—Jesus Himself. How has Jesus revealed Himself to you through your study of His message to the church in Thyatira?

Chapter Six

QUICKENING THE DEAD: REVELATION 3:1-6

The church in Sardis is known as the dead church. For these seven churches in Revelation, there is not only an application for the church as a whole, but also a challenge to us as individuals. We may claim that we are alive, but Jesus knows our works, and He's concerned that we may be heading in a deadly direction.

This is the outline for the church of Sardis:

1. Jesus identifies the church.
2. Jesus gives a description of Himself.
3. Jesus tells them what He knows about them.
4. Jesus tells them what displeases Him.
5. Jesus gives the remedy.
6. Jesus issues a warning.
7. Jesus concludes with a promise.

And to the angel of the church in Sardis write, 3:1

SARDIS

The city of Sardis was about thirty miles southeast of Thyatira. Notice, each of the churches addressed in Revelation 2 and 3 were about the same distance from one another. (See map on page 23.)

Sardis was considered impregnable. The city was situated about 1,500 feet above the roads that led to it. It was said that even children could defend the city of Sardis. [20]

When King Cyrus and his army surrounded the city from their position below, Cyrus discovered that there was no way up the mountain. He offered a reward to any soldier who could figure out a way in. It just so happened one day as a soldier just sat and surveyed the mountainside, he noticed one of the Sardis guards drop his helmet, who then walked down a path to retrieve it. Cyrus' soldier carefully marked that path. Later that night, he and a group of soldiers climbed the pathway and found the city of Sardis unguarded and asleep. The saying soon became widespread, "Sardis was taken as a thief in the night."

> These things says He who has the seven Spirits of God 3:1

THE SEVEN SPIRITS OF GOD

History tells us that the people of Sardis believed the gods used to manifest their life-giving power from their hot springs and that's where they went to get life.

Remember what Jesus said on the last day of the Feast of Tabernacles?

> "Jesus stood and cried out, saying, 'If anyone thirsts, let him come to Me and drink. He who believes in Me, as the Scripture has said, out of his heart will flow rivers of living water.' But this He spoke concerning the Spirit, whom those believing in Him would receive; for the Holy Spirit was not yet given, because Jesus was not yet glorified." (John 7:37-39)

Jesus presented Himself to the church of Sardis as "He who has the seven Spirits of God" (the Holy Spirit). Two things that were happening to the city as a whole were also happening to the church in Sardis: a reliance on past glory and a dependence on the wrong source for life.

In its earlier days, Sardis was one of the most prominent cities in Asia. But at the time of John's writing, it was a shell of what it used to be. So not only were the inhabitants of the city living on their former reputation, but so was the church. Their finest achievements lay in the past. But Jesus didn't say, "It's over, move on." He had very different advice for them.

A REMINDER

As we have seen with the other churches, Jesus begins His message to the church of Sardis with a description of Himself, letting them know something they had either forgotten about Him or would benefit from being reminded.

He has them. He holds. He possesses the character and strength of the seven Spirits of God which we learned, when we studied Revelation 1:4, speaks of the Holy Spirit. As I've mentioned before, out of the 400 verses in Revelation, 278 refer to the Old Testament. So, in understanding the seven Spirits of God, we would be wise to consult what God has already said, and we find it in the book of Isaiah.

> "There shall come forth a Rod from the stem of Jesse, and a Branch shall grow out of his roots. The Spirit of the Lord shall rest upon Him, the Spirit of wisdom and understanding, the Spirit of counsel and might, the Spirit of knowledge and of the fear of the Lord." (Isaiah 11:1-2)

This is talking about Jesus. The church in Sardis needed to be reminded of this description of Jesus because they had lost sight of the ministry of the Holy Spirit. That is what separates a church that is alive and a church that is dead—not attendance, not ministries, not even verse-by-verse Bible teaching, but a dependence upon the work of the Holy Spirit.

I want to park on this because my greatest concern for the church today is that we are losing a dependency upon the power and moving of the Holy Spirit, which puts us in real danger of becoming like the church in Sardis. Dead.

Let's look at each of the seven Spirits of God:

1. THE SPIRIT OF THE LORD MUST REST UPON US

We should get the sense of abiding. Remember what Jesus said in John 15:5.

> "I am the vine, you are the branches. He who abides in Me, and I in him, bears much fruit; for without Me you can do nothing."

Jesus perceived that the church in Sardis thought they were doing much, but they were really doing nothing of value, nothing demonstrating spiritual life.

2. THE SPIRIT OF WISDOM

This would be the proper, supernatural application of knowledge.

3. THE SPIRIT OF UNDERSTANDING

A supernatural insight and discernment; the ability to see something more clearly.

Sometimes when I'm talking to someone, especially in counseling, I get a feeling I'm missing something—like I'm not being told the whole story. It's the ability to see beyond the outward, to see what's really going on. Often you and I only hear one side of a matter, but if we are sensitive to the Spirit, there will be something unsettling inside. We need to be careful, though, as these checks may be the beginning of a decline into leaning on your own understanding, leading to dead decisions. For me, I have to really watch this one. It's so easy to start leaning on or relying on the checks and drawing conclusions that something just isn't right or that we shouldn't move forward.

A check should be just that—a prompt from the Lord to *check* with Him and get His perspective. If we start heeding the checks, rather than getting the Lord's perspective, it's really easy to start thinking we are spiritually wise, and like Sardis, lean on our understanding and insight from the past.

4. THE SPIRIT OF COUNSEL

Advice that comes from wisdom and understanding.

5. THE SPIRIT OF MIGHT

Spiritual power and strength.

Once I taught at a retreat in California, in what is known as "gold country." I was sick, really sick. My voice was raspy and almost gone. I know what it is like to push through illness and pain to teach. I've done it more times than I can count. But that weekend I didn't feel like pushing. I just wanted to go home. But of course, I couldn't.

The theme of the retreat was titled, "Properly Dressed," based on Colossians 3:12-15: putting off old things, and the behaviors we are to put on as people who are beloved of the Lord. Well, I went there dressed mentally like a Southern Californian—someone who is used to a much faster pace of life.

Those hosting the retreat led me to an office to study and to rest a couple of hours before dinner and the first session. The drapes were closed and I was left with my sickness, my phone, and my laptop. Those who know me, know that should have been enough. I had my Bible too, but it just sat there unopened. I was tired. Unconsciously, I went to my phone and laptop. But much to my surprise, there was no phone service. There was no Wi-Fi. And you know what? I wasn't happy. I was sick, I was weak, and my phone and laptop were as useless as I felt.

Then I heard this honking noise, but not the honking of cars. Out of curiousity, I pulled back the drapes and saw about thirty geese gliding across this absolutely lush green lawn. As I continued to watch, seven or eight deer playfully pranced by. And the backdrop—a glorious golden sunset.

And you know what? God nailed me. Not that being busy is always bad, but it's bad when you need it to feel okay.

Not surprisingly, God enabled me to teach at that retreat and I was very, very aware that I did it in His strength and not mine. Contrary to how fatiguing and physically draining teaching at a retreat can be, I left refreshed, because in my sickness, God gave me time to slow down and see some things I had missed.

We are deceivable. We are very prone to think we are okay when we are not. The things and thinking of this life can get to us and we don't see it.

The *church* in Sardis had taken on the thinking of the *city* of Sardis, that they were alive when they were actually dead. They saw a powerless strength in themselves and didn't realize they were missing the strength provided by the Holy Spirit.

6. THE SPIRIT OF KNOWLEDGE

A revelation by the Holy Spirit. Knowing something you couldn't have known unless the Holy Spirit reveals it.

7. THE SPIRIT OF THE FEAR OF THE LORD

A reverence, a respect for God that is needed to keep me in line and stay concerned about what He thinks about me and my decisions above all else. "The fear of man brings a snare" (Proverbs 29:25). The fear of God keeps us from that trap.

"This fear restrains people from sin" (Zodhiates).[21]

We may say of others, "They have no fear of the Lord." The proof is in the choice to sin.

DEPENDENCE ON THE HOLY SPIRIT

When we do not depend upon the Holy Spirit, we are missing or lacking (1) spiritual abiding (2) spiritual wisdom (3) spiritual understanding (4) spiritual counsel (5) spiritual might (6) spiritual knowledge and (7) spiritual fear. When we don't abide in the Lord, we separate ourselves from real spiritual life.

Now a church that appears alive doesn't just lack these things. They have other things to offer—things that appeal to the ears of man, but not to the spirit of man. They probably have a lot of activity going on. Don't mistake religious activity for spiritual life. They appear to be alive. And if you are thinking about another church right now, don't. May we have ears to hear what the Spirit is saying to us as a church, and as individuals.

and the seven stars: 3:1

THE MESSENGERS OF THE CHURCHES

Jesus has the seven Spirits of God and He has the seven stars. Revelation 1:20 tells us that the seven stars are the messengers of the churches. They are in His hands; He is not in their hands. He is not there for their preferences; they are there for His. He wants to use us; we are not to use Him. Oh, how we need to be reminded of this, and reminded often.

I know your works ... for I have not found your works perfect before God. 3:1-2

INCOMPLETE WORKS

What did Jesus know about this church in Sardis? Their works were not perfect before Him. That word *perfect* has been defined as full, mature, or complete. Because it denotes a fullness—works that are not "perfect" have a hollow place. Hollow places get us in trouble, don't they? They are places open to be filled by other things. Jesus identifies Himself as "having the seven Spirits of God." Throughout the Bible, "seven" denotes fullness. Jesus was full of God—complete—perfect. He is God. He is full. They were not. May we look to Him for our fullness, for our completeness.

that you have a name that you are alive, but you are dead. 3:1

SPIRITUALLY DEAD

I studied several commentaries and they compared the church of Sardis to a chicken with its head cut off. The body still flounders around. It looks alive, but that chicken is dead. I went to YouTube and watched a video. Needless to say, it made me sick to my stomach.

The church of Sardis' name displeases Jesus. "You are alive, but you are dead." The church in Sardis had a name and a reputation that they were alive. People thought they were alive.

Have you ever been caught up in believing your own press? People think you are doing well. People admire you and think your faith is thriving, and you start relying on that. You see no need to examine your life. Why fix something that doesn't *appear* to be broken?

"But you are dead." They weren't physically dead; they were spiritually dead. Not spiritually dead in the sense of unsaved, because in verse 3 Jesus gives them a remedy to remember how they received. If they weren't saved, the remedy would not be to remember how they received, but it would be to receive.

Remember what Paul wrote in 1 Corinthians 13, "Though I speak with the tongues of men and of angels … though I have the gift of prophecy, and understand all mysteries and all knowledge … and have all faith ... though I bestow all my goods to feed the poor, and though I give my body to be burned, but have not love … I am nothing; it profits me nothing" (1 Corinthians 13:1-3). Without love, we are nothing and those things profit nothing. Wouldn't you say that a church that operates in those things is alive? Paul said it's nothing; Jesus said—it's dead. Dead things and dead people profit no one.

THE CHALLENGE

What does the Lord see when you appear to others to be worshiping Him? Don't let this question condemn you, rather may it challenge you.

> "The Lord says: 'These people come near to me with their mouth and honor me with their lips, but their hearts are far from me. Their worship of me is made up only of rules taught by men.'" (Isaiah 29:13 NIV)

Look at the next verse: "Therefore once more I will astound these people with wonder upon wonder; the wisdom of the wise will perish, the intelligence of the intelligent will vanish" (Isaiah 29:14 NIV).

As always, Jesus has a remedy; a fix for dead Christians. What was the remedy? How do you make alive something that is dead? Jesus didn't say, "Move to another church." He didn't say, "Leave it" or as it might apply to us individually, quit trying. Sardis was not a throwaway church and neither are you a throwaway believer—not to Jesus. Ephesians 2:1 says, "And you He made alive, who were dead in trespasses and sins." The word *alive* in the KJV reads "quickened," meaning "bring back to life." God is never willing to give up and bury His people. His goal is to bring life back into us.

> Be watchful, and strengthen the things which remain, that are ready to die. Remember therefore how you have received and heard; hold fast and repent. 3:2-3

Here is Jesus' five-part remedy:

1. BE WATCHFUL

Pay attention. Awake from your sleep. What a great warning to the people of Sardis. They had been sleeping when they were attacked. They weren't watching. Jesus is calling them to wake up, look around, and see what's happening.

Judges 16 tells the story of Samson, who didn't realize that the power of God had left him. Why? He wasn't using it. He had settled for a life that didn't need it. "But he did not know that the Lord had departed from him" (v. 20).

This deadness in Sardis seems to tell us that they weren't experiencing persecution. Life was easy. They could kick back and sleep because their enemy was at the bottom of the mountain—but the enemy did come and Sardis was taken as a thief in the night.

2. STRENGTHEN WHAT REMAINS

Go back to what you know. Strengthen your walk with the Lord. Make it alive. Do what it takes. Feed it. Strengthen what you know—before you forget and lose touch.

3. REMEMBER HOW

Notice, Jesus didn't rebuke the church in Sardis for their doctrine or for tolerating sinful acts or sinful theology. It wasn't what they had lost—it was how they lost it. He doesn't say improve—He says remember how.

Jesus said He had not found their works perfect before God. Were they guilty of the same error as the Galatians—forgetting that they can't fill the spiritual hollow with the works of the flesh? "Are you so foolish? Having begun in the Spirit, are you now being made perfect by the flesh" (Galatians 3:3)?

Remember the Thessalonians.

> "… when you received the word of God which you heard from us, you welcomed it not as the word of men, but as it is in truth, the word of God, which also effectively works in you who believe" (1 Thessalonians 2:13).

The word of God "effectually works" in lives through the power of the Holy Spirit. You and I can't—we just can't live this Christian life without the power of the Holy Spirit. We may look alive out there—but we are dead.

And you know where the deadness seems to be evident and visible? In the home. Because all too often, Christians walk into their homes and take off their self-made cloak of righteousness and hang it in the closet.

I'm thoroughly convinced that most Christian marriages fail because they are Christians in name and not in power; each spouse expecting of the other a life that is alive spiritually, yet neither relying on the power of the Spirit to live that way.

Part of remembering is remembering the cost; what it took to clean us up. All sin is sin, but pride is an awful sin, just as awful as sexual immorality or substance abuse. And how do we get the power to overcome? We stay in a place where we know we need it, and we just ask for it.

In a familiar song titled "How Deep the Father's Love," there is a phrase, "It was my sin that held Him there until it was accomplished." "Until it was accomplished"—these words just grabbed me. Jesus didn't quit and He didn't give up His spirit one millisecond too early. He hung on the cross as long as it took to be sure your sin and my sin was covered.

Jesus' love for you kept Him on the cross and the Father's love for you kept Him from rescuing the Son of His love before your sin was taken care of. Have you ever started out to do something good and then decided the price was too high and quit? Jesus didn't—neither did the Father. Remember the cost. Remember how. It will keep you alive.

4. HOLD FAST

Some airports require taking a tram to get from one terminal to another. Inside the tram, there are poles that go from the floor to the ceiling. Upon boarding, you may hear an announcement like, "Hold on; there will be sudden stops and starts." I know exactly what to do. I don't dismiss the announcement thinking, *I'm not sure what he meant* or *What did he say? The sound was too muffled.* I figure it out. Why? Because I want to keep standing. If I don't hold on, there's a chance I'm going to lose my footing.

Jesus tells us to "hold fast." People who think they can stand in their own power will fall and people that are on the ground are as good as dead.

First Corinthians 10:12 reminds us of this simple truth: "Therefore let him who thinks he stands take heed lest he fall."

It's as if the church in Sardis was saying, "Look at me. I'm standing," but Jesus was not impressed. They had lost focus. That's a big part of the problem. People who think they are alive, when they are actually dead, say, "Look at me," not "Look to Jesus."

Hold fast. Jesus gave this advice to three of the seven churches. Surely, it is significant.

5. REPENT

There it is again. For every church that had a problem, repentance was part of the remedy.

To repent is to agree with God and do an about-face. A walk that is dead, that is not experiencing the flow of the living water of the Holy Spirit is useless. Go back to a walk that is alive.

Slow down. Slow down and write these words out. Be watchful. Strengthen your walk with the Lord. Remember how. Remember the cost. Hold fast. And repent.

Just pick out a few words from Jesus' remedy to the church in Sardis and think about them for a while. You know what all of these words mean. Ask the Lord how they might apply to you. He will tell you if you really want to know.

> Therefore if you will not watch, I will come upon you as a thief, and you will not know what hour I will come upon you. 3:3

WATCH

After Jesus presents the remedy, He issues a threat—the warning of what will happen if they ignore the remedy. Jesus told them to watch. There were consequences if they didn't.

As a city, they knew the consequences. Like a thief in the night, Cyrus' men came while they were not watching. Jesus told them—if you don't watch, I will come and you won't know when.

Is Jesus referring to the rapture? Or is He referring to a time when judgment will come upon them? Both are true.

Jesus is saying to them and to us—be watchful, be awake, be ready because you don't know when I will wrap it all up—you don't know when, like the soldiers of Cyrus, I will come and life will change.

> You have a few names even in Sardis who have not defiled their garments; and they shall walk with Me in white, for they are worthy. 3:4

THE WHITE AND WORTHY

Jesus recognized there were some in Sardis who had not defiled (soiled as with mud or filth) their garments. There was a remnant in the church that were doing well. Do you think you would be among them? Most of us do—that's the deception we need to be careful of. Isaiah 64:6 enhances our understanding, "But we are all like an unclean thing, and all our righteousnesses are like filthy rags; we all fade as a leaf, and our iniquities, like the wind, have taken us away."

Isaiah 64:7 adds, "And there is no one who calls on Your name, who stirs himself up to take hold of You."

Note the word *hold*. Remember Jesus said to "hold fast." The church in Sardis relied upon their reputations and their works rather than relying on the Lord; however, there were a few who had not done that—and Jesus noticed. He did not lump them in with the rest who would suffer the consequences. Rather, they will walk with Him in white. One day, we all will walk with Him in white, but this speaks of those who have chosen to walk with Him now. They will walk with Him in white, living in the benefits of the cleansed life presently.

Matthew Poole, a sixteenth-century English theologian, wrote, "As sin is expressed under the notion of nakedness, so holiness is expressed under the notion of a garment." [22]

Without the garment, there is no holiness. If we remove the emphasis on the Holy Spirit to walk in holiness, we look to other useless means. If we do not teach the demand to be holy, we become carnal. If we do not teach the power to be holy, we become hypocrites.

He who overcomes shall be clothed in white garments, 3:5

A PROMISE TO OVERCOMERS

As with the preceding messages, Jesus concludes with a promise to overcomers—that's all of us who believe. One day, this is what it will be like for each of us who believe:

CLOTHED IN WHITE GARMENTS

In their familiar pagan worship of the day, you could not approach the gods clothed in dirty garments. In Matthew 22, Jesus explained the absolute necessity of the wedding. No garment—no entrance. Jesus is reassuring them, and us here. Jesus will take care of our need for a white garment by clothing us Himself.

One day while snorkeling in Kauai, I saw a turtle. As soon as I did, I shouted for my granddaughter, Zoe. "Zoe, Zoe, turtle—come see!" I screamed so loud that everyone on this little beach heard me and looked up. Then I realized something. Only Zoe could see the turtle because only Zoe had snorkeling gear. The other people just looked at me and did nothing, because there was nothing they could do. When we came back onto shore, Zoe said to me, "They all missed the turtle." To see the turtle, you needed snorkeling gear. Once I shouted, it was too late for anyone to go buy snorkeling gear.

To see the wonders of heaven, you need a white robe. It can only be found in Jesus, and He promises to give one to everyone who comes to Him now.

and I will not blot out his name from the Book of Life; 3:5

THE BOOK OF LIFE

In John's day, a king kept an accurate register. If a man committed a crime against the state, or if he died, his name was erased. Knowing this, Jesus in essence said, the king might blot out your name for something you've done, but I will *not.* The sense of the word *not* is—I will never, I will not ever take your name off My list.

WHOSE NAMES ARE NOT IN THE BOOK OF LIFE?

1. Whoever has sinned against God.

"And the Lord said to Moses, 'Whoever has sinned against Me, I will blot him out of My book.'" (Exodus 32:33)

2. Those who worship the Antichrist.

"All who dwell on the earth will worship him, whose names have not been written in the Book of Life of the Lamb slain from the foundation of the world." (Revelation 13:8)

3. Anything that defiles or causes an abomination or a lie.

"But there shall by no means enter it anything that defiles, or causes an abomination or a lie, but only those who are written in the Lamb's Book of Life." (Revelation 21:27)

4. Anyone who takes away from the words of the book of this prophecy (Revelation).

"And if anyone takes away from the words of the book of this prophecy, God shall take away his part from the Book of Life, from the holy city, and from the things which are written in this book." (Revelation 22:19)

WHAT HAPPENS TO THOSE NOT IN THE BOOK OF LIFE?

They will be cast into the lake of fire.

"And anyone not found written in the Book of Life was cast into the lake of fire." (Revelation 20:15)

WHOSE NAMES ARE WRITTEN IN THE BOOK OF LIFE?

Fellow workers.

"… be of the same mind in the Lord. And I urge you also, true companion … who labored with me in the gospel … and the rest of my fellow workers, whose names are in the Book of Life." (Philippians 4:2-3)

"He who overcomes." (Revelation 3:5)

WHEN ARE THEY WRITTEN IN THE BOOK?

They have been there since the foundation of the world.

"All who dwell on the earth will worship him, whose names have not been written in the Book of Life of the Lamb slain from the foundation of the world." (Revelation 13:8)

"The beast that you saw was, and is not, and will ascend out of the bottomless pit and go to perdition. And those who dwell on the earth will marvel, whose names are not written in the Book of Life from the foundation of the world, when they see the beast that was, and is not, and yet is." (Revelation 17:8)

NAMES OF SAVED AND UNSAVED

Are names written in of those who are saved or are names blotted out of those who are not? There are several theories, but then we'd be jumping from what God says to what people think. And isn't that what was so displeasing about the church in Sardis? What matters is this incredible promise: "He who overcomes shall be clothed in white garments, and I will not blot out his name from the Book of Life.

> but I will confess his name before My Father and before His angels. He who has an ear, let him hear what the Spirit says to the churches. 3:5-6

CONFESS

One of the definitions of *confess* is "acknowledge as belonging to." Jesus will one day say to the Father, "She's mine." The result of really taking that in should have had an impact on the dead believers in Sardis. And it should have an impact on us. It should provoke in us an appreciation that results in living lives all about Him.

CLOSING THOUGHTS

On the day of Pastor Chuck's memorial service, I arrived at the San Diego airport at 2:00 p.m. I was flying in from the retreat I taught at in Central California. Dale met me with a change of clothes and I changed in the airport restroom. From there we drove to Anaheim, only to find lines and lines of people wrapped around the Honda Center. It seats approximately 18,000 people and it was nearly filled. Thankfully we had reserved seats and we were able to walk right in. I could have been easily deceived into thinking *we had a name that was alive*, compared to the others who had to wait in line. But it was the kindness of Pastor Chuck's family to have a special guest list for Calvary Chapel pastors and their family.

We saw a lot of people we had grown up with spiritually and people we had ministered with and we reminisced about years gone by. Throughout the night, pastors shared their testimonies on stage, mostly from the beginning Calvary days. They shared memories of Pastor Chuck over and over again, telling about how he sought the moving of the Holy Spirit.

Intermittently between the testimonies, different musical artists and bands performed, starting with Love Song, one of the first Maranatha groups, and Parable, and Malcolm and Alwyn. In almost every group we have a friend, and it stirred a lot of good memories. As the night progressed, I found myself wonderfully touched by the Holy Spirit as we worshiped with new groups that God is using now, like Jeremy Camp and Phil Wickham. Phil's parents are our friends; he has his mother's lungs and his father's gift of playing the guitar. It was so awesome to sense the presence and moving of the Holy Spirit just as strongly as I ever remember Him working. I didn't long for the "good old tent days" because the Holy Spirit was moving powerfully right then. And all I could say was, "Wow!"

That's what Jesus wants for us. Not a glorying in what He did in our lives in the past, not a reliance on what people think of us, not a dependency on our own knowledge or skills, but He wants us alive simply and only because the Holy Spirit of the living God is filling us with Himself, and that filling is flowing out to people who are dying to see and experience real life.

Just as Jesus quickened the church of Sardis to life, He quickens you and me too. Jesus doesn't say, "It's over, move on." He wants us to be watchful and strengthen the things that remain. You and I are not throwaways; we're keepers. We are meant to be vessels filled and used by the Spirit of the LIVING God!

REFLECTION QUESTIONS

(For more extensive study questions visit CathyDickinson.com)

1. Jesus identified Himself to the church in Sardis as, "He who has the seven Spirits of God" (v. 1). What two things were happening to the *city* as a whole that were also happening to the *church* in Sardis?

2. Give a brief description of each of the Seven Spirits of God (the Holy Spirit).

The Spirit of the Lord:

The Spirit of Wisdom:

The Spirit of Understanding:

The Spirit of Counsel:

The Spirit of Might:

The Spirit of Knowledge:

The Spirit of the Fear of the Lord:

3. What separates a church or individual that is spiritually alive from one that is spiritually dead? When we do not abide in the Lord we separate ourselves from real spiritual life.

4. The church in Sardis appeared to be alive, but they were dead. As believers, we can appear to be alive and yet be dying spiritually. How are you challenged by this truth?

Don't mistake religious activity for spiritual life. I must actively pursue a relationship with Jesus "works" don't cut it - they are to glorify Him

5. Jesus pointed out that their works were not perfect (mature, full, complete) before God. Their works were hollow, at least to some degree. What might that practically look like in an individual's works? In a church's works? Actively laying a plan before God and seeking His direction. Seeking the scripture and prayer. Waiting for God to move - not me moving. All acts will be done in love

6. Jesus gave five instructions to the church in Sardis, and we were encouraged to slow down and ponder each one before the Lord. Share how they apply to you personally.

Be watchful: I need to pay attention and guard my time with the Lord. Seeking Him first.

Strengthen what remains: He died for me and gave me a new life - am I strengthening that walk - do I seek him.

Remember how: Receive the word of God - pray for an infilling of the Holy Spirit and love for Him.

Hold fast: Don't quit. Remember the cost Jesus paid for me and cling to Him.

Repent: Not be lazy or self-serving.

7. While all overcomers will one day be clothed in white, Jesus acknowledged the few in Sardis that "had not defiled their garments"—they would "walk with Him in white." What does it mean to walk in white with Jesus now? Rely on Jesus - He is the one who holds me. To be clothed by Him means to live for Him and obey Him. Serve Him in truth and love and obedience

8. "He who has an ear, let him hear what the Spirit says to the churches." What is the Spirit saying to you through this message? Be disciplined listen to what He wants me to do.

Chapter Seven

WILL JESUS FIND FAITH IN YOU? REVELATION 3:7-13

Jesus had no words of rebuke for the church in Philadelphia, even though they couldn't have been perfect. He only had encouragement. I'm so glad Jesus isn't a nitpicker, aren't you? He sees things that please Him and He sees their struggle. He also sees how they handle their struggle.

As we look at the church in Philadelphia, personally ask yourself this question: "What is Jesus looking for in me when I struggle?"

This is the pattern for the church of Philadelphia:

1. Jesus identifies the church.
2. Jesus introduces Himself.
3. Jesus tells them what He knows.
4. Jesus tells them what pleases Him.
5. Jesus tells them what He will do.
6. Jesus gives a warning.
7. Jesus gives promises.

And to the angel of the church in Philadelphia write, 3:7

PHILADELPHIA

The church in Philadelphia was the youngest of the seven addressed by Jesus in Revelation. It was about thirty miles from Sardis (See map on page 23.)

The city was founded about 150 BC by King Attallus of Pergamum. He was known for his great love for his brother and so was nicknamed Philadelphus, which means "lover of a brother," and the city was named Philadelphia to honor him. [23]

It is significant in Scripture when God specifically gives someone a name. Although Christians are called to have a brotherly love for one another six times in the New Testament, there is nothing that would indicate that the church in Philadelphia was known for its love of the brethren. Jesus didn't address it here, so our study of the message to the church in Philadelphia will not be about the need for brotherly love in the church.

As we have seen with each individual church we have studied so far, Jesus used their secular history to drive home His message to them. Here's what is significant about the history of the city of Philadelphia. It was a city prone to earthquakes—bad ones—bad enough to level just about the whole city except for the pillars that held up the buildings. That caused a fear to develop in the people. When an earthquake occurred, they would flee the city and live in tents until they felt it was safe to return.

Philadelphia was built with the deliberate intention to be a missionary city—not for the gospel, but for the Greek culture. Anyone who was not Greek was considered a barbarian, so Philadelphia was established as a center for those who wanted to learn the Greek culture.

> These things says He who is holy, He who is true, 3:7

Unlike the other descriptions of Jesus given to the other churches, this description of Jesus is not found in Revelation 1. Most of the descriptions are referenced from the Old Testament.

The believers in the church in Philadelphia lived in a world that challenged their faith. So do we. Jesus' description of Himself is meant to help us too. That's why it was so crucial for Jesus to remind them—He is holy. He is true—genuine.

HE WHO IS HOLY

The Old Testament is very clear that only God is *He who is holy*. Psalm 16:10 reminds us that Jesus is the Holy One of God. "For You will not leave my soul in Sheol, nor will You allow Your Holy One to see corruption." The demons knew it too. According to Mark 1:24 they said, "Let us alone! What have we to do with You, Jesus of Nazareth? Did You come to destroy us? I know who You are—the Holy One of God!"

Mary knew it. "And the angel answered and said to her, 'The Holy Spirit will come upon you, and the power of the Highest will overshadow you; therefore, also, that Holy One who is to be born will be called the Son of God" (Luke 1:35).

Peter knew it when he spoke to the men of Israel. "But you denied the Holy One and the Just, and asked for a murderer to be granted to you" (Acts 3:14).

Jesus is He who is holy—the One who has been set apart to be our example. In His holiness, Jesus set the example that He must be about His Father's business. We are to be holy as He is holy; His way is always the right choice. Our choices should be made based on Him, rather than on ourselves or the world around us.

HE WHO IS TRUE

There are two Greek words which might be translated as "true." One means "true and not false;" the other means "true and not fake." It is the latter that is used here in Revelation. Jesus is the real God. He is genuine. He is the original; not a copy, not a fake.

There are many verses that declare "He who is true" is God in the Old Testament. Here is just one account in Exodus when Moses wanted to see God. This is what God declared about Himself: "And the LORD passed before him and proclaimed, 'The LORD, the LORD God, merciful and gracious, longsuffering, and abounding in goodness and truth" (Exodus 34:6).

John makes this declaration of Jesus: "And we know that the Son of God has come and has given us an understanding, that we may know Him who is true; and we are in Him who is true, in His Son Jesus Christ. This is the true God and eternal life" (1 John 5:20).

Everything Jesus says about heaven, hell, love, salvation, judgment—everything is true and can be depended upon. You and I go to sleep at night fully believing that morning will follow. The words of Jesus are just as sure. We can trust Him to do what He says.

> He who has the key of David, He who opens and no one shuts, and shuts and no one opens: 3:7

HE HOLDS THE KEY OF DAVID

This is a prophecy about Jesus in the book of Isaiah.

> "The key of the house of David I will lay on his shoulder; so he shall open, and no one shall shut; and he shall shut, and no one shall open." (Isaiah 22:22)

In the days of King Hezekiah, "the key of David" was given to the king's servant Eliakim. This key represented authority, access; not just to let oneself in, but also to let others in. No one got in to see the king without gaining access through his servant. This verse clearly speaks of access to the King. Jesus possesses the authority and the power.

Do you want entrance into the kingdom? Jesus has the key—the only key. Notice, there is only one. "Jesus said to him, 'I am the way, the truth, and the life. No one comes to the Father except through Me'" (John 14:6).

We have the assurance that when He opens a door, no one can shut it and when He closes a door, no one can open it. Jesus is the One who grants access to God in heaven and He is the One who will deny it. No one else has the key.

> I know your works. 3:8

JESUS KNOWS YOUR HEART

We live in a day when there is much known about us. The other day as I searched YouTube, it had suggestions for me based on what it knew about me. Christian videos, beach videos, and cell phone apps. YouTube knows me well—although it missed one thing that is very important to me—family. YouTube walks amongst the Internet; Jesus walks amongst our hearts.

Recently, Dale and I hung a couple of pictures and afterwards Dale commented, "This looks more and more like a grandparent's house." If you looked around our house, you'd see things about Jesus, things about the beach, techy stuff, and family—that's what you would discern is important to me. Dale lives in the same house, but he doesn't nearly have the love for the beach or techy stuff that I have. Only two are true—Jesus and family. But Jesus knows. Jesus would not walk in our house and look at the things on my wall to know what's important to me. He would look at the things in my heart.

> See, I have set before you an open door, and no one can shut it; 3:8

THE STRUGGLE

They had an open door set before them but they were having trouble with certain Jews—Jews who said they were Jews, but lied; rather they were "of the synagogue of Satan" (v. 9). What these Jews did at that time was deny any believing (Christian) Jew access to the synagogue, rejecting them as heretics. They shut the doors to what they called God's house. Jesus let the believers in Philadelphia know that He was the One who opened the doors to His house and that no one could keep them out.

Now that's the interpretation I like. We know the former interpretation is true—Jesus is the only One who can open the door to heaven. However, there's another interpretation based on the intentions of the founding of the city of Philadelphia. Remember, Philadelphia was to be a missionary city for the Greek culture. Jesus could very well mean that He was opening a door for them for true missionary work. In the New Testament, when Paul spoke of the Lord opening doors, it always referred to opportunities of ministry.

Historically, we do not know if Jesus opened the door of ministry opportunity to the Philadelphian believers or not. We can assume He did since that's the purpose of the church. But is it the message He was speaking to them about here? He doesn't tell them they are to do anything about the open door.

> for you have a little strength, 3:8

LITTLE STRENGTH

The church of Philadelphia had little power or influence in the city. They weren't real important in the eyes of others.

The amount of strength we have means nothing to the Lord. It's what we use of His strength that is important. Jesus is certainly not saying be like the little train "I think I can, I think I can." You can do it—you've got a little strength, use your little strength.

Ever think of yourself like that? Who am I? I have little strength. How can I make a difference? Then you're in good company. Remember when God called Moses to be the deliverer of His people? That's what Moses thought. He actually said, "Who am I that I should go to Pharaoh, and that I should bring the children of Israel out of Egypt?" (Exodus 3:11).

David said to Saul, "Who am I, and what is my life or my father's family in Israel, that I should be son-in-law to the king?" (1 Samuel 18:18).

King Solomon said, "Now, O LORD my God, You have made Your servant king instead of my father David, but I am a little child; I do not know how to go out or come in" (1 Kings 3:7).

And Jeremiah said, "Ah, Lord GOD! Behold, I cannot speak, for I am a youth" (Jeremiah 1:6).

Here is what God has to say about our *little strength*.

> "But God has chosen the foolish things of the world to put to shame the wise, and God has chosen the weak things of the world to put to shame the things which are mighty; and the base things of the world and the things which are despised God has chosen, and the things which are not, to bring to nothing the things that are." (1 Corinthians 1:27-28)

God doesn't say, "I will multiply the strength you have." He says, "Use Mine."

Apply this to how you are handling your struggle. What is your attitude toward your strengths or lack of them?

> have kept My word, 3:8

KEEP HIS WORD

It is in the tough times that it is toughest to keep God's Word. They observed it—they kept their eyes on it. I love that. How often do you think you would stray or flounder if you just kept your eyes, your attention, on God's Word? They kept it. They followed it. They didn't pick and choose when they would follow His Word or what parts of His Word they would keep.

> and have not denied My name. 3:8

DON'T DENY HIS NAME

There are lots of ways to deny Jesus' name.

In Titus 2 we are told how we should behave as wives, wrapping it up with, "to be discreet, chaste, homemakers, good, obedient to their own husbands, that the word of God may not be blasphemed" (Titus 2:5).

When we blaspheme, we hurt the reputation of someone. That's a way of denying who He is—by walking in a way that misrepresents Him. It's especially tempting to bail on walking in His way when we are struggling. What does this tell others? It tells them that the God you claim to follow isn't big enough or caring enough for you to trust Him in your struggle.

> Indeed I will make those of the synagogue of Satan, who say they are Jews and are not, but lie—3:9

THE SUFFERING

The church of Philadelphia suffered from Jews who were of the synagogue of Satan. They suffered from liars. We addressed this when we looked at the church of Smyrna. It's interesting that this is the only other church that didn't receive a rebuke from Jesus, an indicator that this sort of persecution is a result of believers being effective and not giving in to their struggle.

These Jews, who were not Jews, were people whose claim to David did not give them the key to David's kingdom. Jesus in essence said, "I have the key and I have opened the door to anyone who comes to Me," not those who simply claim to be of David's people.

These certain Jews may claim that the kingdom belongs to them, but Jesus is reminding the believers in Philadelphia, "Most assuredly, I say to you, I am the door of the sheep. All who ever came before Me are thieves and robbers, but the sheep did not hear them. I am the door. If anyone enters by Me, he will be saved, and will go in and out and find pasture" (John 10:7-9).

> indeed I will make them come and worship before your feet, and to know that I have loved you. 3:9

WHAT JESUS WILL DO

Jesus tells them what He would do for them—and for us. There are two possible interpretations worth noting.

This group of Jews in the city of Philadelphia who were claiming to know God would one day come to know that what these believers were declaring about Jesus was true. They would be transformed from enemies into worshipers of God and worship the Lord right alongside them.

Many times, the Jews who most fervently opposed Christianity, Paul being a great example, were the ones who ended up embracing it. I remember so well when Dale and I first came to our church and taught on the gift of tongues, those who opposed us the most, and opposed us greatly, now speak in tongues themselves. Often when we see great resistance, it is because a person is fighting the work of the Holy Spirit.

Secondly, we also know that anyone who opposes Jesus will one day bow before Him, acknowledging that He is Lord. It may refer to that day. And the Jews were expecting that day. Imagine being a new Christian and God's supposed people (these Jews) telling you that you've got it all wrong. Look at what Isaiah 60:14-16 says, speaking of the city of God:

> "Also the sons of those who afflicted you shall come bowing to you, and all those who despised you shall fall prostrate at the soles of your feet; and they shall call you The City of the LORD, Zion of the Holy One of Israel. Whereas you have been

> forsaken and hated, so that no one went through you, I will make you an eternal excellence, a joy of many generations. You shall drink the milk of the Gentiles, and milk the breast of kings; you shall know that I, the LORD, am your Savior and your Redeemer, the Mighty One of Jacob."

Who afflicted Jerusalem? The Gentiles. The Jews were all ready to see the Gentiles bow down before them and acknowledge they were God's people. But here Jesus has turned the tables and is reassuring the believers—the ones who are truly His. Those who say they are not will one day see how much God loves His own.

> Because you have kept My command to persevere, 3:10

PERSEVERE

Literally, according to the Greek scholar Kenneth Wuest, "Because you safeguarded the Word by observing it, which to observe requires the endurance which is Mine." [24] This has the sense of how they kept His Word. The word *endurance* is translated from the Greek word *hupomone* and is helpful in describing how they kept His word: constancy under suffering in faith and duty.

We shouldn't fail to notice two very important words that describe how they handled their struggles—they *kept* His Word, and they *kept* His command to persevere. They were steadfast and unwavering. Secondly, Jesus' use of the word *My*. Jesus said they "have kept *My* Word, and have not denied *My* name," and "have kept *My* command to persevere." His Word, His name, His command. They were about Jesus. In their struggle, they were about Him—that's key! Jesus noticed they were living for Him by valuing His Word, His name, and His example; that's faithfulness.

Jesus said, "When the Son of Man comes, will He really find faith on the earth?" (Luke 18:8). If He came today, would He find you as He found the church in Philadelphia, faithful? If not, why not?

> I also will keep you from the hour of trial which shall come upon the whole world, to test those who dwell on the earth. 3:10

JESUS WILL KEEP US

If you can make this mean anything but the tribulation, I want to know. It is a particular time of trial that will come upon the whole world. Nothing else fits. It had not come yet. It will come. He who says these things is Holy and True. They could (and we can) depend on who He is and what He says.

The purpose of the hour of trial is "to test those who dwell on the earth." This phrase is mentioned eight times in Revelation and it always refers to unbelievers.

> "The Lord knows how to deliver the godly out of temptations and to reserve the unjust under punishment for the day of judgment." (2 Peter 2:9)

Yes, God has unleashed His wrath upon His people before. We see it often in the Old Testament. But the purpose of this period of time is to unleash His wrath upon unbelievers. Jesus assures us to keep us from this time of trial, and we'll cover a lot more about this and the rapture when we get to chapter 4 of Revelation.

> Behold, I am coming quickly! 3:11

Look for Jesus, not for the Antichrist. Those words were always intended to encourage the believer to hang in there and prepare for His coming. They were not told to us to prepare for the tribulation.

> Hold fast what you have, that no one may take your crown. 3:11

HOLD FAST FOR THE CROWN

Jesus had only one instruction for them, a warning, and He says it to a church that is suffering. Crowns are usually rewards. If you and I don't hold fast, if we don't remain faithful when times get hard—what a waste.

I try to look at every struggle with this goal: to get a "well done" for how I've handled it. If I fail to keep His Word, if I act in a way that denies His name, if I do not persevere, there will be no crown for that struggle. There will be no "well done."

> He who overcomes, I will make him a pillar in the temple of My God, 3:12

PILLARS

Oh how significant those words would be to believers in Philadelphia who knew all about pillars—pillars were strong—pillars could not be knocked down. And in their day, names of important people were written on pillars.

In contrast to those of the city who appeared to have stability and strength, it will be revealed that they, the overcomers in Christ, are the pillars.

> and he shall go out no more. 3:12

STABILITY

Again we have the promise of stability. Earthquakes had caused them to go out from the city for protection, then back in, then out again. Life in God's kingdom will not be like that. They will be *in* all the time, safe and secure.

> I will write on him the name of My God and the name of the city of My God, the New Jerusalem, which comes down out of heaven from My God. And I will write on him My new name. 3:12

THE NAME OF MY GOD

Satan, the imitator, will mark his people with his mark. Jesus, the True, will mark His people with His.

Written names indicate ownership. You label that which is yours. So, God writes His name on you to acknowledge that He has claimed you as His. The church of Philadelphia had not denied Him—He would not deny them.

For those who don't know Him, do you know what words they will hear? "I never knew you; depart from Me" (Matthew 7:23). No one with His name written on them will ever hear those words. My grandkids will never hear me say those words either. When we go to Disneyland, I write my phone number and name on my grandkids' arms—if they get lost, call me—they belong to me.

THE NAME OF THE CITY OF MY GOD

This makes me think of when I go to the airport and check in my luggage and the destination is written all over the tags. I think of the many places I have traveled, and the words "*San Diego* are my favorite. When my luggage is labeled San Diego, that's where it's going. That's my city. When God's city is written on you, that's your destination. That's your city—forever—and He loses no one. We are citizens of the New Jerusalem, which comes down out of heaven because Jesus opened the door. He will not shut you out.

JESUS' NEW NAME

This denotes a yet unrevealed aspect of the character of Jesus, a new quality that will be revealed. We think we know Him now, yet there's a sense here that however deeply or well we know Him, it will pale when we see Him as He is—I just can't imagine. I try, but I know I fall so short in thinking about what I will understand about Jesus that I don't understand.

We learned in Revelation 2:17 that we will get a stone with a new name written on it. Now we find out that Jesus will have a new name too—at least new to us. Maybe it's new because no one has ever called Him that name before; but one day you will. One day I will. He will write His new name on us.

> He who has an ear, let him hear what the Spirit says to the churches. 3:13

CLOSING THOUGHTS

The crux of this message for us is in the example of how the church in Philadelphia handled their struggle. This is how Jesus would have you handle your struggle. This is what pleases Him and every believer can do the same.

Whether you handle the struggles well or not, if you are a believer, Jesus is still going to open the door for you; He's still going to write His name on you. But if in the times of struggle you don't keep to the things of Jesus and continue to be about Jesus, you'll have His name but not His praise. That's a tough statement. I almost deleted it, but it's His word of encouragement to Philadelphia. If they "hold fast" they'll have both. We can't deny that it is also a word of warning, not of punishment, but of missing out on what God desires to do.

The church in Philadelphia was not the church of brotherly love. The church in Philadelphia was the church of faithfulness. And Jesus knew it.

REFLECTION QUESTIONS

(For more extensive study questions visit CathyDickinson.com)

1. Jesus chose to use Old Testament descriptions of Himself in the message to the church in Philadelphia. Write what you learned about each description below:

He who is holy:

He who is true:

He who has the key of David:

He who opens and no one shuts, and shuts and no one opens:

2. Jesus said to the believers in Philadelphia, "for you have a little strength." What is your attitude about your strengths or lack of them?

3. The church in Philadelphia kept His Word. Take some time to ask the Lord to shed light where, in your struggle, you have taken your eyes off of the truth of His Word.

4. They did not deny His name. What are some ways we can deny His name when suffering or in the midst of a struggle?

5. Jesus commended these believers for their faithfulness to Him and to His Word in their struggle. In verse 10, he also commended them for keeping His command to persevere. Share what you learned about perseverance.

6. In verse 11, Jesus encouraged the believers in Philadelphia with the statement, "Behold, I am coming quickly!" How is this encouraging to you personally?

7. "Hold fast what you have, that no one may take your crown" (v. 11). This was a word of encouragement to the church in Philadelphia (and to us) but it can also be a word of warning. What is the warning and how are you challenged by it?

8. Jesus promises to those who overcome to write names on them (v. 12). Fill in the blanks and record the significance of the name that He will write on you.

The name of My ________________

What is the significance?

The name of the ________________ of My God

What is the significance?

My (Jesus') ________________ name

What is the significance?

Notes

Chapter Eight

DO YOU KNOW WHAT YOU NEED? REVELATION 3:14-22

This is the outline for the church of Laodicea:

1. Jesus identifies the church.
2. Jesus introduces Himself.
3. Jesus tells them what makes Him sick.
4. Jesus counsels them.
5. Jesus corrects them.
6. Jesus extends an invitation.
7. Jesus gives the promise.

And to the angel of the church of the Laodiceans write, 3:14

LAODICEA

The meaning of *Laodicea* is something like "the people rule," but it didn't get its name because it had that kind of attitude. The city was called Laodicea simply because it was named after the wife of the king who established it. (See map on page 23.)

Laodicea was about forty-five miles southwest of Philadelphia and was one of three cities clustered together with Colossae and Hierapolis. Three main trade routes went through the city, similar to a freeway interchange. Laodicea was a very rich and prosperous city and known for four things—four things which Jesus addressed in His message to them.

1. LUKEWARM WATER

During certain times of the year, Laodicea's water supply would dry up, so they would get water from the two adjacent cities. Colossae was known for having cold water and Hierapolis was known for having hot springs, but by the time it traveled from either city via aqueduct it became lukewarm.

2. ABUNDANCE OF GOLD

Their wealth caused them to be self-sufficient. In AD 60 when an earthquake completely destroyed the city, they refused aid from Rome and rebuilt the city with their own resources. That's hard for us to fathom. We can't imagine a city turning down federal aid today, but they did. Apparently that was rare back then too because Tacitus, a Roman historian, wrote this: "Laodicea arose from the ruins by the strength of her own resources and with no help from us." [25] The Laodiceans were very proud of that fact.

3. BLACK WOOL

The city was renowned for producing a fine, soft, and shiny black wool from the sheep that grazed in the area. It was a great center for the manufacturing of clothing, especially for warm outer garments.

4. EYE SALVE

Laodicea was also famous for their medicinal eye salve known to cure eye defects. They manufactured a powder and placed it in capsules, and the people would add oil or water to it or wrap it in dough, and put it on their eyes.

To this city with lukewarm water, which was rich with gold, black garments and eye salves, Jesus presented Himself as:

> These things says the Amen, the Faithful and True Witness, the Beginning of the creation of God: 3:14

THE AMEN

> "For all the promises of God in Him (Jesus) are Yes, and in Him Amen, to the glory of God through us." (2 Corinthians 1:20)

Jesus Himself is the confirmation of God's promises. There are nearly 3,600 promises in the Bible. Some are directed specifically to one person, such as the promise to Sarah that she would have a child when she was ninety years old. It's doubtful any of us would want to claim that one! There was the promise to Joshua to march around the city of Jericho seven times, and on the seventh day the wall of the city fell flat. And of course, there were promises of destruction made to the nation of Israel as a whole. We don't want those either. But most of the 3,600 promises are made to each and every person who belongs to the Lord.

Time has proven, and continues to prove, that God is faithful to do what He has said. Likewise Jesus, in rising from the dead as He said He would, is also proof—"the Amen" of what God has said.

I found this site called DailyBiblePromise.com. It will email a promise to you every day. If you visit the site, many of God's promises are listed according to topics. If you start your day reminded of just one of His promises, it may help you to keep the right focus.

The believers in Laodicea didn't appear to have been a people steeped in God's promises.

THE FAITHFUL AND TRUE WITNESS

A witness is someone who declares what they see. Jesus is "the Faithful and True Witness" of what He sees. When He declares that He sees this church of the Laodiceans as lukewarm, then they most certainly are lukewarm. Do you ignore the conviction of the

Holy Spirit when He points out something about you? Excusing it away or justifying it? He is reminding those in the church of the Laodiceans that what He sees is absolutely accurate, just as what He promises is absolutely certain.

THE BEGINNING OF THE CREATION OF GOD

Paul used the same description of Jesus in his letter to the Colossians, giving a little more explanation: "He is the image of the invisible God, the firstborn over all creation. For by Him all things were created that are in heaven and that are on earth, visible and invisible, whether thrones or dominions or principalities or powers. All things were created through Him and for Him" (Colossians 1:15, 16).

Jesus is the source of creation. He is the power by which creation began. "In the beginning was the Word, and the Word was with God, and the Word was God. He was in the beginning with God. All things were made through Him, and without Him nothing was made that was made" (John 1:1-3).

Jesus was making it very clear to the church of Laodicea that He is the source they should depend upon. The city residents didn't need Rome and apparently the Christians were living like they didn't need Jesus.

> I know your works, that you are neither cold nor hot. I could wish you were cold or hot. 3:15

DEVOID OF GOOD QUALITY

They were neither cold nor hot and Jesus declares that either of those conditions would be better than lukewarm. Most of us have been taught that hot represents fervency for the Lord—someone who is on fire for Him, and that cold represents someone who is cold to the things of the Lord—perhaps not even saved.

The word *cold* here literally means "cold." However, since Jesus did say that in the last days, "because lawlessness will abound, the love of many will grow cold" (Matthew 24:12), we can't rule out entirely the possibility that this is referring to their spiritual condition.

Zodhiates, my favorite Greek scholar, says this about the meaning *cold* here: "It does not represent spiritual lifelessness or an absence of zeal. Rather, it signifies a good quality and is analogous to one of the two conditions (hot or cold) in which water proves beneficial." [26]

Some say Jesus is speaking to unbelievers, mostly based on the things Jesus counsels them to "buy" in verse 18 and His invitation to "open the door" in verse 20. Again, maybe. It's hard enough for believers to understand what Jesus meant by things like "gold refined" and "white garments" and "eye salve," let alone unbelievers. An unbeliever simply needs to be told that Jesus died for their sins and be challenged to surrender to that fact.

We certainly would be in error to write these words off as not applying to us, wouldn't we. Since you and I are prone to the same false thinking and wrong dependencies as they were, we are going to approach this as a message to the believer.

Let's look again at what Zodhiates said about the word *cold*: "It does not represent spiritual lifelessness or an absence of zeal. Rather, it signifies a good quality and is analogous to one of the two conditions (hot or cold) in which water proves beneficial."

Cold water is refreshing. Hot water is soothing. To say that one's life is neither cold nor hot is to say it is devoid of any good quality. Taken in the context of the city of Laodicea that was drawing from the cold water of Colossae and the hot water of Hierapolis, it would seem that Jesus was pointing out that there were good things about cold water and good things about hot water but Laodicea had neither. If we interpret cold as hardened or unsaved, as many do, are we to believe Jesus would rather have someone go to hell than be lukewarm? Certainly not!

COMPROMISED

Those in the church of the Laodiceans were neither cold nor hot. They were lukewarm. How does water become lukewarm? It becomes the temperature of the surrounding environment. The cold water from Colossae and the hot water from Hierapolis became lukewarm as it was mixed with the environment. It was no longer purely cold or purely hot. Later in verse 17, Jesus calls these believers "miserable." It is *miserable* to be lukewarm. A lukewarm Christian has too much of the world to be happy in Jesus and too much of Jesus to be happy in the world.

To help you get a hold of the seriousness of this idea of a lukewarm Christian, take a moment to rate your relationship with the Lord right now. Solely for the purpose of rating ourselves, let's say that cold is bad. Cold would be a 1, 2, or 3 and hot would be an 8, 9, or 10. That leaves lukewarm in the middle at 4, 5, 6, or 7. Where would you put yourself on the scale? If you are anywhere in the middle, even 7, think about it—consider it—this message may be for you. Or perhaps you don't think that you are that bad? Neither did they.

Although Jesus will only judge those who reject Him, He has some very strong words for those who belong to Him, but who live apart from Him as far as their daily choices and attitudes.

> So then, because you are lukewarm, and neither cold nor hot, I will vomit you out of My mouth. 3:16

WHAT MAKES JESUS SICK?

When Jesus said, "I will," He is saying, "I am about to" or "I am ready to." Think about what it's like when you know you are about to vomit. Something inside of you isn't agreeing with you and your body says, "It's got to go! It cannot stay!" This is such a strong statement coming from Jesus that it's hard to perceive. I can imagine it being said to unbelievers, but then, I don't think they were ever in His mouth, ever a part of Him. But to believers, those are harsh words.

What is Jesus saying? He loved the church of Laodicea, which we will see in verse 19, yet they made Him sick. Let's look at what the Laodiceans were doing that caused Jesus to be sickened.

> Because you say, "I am rich, have become wealthy, and have need of nothing"—and do not know that you are wretched, miserable, poor, blind, and naked—3:17

NEEDING NOTHING

That's how "The Faithful and True Witness" saw them.

Jesus saw the church in Smyrna as rich when they saw themselves as poor. He had only praise and encouragement for them. What a contrast Laodicea was to this church. It's likely that the rest of the world admired the citizens of Laodicea for their self-sufficiency. Certainly their children were taught that's the way to be. God helps those who help themselves, right? Maybe that's where this lie started. At least it was perpetuated there.

When our granddaughter Janae was two, and she was very two, she let us know she could do it "by self." But one day at the park she got herself in a precarious position on the bars and she knew it, so she cried out, "Grammy, Grammy, help me!" I didn't ignore her and think, *Oh, how weak you are; try harder.* I was thrilled that she called out to me and I responded to her call. Maybe you haven't gone so far as to say, "I have need of nothing," but do you ever cry out to the Lord and plead, "Help me! I am poor and needy"? He will respond to you if you do.

David, who had a heart after God's heart, readily admitted, "I am poor and needy" (Psalm 86:1). Oh, how God loves that. The opposite of that is Laodicean thinking—it's pride. Pride makes Jesus sick, very sick. God hates pride because pride says, "I need nothing." Our God is continually saying to us, "Call on me."

PRIDE

Several years ago, Gisela Yohannan taught about Paul's thorn in the flesh and how he finally realized that when he was weak, God was strong. Then Gisela challenged us to consider how much of our own strength do we rely upon.

She basically asked, "Are you pretty strong? Maybe so strong that you have about eighty percent of what it takes, so you only call on God to fill the twenty percent gap? If so, then what *you* have accomplished is eighty percent *you* and twenty percent God." Yes, God calls us to use our gifts, even our strengths, but He never calls us to depend on them, relax in them, or pride ourselves about them.

Paul concluded, "When I am weak, then I am strong" (2 Corinthians 12:10). The weaker Paul was, the stronger God would show Himself on Paul's behalf. Showing Himself strong in our weakness, contrary to what the world and our flesh would tell us, is what pleases our Lord. We are to walk in His strength, not ask Him to fill the gap.

"In Him we live and move and have our being" (Acts 17:28). That's the attitude that pleases God. Walking in His strength begins with an awareness of His presence in our lives and paying attention to Him.

The Bible tells us "no one is good" (Luke 18:19). It tells us that the works of our flesh are "like filthy rags" (Isaiah 64:6). "Those who live according to the flesh set their minds on the things of the flesh" (Romans 8:5). And "nothing good dwells" in our flesh (Romans 7:18). The question to ask yourself is, "Do I really believe that? Or is there a part of me that believes the lie that I'm basically good?"

When we lean on our own understanding, strength, and desires, aren't we essentially saying that we're good? How is that thinking any different from those in the church in Laodicea?

JESUS' COUNSEL

Jesus has some counsel for them—three pieces of advice that they would have understood because of their situation.

> I counsel you to buy from Me gold refined in the fire, that you may be rich; 3:18

1. REFINEMENT

I thought of the gold nuggets they might have had. I pulled up pictures of both a nugget and of refined gold. The nugget looked pretty nice, but refined gold was beautiful. What does refining do? Refining exposes the genuineness.

First Peter 1:7 says this: "that the genuineness of your faith, being much more precious than gold that perishes, though it is tested by fire, may be found to praise, honor, and glory at the revelation of Jesus Christ."

They thought they were fine and didn't think they needed refining. Why did they think that? Because they were rich with material possessions. Might you or I think the same thing? Maybe not in words, but in actions perhaps we've said, "I don't need to seek the Lord today—I'm fine. Things are going well." I know I have. How is that any different from the believers in Laodicea?

For more understanding and insight into God's call to buy from Him, look at this passage from Isaiah.

> "Why do you spend money for what is not bread, and your wages for what does not satisfy? Listen carefully to Me, and eat what is good, and let your soul delight

itself in abundance. Incline your ear, and come to Me. Hear, and your soul shall live; and I will make an everlasting covenant with you—for My thoughts are not your thoughts, nor are your ways My ways, says the Lord. For as the heavens are higher than the earth, so are My ways higher than your ways, and My thoughts than your thoughts." (Isaiah 55:1-3, 8-9)

Jesus counsels, "Buy from Me gold refined in the fire, that you may be rich." He is basically saying, "Come to Me. I have riches above and beyond what you could ever imagine and they are yours for the asking." Why is Jesus telling them this? He tells them for their good, that they may truly be rich.

> and white garments, that you may be clothed, that the shame of your nakedness may not be revealed; 3:18

2. WHITE GARMENTS

They had been making quite a profit from people buying their black garments, but listen to the rejoicing heart of Isaiah: "I will greatly rejoice in the LORD, my soul shall be joyful in my God; for He has clothed me with the garments of salvation, He has covered me with the robe of righteousness, as a bridegroom decks himself with ornaments, and as a bride adorns herself with her jewels" (Isaiah 61:10).

Notice the phrase *decks himself.* That's pretty flashy. Their wool might have been shiny, but Jesus' garments are going to be flashy. What are you wearing now? The ways of the world or His righteousness? Or perhaps you are wearing a little bit of both, and if you are, then you probably clash and that makes our Lord sick. Why is Jesus telling them this? For their good—"that the shame of your nakedness may not be revealed."

Look at the quote from Matthew Poole again from chapter six, "As sin is expressed under the notion of nakedness, so holiness is expressed under the notion of a garment." [27] We don't want to be seen without Jesus' holiness covering us. It's shameful. We want others to see Jesus' character, not our own.

> and anoint your eyes with eye salve, that you may see. 3:18

3. SPIRITUAL SIGHT

I read when archaeologists excavated the ruins in the ancient city of Laodicea, they found nothing in the ground but dirt, nothing that indicated there was a miracle eye dust. So maybe it was a hoax. Laodicea had this eye salve that supposedly helped with sight or soothed the eyes, but they weren't seeing all there was to see. I couldn't help but think of the blind man whose sight was restored when Jesus took simple mud from the ground, spit on it, and applied it to the man's eyes. Jesus wanted to give them spiritual eyes to see beyond what was right in front of them, much more than soothe.

Let's look at what Peter had to say in support of this. First, Peter points out,

> "As His divine power has given to us all things that pertain to life and godliness, through the knowledge of Him who called us by glory and virtue, by which have been given to us exceedingly great and precious promises, that through these you may be partakers of the divine nature, having escaped the corruption that is in the world through lust." (2 Peter 1:3-4)

Peter concludes, "For he who lacks these things is *shortsighted, even to blindness*, and has forgotten that he was cleansed from his old sins" (2 Peter 1:9).

Spiritual things are spiritually understood or seen. Why did Jesus counsel them to anoint their eyes with salve from Him? So that they may *spiritually see.*

> As many as I love, I rebuke and chasten. 3:19

A LOVE CORRECTION

Let's summarize what Jesus said about those in the church of the Laodiceans. They were lukewarm, wretched, miserable, poor, blind, and naked. Wow! Maybe He *was* talking to unbelievers. Jesus was telling them, "You think you are self-sufficient and don't need anything? I see it very differently. You need My refining work, you need My righteousness, and you need My eyes because you can't see that you are poor, naked, and blind."

Has Jesus ever called you those things? We often respond in one of two ways. (1) We can't imagine it and continue to function in our pride, or (2) we believe it and move to a mode of condemnation. But ah, Jesus follows up with these words, "As many as I love, I rebuke and chasten" (Revelation 3:19).

PHILEO

God *agape* (unconditionally loves) the whole world—both unbelievers and believers. But the Greek word for *love* used here is not *agape*; it is *phileo. Phileo* is a responsive kind of love, an "I like you" kind of love. God only links that kind of love with believers—those that are His. *Phileo* love is an "I want the best for you" kind of love. Yes, God wants the best for everyone, but He is not working toward the best for someone who isn't His. He doesn't work all things out for their good and He doesn't chasten them or rebuke them with the purpose of getting them back on track with Him.

This reminds me of a time when our three grandsons spent the night. We all slept on the floor and couches in the family room. At one point I found myself just staring at them while they were sleeping and praying for them. I want the best for them. If you asked me why I love them so, I think my answer would be, "Just because they are mine; they are my grandsons." You could lay a child down next to those three boys who was absolutely perfect and I would not have the feelings toward that child that I do for my grandsons. God doesn't *phileo* love perfect people. He *phileo* loves those who are His, simply because they are His.

My grandsons have certainly done things that have grossed me out to the point of me saying, "Stop that!" or "Take that away!" or "I'm going to vomit!" or "That's got to go!" But even though they make me sick sometimes, it doesn't affect or diminish my love for them in any way.

WHAT'S YOUR RESPONSE?

What do you do when God convicts you, even to the point of revealing your wretchedness to you? Do you give up? Do you feel like you just can't pull out of the way you are, so why try? Jesus has a message for you and it's this—I love you! And My rebuke and My chastening are proof of that.

> "And you have forgotten the exhortation which speaks to you as to sons: My son, do not despise the chastening of the LORD, nor be discouraged when you are rebuked by Him; for whom the LORD loves He chastens, and scourges every son whom He receives. If you endure chastening, God deals with you as with sons; for what son is there whom a father does not chasten? But if you are without chastening, of which all have become partakers, then you are illegitimate and not sons. Furthermore, we have had human fathers who corrected us, and we paid them respect. Shall we not much more readily be in subjection to the Father of spirits and live? For they indeed for a few days chastened us as seemed best to them, but He for our profit, that we may be partakers of His holiness. Now no chastening seems to be joyful for the present, but painful; nevertheless, afterward <u>it yields the peaceable fruit of righteousness</u> to those who have been trained by it." (Hebrews 12:5-11)

The New Living Bible states it this way: "there will be a peaceful harvest of right living." Then Jesus says a very important word: "Therefore." Therefore what? Wallow in your failure? Stay stuck in the way you are? Certainly not!

> Therefore be zealous and repent. 3:19

BE ZEALOUS

To be zealous is to have an intense desire. Zealousness comes from hanging out by the fire—His refining fire. Get out of the lukewarm water of your flesh or of the lukewarm water of the world and get into the hot cleansing waters of repentance. Drink deeply of the cool refreshment of His Holy Spirit.

> Behold, I stand at the door and knock. If anyone hears My voice and opens the door, I will come in to him and dine with him, and he with Me. 3:20

JESUS COMES TO US

An unknown fourteenth-century author had this to say about this passage:

"Love for men emptied God. For He does not remain in His place of glory and summon to Himself the servant whom He loved; but goes Himself and seeks him; and He who is rich comes to the dwelling of the poor, and discloses His love. He does not withdraw from him who repels Him, nor is He disgusted at his insolence; but pursuing him, remains sitting at his doors, that He may show him the One who loves him." [28]

Jesus came to us. God comes to you. The idea of Jesus at the door applies to the sinner and the saint just the same.

BONDING TIME

The word *dine* in verse 20 refers to having supper. Supper was the last meal of the day and it was the time when they settled in and took their time eating and enjoying fellowship. We hardly know what that means today.

I heard a joke about a mom calling out, "Time for dinner" and the kids ran, put on their jackets, and got in the car, ready to go to the nearest take out. When our son and daughter were in high school, I used to take them out individually for lunch. My son once said to me, "Can we just eat lunch and go or does this have to be a bonding time?"

The believers in Laodicea didn't want to bond with Jesus. They didn't think they needed it. Nothing compares to slowing down and dining with Jesus. He's waiting—waiting for us to hear His call and respond. The word *hear* in verse 20 means to "listen with the intent to respond." When my granddaughter, Janae, knocks on my door, she doesn't come to dine with me or spend time with me. She knocks. I open the door and she heads right for the cupboard with the fruit snacks and then back out the door she goes. Are you like that? What have You got for me, God? Did you taste the Word today? When? When you were in the shower? When you were in the car? Did you quickly read a devotional or a few verses? Did you hear Him knocking when the alarm went off? Or did you hit the snooze button?

OPEN THE DOOR

In the church of the Laodiceans we see a people who were too preoccupied with their own lives to need Jesus. Jesus extended an invitation. He was calling to them and He's calling to us, "Come to Me, need Me, spend time with Me."

There's a famous picture of Jesus knocking on a door, but the door has no latch, no doorknob or handle. When asked where the door latch was, the artist responded, "It's on the inside."

The choice to open the door is ours. Jesus never plays ding-dong ditch. He doesn't knock and then go away when you open. He says, "I WILL come in to him and dine with him, and he with Me." We are offered mutual dining with the One who is the AMEN.

> To him who overcomes I will grant to sit with Me on My throne, as I also overcame and sat down with My Father on His throne. 3:21

A PROMISED THRONE

Jesus concludes with His promise to him who overcomes—to all who belong to Him. This is what He who is Faithful and True declares: "I will grant to sit with Me on My throne, as I also overcame and sat down with My Father on His throne." A throne is usually a one-seater. I don't know what His throne is going to be like, but God reveals a little bit about it as we continue to study Revelation.

Consider the request John's mother made of Jesus when she asked if John and his brother, James, could sit one on His right hand and one on His left in His kingdom. But Jesus said, "…to sit on My right hand and on My left is not Mine to give, but it is for those for whom it is prepared by My Father" (see Matthew 20:20-23).

I wonder what John was thinking when Jesus made this promise to all overcomers. Jesus had said it wasn't His to give. Now that Jesus has ascended to His throne, He is giving it. And He's giving it to *all* of us that are His. I don't really know what that means. I would think the throne is the best place and Jesus wants to share it with us. Wow! Just wow!

> He who has an ear, let him hear what the Spirit says to the churches. 3:22

CLOSING THOUGHTS

To all of the seven churches, Jesus had this to say to each one: "He who has an ear, let him hear what the Spirit says."

> To the church of Ephesus the Spirit had said they had lost their first love.
>
> To the church in Smyrna the Spirit had challenged them to do what God had called them to do despite the cost.
>
> To the church in Pergamos the Spirit had said they were compromising.
>
> To the church in Thyatira the Spirit had said they allowed unbiblical teaching in their lives.
>
> To the church in Sardis the Spirit had said they had left their dependence on the Holy Spirit.
>
> To the church in Philadelphia the Spirit had said they handled their struggles faithfully.
>
> To the church of the Laodiceans the Spirit had said they were lukewarm and didn't even know it.

It's easy to find ourselves in each one of these. What is the Holy Spirit saying to you? Where have you been challenged?

REFLECTION QUESTIONS

(For more extensive study questions visit CathyDickinson.com)

1. What did you learn about Jesus' introduction as "the Faithful and True Witness"?

2. What does the statement "you are neither cold nor hot" mean?

3. A lukewarm Christian is miserable, having too much of the world to be happy in Jesus and too much of Jesus to be happy in the world. Share when you have seen or experienced the truth of this statement?

4. What did the believers in Laodicea say that made Jesus sick? How can you prevent the same attitude from creeping into your own life?

5. Which one of Jesus' three pieces of counsel to the church of the Laodiceans challenges you the most and why?

6. Jesus rebuked and chastened the church of Laodicea. What is your natural default response to His rebuke?

7. When you consider His message to the believers in Laodicea and that His chastening rebuke is proof of His love for you, how will this affect your response in the future?

8. Take some time to pray and consider the truth that Jesus wants to dine with you and enjoy fellowship with you. Whatever your current dining time with Jesus is like, how are you challenged to make this time more intimate with Him than it is now?

9. What was revealed to you about Jesus through the study of His message to the church of the Laodiceans?

10. Which one of the seven churches do you most identify with? Why? Write and commit to the remedy and counsel Jesus gave to that church.

Chapter Nine

THE RAPTURE OF THE CHURCH

"Write the things which you have seen, and the things which are, and the things which will take place after this" (Revelation 1:19).

AFTER THIS

In chapters 2 and 3 of Revelation, we saw "the things which are," the letters to the churches. We saw the condition of the churches that existed then and we also saw similarities to the church and to us as individuals today. These are "the things which are."

The remaining chapters in Revelation reveal "the things which will take place after this." From this point on, we will be approaching our study from a pre-tribulation rapture vantage point, the belief that the church will be caught up into heaven before the tribulation begins. So before diving further into Revelation, I want to explain what the rapture is and the basis for the belief that it takes place pre-tribulation. Here is a brief overview.

RAPTURE

The term *caught up* in Latin is *rapturos*. It literally translates as "snatched up." It is from this Latin word that we get our word "rapture."

"For the Lord Himself will descend from heaven with a shout, with the voice of an archangel, and with the trumpet of God. And the dead in Christ will rise first. Then we who are alive and remain shall be caught up together with them in the clouds to meet the Lord in the air. And thus we shall always be with the Lord." (1 Thessalonians 4:16-17)

"Behold, I tell you a mystery: We shall not all sleep (die), but we shall all be changed—in a moment, in the twinkling of an eye, at the last trumpet. For the trumpet will sound, and the dead will be raised incorruptible, and we shall be changed." (1 Corinthians 15:51-52)

There will be a time when, at the sound of a trumpet, in the twinkling of an eye (faster than a blink) Jesus will come for His people. The bodies of those who have already died will be raised up; those who belong to Jesus and are alive will be caught up together with them to meet the Lord in the air and be forever with Him.

WHEN IS THE RAPTURE?

The question that arises in the study of Revelation is not, "IS there a rapture?" but rather, "WHEN will the rapture occur?" There are those who believe that the rapture will occur before the tribulation. Some believe that the rapture will occur about halfway into the tribulation and still others believe the rapture will occur at the end of the tribulation. The one thing these viewpoints all have in common is that they are embraced by godly, well-studied people. There is controversy within the body of Christ about the timing of the rapture.

It is my understanding, and I emphasize *my understanding*, that most evangelical Christians, including Calvary Chapels, believe that the rapture will occur before the tribulation. I have tried to see the other views, but there are pre-tribulation points that cannot be dismissed, while there are other verses that cause us to wonder how post-tribulation fits.

Because the timing of the rapture is not a for sure thing, I considered leaving it out of our study of Revelation. But my guess is, when we get to chapters 6-19 where God is pouring out His wrath, the most predominant question you would have is, "Am I going to have to go through that?" And the result of not having that question answered would, I think, be much fear—even if you had the faith to comfort yourself with the Lord's promise that He will never leave you nor forsake you. That's why it's important we approach Revelation with an idea of where we are going to be during a time on earth that will be worse than anyone has ever experienced to date.

PRE-TRIBULATION RAPTURE

Here is the basic reasoning behind the belief of the pre-tribulation rapture:

1. GOD DID NOT APPOINT US TO WRATH

> "For God did not appoint us to wrath, but to obtain salvation through our Lord Jesus Christ." (1 Thessalonians 5:9)

The tribulation is the time God has appointed to pour out His wrath. Biblically, wrath and anger are two different things. Anger is quick—quick to feel and quick to be expressed. Wrath is the result of a building up and is not expressed explosively. As we will see in Revelation, it is well-planned and well-thought out by the Lord. It has been building over the millennia as God has not missed the commission of one sin. He has seen all the awful depravity of man over and over and over again. He has seen man choose his own ways over those of the Lord's again and again. God not only sees it, God *ponders* what He sees. He weighs it out. He really thinks about it. "For the ways of man are before the eyes of the LORD, and He ponders all his paths" (Proverbs 5:21). We will see this wrath more clearly when we get to later chapters which discuss the time of the tribulation.

First Thessalonians says this: "...to wait for His Son from heaven, whom He raised from the dead, even Jesus <u>who delivers us from the wrath to come</u>" (1 Thessalonians 1:10).

Jesus promised the church of Philadelphia, "Because you have kept My command to persevere, I also will keep you from the <u>hour of trial which shall come upon the whole world</u>, to test those who dwell on the earth" (Revelation 3:10).

2. THE RAPTURE IS A COMFORT TO BELIEVERS

When the rapture is mentioned, it is meant to be a comfort to believers. Right after Paul wrote about the rapture in 1 Thessalonians 4:16-17, he wrote, "Therefore comfort one another with these words" (1 Thessalonians 4:18). Paul continued to write to reassure them that they were not going to be in the tribulation because "God did not appoint us to wrath" (1 Thessalonians 5:9). "Therefore comfort each other and edify one another, just as you also are doing" (1 Thessalonians 5:11).

The thought of being taken up, out of this earth to be with Jesus forever, is a very comforting truth. But for me, a lot of that comfort would be lost if it came with the prospect of living in a time of God pouring out His wrath. Yes, in this world we will experience tribulation—but not God's wrath.

3. THE CHURCH IS NOT MENTIONED AFTER REVELATION 3

The church is referred to nineteen times in Revelation prior to chapter 4, but not again throughout the chapters that deal with the tribulation. It's impossible to give a specific scriptural reference to prove that, but as we study the remaining chapters it will be apparent that the church is absent. It's just not there.

4. THE TRIBULATION IS FOR ISRAEL, NOT THE CHURCH

Daniel 9 speaks of the 490 years that God will deal with Israel. From the time of the going forth of the commandment to rebuild the temple to the coming of the Messiah would be 483 years. That leaves seven years remaining. Study it. It would be hard to make that seven years refer to anything but the seven years of tribulation.

Speaking of the tribulation, Jeremiah wrote: "Alas! For that day is great, so that none is like it; and it is the time of Jacob's (Israel's) trouble, but he shall be saved out of it" (Jeremiah 30:7). The tribulation is Israel's last opportunity to be redeemed.

"For I do not desire, brethren, that you should be ignorant of this mystery, lest you should be wise in your own opinion, that blindness in part has happened to Israel until the fullness of the Gentiles has come in" (Romans 11:25). We are living in the time of the Gentiles; the time between the first coming of the Messiah and the rapture. When the time of the Gentiles is over, it will again be the time for Israel.

5. THE RAPTURE IS IMMINENT

This is my personal favorite and it's the one that the mid-tribbers and post-tribbers can't explain away. *Imminent,* meaning that the rapture can happen at any time and no one knows when that time will be.

> "But know this, that if the master of the house had known what hour the thief would come, he would have watched and not allowed his house to be broken into." (Matthew 24:43; Luke 12:39)

> "For you yourselves know perfectly that the day of the Lord so comes as a thief in the night." (1 Thessalonians 5:2)
>
> "Remember therefore how you have received and heard; hold fast and repent. Therefore if you will not watch, I will come upon you as a thief, and you will not know what hour I will come upon you." (Revelation 3:3)
>
> "But of that day and hour no one knows, not even the angels in heaven, nor the Son, but only the Father." (Mark 13:32)

If the timing of the rapture was mid-trib or post-trib, we could count the days and therefore know the day of Christ's return. Mid-tribulation would be three-and-a-half years after the Antichrist signs an alliance with Israel. Post-tribulation would be 1,290 days from the mid-tribulation mark when the Antichrist takes the daily sacrifice away. Both of those are dependent on something happening before the rapture. The Bible clearly teaches we are to be ready because it could happen at *anytime*.

THE PARABLE OF THE VIRGINS

Consider the parable of the wise and foolish virgins.

> "Then the kingdom of heaven shall be likened to ten virgins who took their lamps and went out to meet the bridegroom. Now five of them were wise, and five were foolish. Those who were foolish took their lamps and took no oil with them, but the wise took oil in their vessels with their lamps. But while the bridegroom was delayed, they all slumbered and slept. And at midnight a cry was heard: 'Behold, the bridegroom is coming; go out to meet him!' Then all those virgins arose and trimmed their lamps. And the foolish said to the wise, 'Give us some of your oil, for our lamps are going out.' But the wise answered, saying, 'No, lest there should not be enough for us and you; but go rather to those who sell, and buy for yourselves.' And while they went to buy, the bridegroom came, and those who were ready went in with him to the wedding; and the door was shut.
>
> "Afterward the other virgins came also, saying, 'Lord, Lord, open to us!' But he answered and said, 'Assuredly, I say to you, I do not know you.'
>
> "Watch therefore, for you know neither the day nor the hour in which the Son of Man is coming." (Matthew 25:1-13)

WATCH FOR THE BRIDEGROOM

Five were ready for the coming of the bridegroom; five were not. At the end of the parable, did Jesus exhort them to have oil in their lamps because a time was coming when they would not be able to buy or sell? No. His exhortation was, "Watch therefore, for you know neither the day nor the hour in which the Son of Man is coming."

Scripture tells us to watch for the coming of Jesus, not to watch for the revealing of the Antichrist. We are told to be ready for Jesus' coming, not stock up for the hard times to come!

THE JEWISH WEDDING

The parable of the virgins is so important. The Jews of the day would have understood it much better than we do as it clearly represented the way they celebrated weddings. Look at the steps to a Jewish wedding and marvel at how closely it relates to Jesus coming for His bride, the church.

1. THE BETROTHAL

The prospective groom would travel from his father's house to the house of the prospective bride. Jesus left His Father's house in heaven to come to our house on earth.

2. THE GROOM PAYS THE PRICE FOR THE BRIDE

In paying the purchase price for the bride, he established his commitment to her. Jesus paid for you and me with the price of His blood shed on the cross.

We have this wonderful promise in Ephesians 1:13-14, "You were sealed with the Holy Spirit of promise who is the guarantee of our inheritance until the redemption of the purchased possession, to the praise of His glory."

The moment someone receives Jesus and the price He paid for them, God seals the believer with the Holy Spirit "Who is the <u>guarantee</u> of our inheritance until the redemption of the purchased possession." This word *guarantee* is the Greek word that is also translated as engagement ring. We, as believers, now live in that state of betrothal or engagement.

3. THE GROOM RETURNS TO HIS FATHER'S HOUSE

The prospective groom would then return to his father's house and stay for an extended period of time and he would prepare their living accommodations at his father's house. The future bride and groom would live on his father's property.

> "In My Father's house are many mansions; if it were not so, I would have told you. I go to prepare a place for you." (John 14:2)

4. THE GROOM RETURNS FOR HIS BRIDE

The groom would come for his bride, but not at a time he or she knew. Only when his father determined it was time, then the groom would return for his bride. The groom did not know—as Jesus said He did not know. Therefore, the bride was to be always ready, always anticipating the coming of her groom and her wedding day.

> "And if I go and prepare a place for you, I will come again and receive you to Myself; that where I am, there you may be also." (John 14:3)

5. THE GROOM TAKES HIS BRIDE TO HIS FATHER'S HOUSE

The groom returns with his bride to his father's house. The bride undergoes a ritual cleansing prior to the wedding ceremony to get ready for her groom. This period of time could be up to seven days.

After Jesus raptures the saints, He will bring them into His chambers. The tribulation saints will join them after their death, because they repented and cleansed themselves with the blood of the Lamb. This seven days matches the seven years of tribulation.

> "Come, my people, enter your chambers, and shut your doors behind you; hide yourself, as it were, for a little moment, until the indignation is past. For behold, the Lord comes out of His place to punish the inhabitants of the earth for their iniquity; the earth will also disclose her blood, and will no more cover her slain." (Isaiah 26:20-121)

6. THE MARRIAGE SUPPER

When the bride has made herself ready, the groom and bride marry and there is a marriage feast and celebration.

> "Let us be glad and rejoice and give Him glory, for the marriage of the Lamb has come, and His wife has made herself ready… Then he said to me, "Write: 'Blessed are those who are called to the marriage supper of the Lamb!'" And he said to me, "These are the true sayings of God." (Revelation 19:7, 9)

7. THE GROOM PRESENTS HIS BRIDE

After the celebration, the bride is brought forth with her husband to a public place—for all to see. This parallels Jesus bringing His church to earth with Him at the second coming.

> "Then one of the seven angels who had the seven bowls filled with the seven last plagues came to me and talked with me, saying, 'Come, I will show you the bride, the Lamb's wife.' And he carried me away in the Spirit to a great and high mountain, and showed me the great city, the holy Jerusalem, descending out of heaven from God, having the glory of God. Her light was like a most precious stone, like a jasper stone, clear as crystal." (Revelation 21:9-11)

Now that's beautiful and incredible; mid-trib and post-trib thinking mar that whole picture.

CLOSING THOUGHTS

God did not pour out His wrath until His people were safe. Consider these Scriptures:

> "But as the days of Noah were, so also will the coming of the Son of Man be. For as in the days before the flood, they were eating and drinking, marrying and giving in marriage, <u>until the day that Noah entered the ark</u>." (Matthew 24:37-38)

> "Likewise as it was also in the days of Lot: They ate, they drank, they bought, they sold, they planted, they built; but on the day that Lot went out of Sodom it rained fire and brimstone from heaven and destroyed them all. Even so will it be in the day when the Son of Man is revealed." (Luke 17:28-30)

For a more detailed teaching on what the rapture is and our basis for believing there is a rapture, read 1 Corinthians 15 and all of 1 and 2 Thessalonians. You can also listen to a message I taught from 1 Thessalonians 4:13-18, "Words of Comfort." [29]

REFLECTION QUESTIONS

(For more extensive study questions visit CathyDickinson.com)

1. Give a brief description of what the rapture is.

2. The rapture is to be used to comfort believers and we are told to comfort others with the comfort we've received. What comfort have you personally received when you considered a pre-tribulation rapture?

3. Considering that you, as a believer, are the "bride of Christ," take some time to soak in the steps of a Jewish wedding. Record your thoughts and end with a prayer of praise and thanksgiving.

S.May

Chapter Ten

THE THRONE OF HEAVEN: REVELATION 4

> After these things I looked, and behold, a door standing open in heaven. And the first voice which I heard was like a trumpet speaking with me, saying, "Come up here, and I will show you things which must take place after this." 4:1

While John saw it perfectly, he couldn't describe it perfectly. He had to describe heavenly things with earthly words. How would we describe the ocean to someone who lived in the desert or a sunset to someone who had never seen the sky?

We, like John, would be left trying to relate what we've seen with what others have been exposed to and very often resorting to words such as "like" in an effort to compare with the incomparable.

AN OPEN DOOR

John saw "a door standing open." Did you think there was a gate? How many times have we heard about Saint Peter standing at the entrance of heaven, guarding the pearly gates, asking questions of the deceased to see if they passed the test to enter in? Let's not forget that Jesus passed the test for us and the way has been made open for all who belong to Him.

MAN'S ACCOUNT OR GOD'S?

What if we stopped right here in our study and I had you draw the open door to heaven and what you imagined was beyond that door? What would you draw? Would you draw a lot of clouds and people looking like angels playing harps? Perhaps some envision a perfect earth. That's what the Jehovah's Witnesses promise—no Jesus—just a perfect earth.

Some who claim to have had near-death experiences have written bestsellers and tell us there's a tunnel with a bright light at the end and loud sounds. Christians and non-Christians alike flock to read these books hoping to get a glimpse of heaven for themselves and maybe get answers to some of their questions: *Will I see my loved ones? Will I know my loved ones? Will I be able to fly? How old will I be?* We look to these accounts to tell us what heaven is like. Maybe they are credible; maybe they are not.

God has chosen to reveal what He wants us to know right now. While He wants us to understand some things about our eternal home, prepare yourself that you may have some unanswered questions. We don't have all the answers. God has given to us, in His Word, what He wants us to know about heaven. His revelation of heaven is faithful and true. Are we as interested in what God has declared or are we more interested in a *New York Times* bestseller?

GOD'S ACCOUNT

> Immediately I was in the Spirit; and behold, a throne set in heaven, and One sat on the throne. 4:2

John saw "One who sat on the throne"—the Father— but he didn't describe a physical body. "God is Spirit, and those who worship Him must worship in spirit and truth" (John 4:24).

He doesn't seem disappointed that he hasn't seen his loved ones. John is in awe and he does the best he can to describe to us what he saw. What did John say about the One on the throne?

> And He who sat there was like a jasper and a sardius stone in appearance; 4:3

Jasper is later described in Revelation as clear as crystal, more like a glorious diamond, bright and beautiful. A sardius stone is a deep, deep, ruby red. Of course we think about the cleansing power of the blood, but we aren't told about the significance of these stones. They do represent the first and last of the tribes of Israel, as told to us in Revelation 21, but that's not really helpful. Rather we could say that the first and last tribes of Israel may represent these stones in heaven.

> and there was a rainbow around the throne, in appearance like an emerald. 4:3

John saw a rainbow *around* the throne. It is my understanding that a rainbow is actually a circle; we just don't see the whole thing. One commentator wrote that the circle of a rainbow could be seen from an airplane. We don't know precisely, but something encircled the throne that was *like* a rainbow, that was green *like* an emerald. Some translate it as a halo.

God created colors. When we gaze at sunsets, flowers, multi-colored birds and fish, and the blues of the ocean, we're amazed that the earth is so colorful. There is no way heaven is going to be less vibrant. There is no way heaven won't be wonderful to you.

In a program I watched recently, it said that our brain can take in or identify only a very small amount of the spectrum of colors that are out there. In heaven, we will be able to take them all in with perfect clarity. Oh, how confined John must have felt, "I saw a rainbow that was like an emerald." That's the best he could do, but when we see it we will know and smile at how far John's descriptions fell from heaven's realities.

> Around the throne were twenty-four thrones, and on the thrones I saw twenty-four elders sitting, clothed in white robes; and they had crowns of gold on their heads. 4:4

There are three points to support that these twenty-four elders are representatives of the church.

1. JOHN CALLED THEM ELDERS

Angels are never called elders. John's experience would have been that elders were leaders or representatives of God's people.

2. THEY POSSESSED PROMISES TO OVERCOMERS

John used three terms to describe these elders: they sat on thrones, they were clothed in white robes, and they had crowns—these are crowns of victory for overcoming. These are all promises that Jesus made to overcomers in His messages to the churches in Revelation 2 and 3.

3. THEY WERE REDEEMED

We see these elders again in Revelation 5 worshiping and singing a song to the Lamb.

"And they sang a new song, saying … 'For You were slain, and have redeemed us to God by Your blood out of every tribe and tongue and people and nation, and have made us kings and priests to our God; and we shall reign on the earth'" (Revelation 5:9-10). We will also see them at other times in Revelation. When the four living creatures worship, the elders join them.

Remember John's description of Jesus in Revelation 1:5 "Him who loved us and washed us from our sins in His own blood." Only believers can be redeemed and represent all of us who have been redeemed by His blood; therefore, these elders are not angels.

> And from the throne proceeded lightnings, thunderings, and voices. 4:5

Israel had seen and heard God's display of lightning and thunder and they trembled at the power. Other than a bomb, what makes a more powerful sound than thunder? It is believed that these lightnings and thunderings are a sign that judgment is about to begin. Because God is holy, He must also judge, and indeed it will begin with the opening of the first seal when we get to Revelation chapter 6.

> Seven lamps of fire were burning before the throne, which are the seven Spirits of God. 4:5

These lamps do not represent the lampstands or candlesticks of the seven churches mentioned in Revelation 1. In the Greek language, these are two separate words. This word *lamp* is more accurately translated as "torch," and they "are the seven Spirits of God," which is the Holy Spirit. We learned this when we studied Revelation 1: "Grace to you and peace from Him who is and who was and who is to come, and from the seven Spirits who are before His throne" (Revelation 1:4).

> Before the throne there was a sea of glass, like crystal. 4:6

The closest I can relate to a sea of glass is a lake in Maine that I saw during the fall. It was so still; it reflected all of the autumn trees. I wonder if this sea of glass reflected the glories of the throne.

> And in the midst of the throne, and around the throne, were four living creatures full of eyes in front and in back. The first living creature was like a lion, the second living creature like a calf, the third living creature had a face like a man, and the fourth living creature was like a flying eagle. The four living creatures, each having six wings, were full of eyes around and within. 4:6-8

Creatures is probably an inadequate word. John describes them as living beings of some sort.

Ezekiel saw something similar, but each one had these four faces. It's possible he saw them from a different perspective than John. We'll look at them when they come up again in a later chapter, because at this point in time, John was more interested in the "One on the throne." So were the elders and the living creatures. Look at their response to Him—

> And they do not rest day or night, saying: "Holy, holy, holy, Lord God Almighty, Who was and is and is to come!" 4:8

HOLY, HOLY, HOLY

In Isaiah 6:3, when Isaiah saw the Lord sitting on the throne, he heard the same words, "Holy, holy, holy." This scene opens our spiritual eyes to see the first two phrases of the Lord's Prayer in a deeper way. "Our Father in heaven, hallowed be Your name" (Matthew 6:9). Our Father God is in heaven, sitting upon His throne, and holy is His name! Jesus said we are to pray, "Your kingdom come. Your will be done on earth as it is in heaven" (Matthew 6:10).

Since studying Revelation, the Lord has taken me deeper as I pray those first two phrases. I never cease to be amazed that there's always a deeper place. Father in Heaven, Your name is holy. To acknowledge Him as holy is to say that He is perfect in all of His ways. Everything—EVERYTHING—He does is perfect, because there's just nothing wrong about Him. He is light. He is glory. He is majesty.

> Whenever the living creatures give glory and honor and thanks to Him who sits on the throne, who lives forever and ever, the twenty-four elders fall down before Him who sits on the throne and worship Him who lives forever and ever, and cast their crowns before the throne, 4:9-10

CASTING CROWNS

When the creatures worshiped, the twenty-four elders worshiped. These creatures were worship leaders—blessed worship leaders—because the elders joined in their worship giving "glory and honor and thanks to Him who sits on the throne." The elders then fell down before Him and cast their crowns.

The Greek word *cast* used here means "to throw with abandonment." It's doubtful that they had worn the crowns very long. How long would it take in heaven to understand that the crowns belong to Him, who by His grace worked great things in us and through us? Certainly, these twenty-four elders didn't cast them before the throne and put them back on later. Casting their crowns before the throne was a one-time thing.

These elders represent you, believer. One day you will bow. One day you will sing. One day you will cast your crown before the throne, acknowledging everything good you ever did was because of Jesus.

> saying: Thou art worthy, O Lord, to receive glory and honour and power: for Thou hast created all things, and for Thy pleasure they are and were created. 4:10-11 (KJV)

WORSHIP

You and I are going to understand things in heaven that we don't comprehend now, but for now, here is a question to ponder: What more do we need to know about the Lord before we will truly worship Him? If we hold back in our worship now, when the time comes for us to join the elders in worshiping Him, I think we will experience a regret of sorts—the kind of regret we have when we discover something wonderful that we could have been experiencing all along. We will realize we could have been experiencing the joy, and the exhilaration, and the freedom of worshiping the Lord all along, but we missed out, because we held back.

The simple fear of man stifles our freedom in worship. There are some people who love for people to look at them while they worship. These are the ones the church ushers have to calm down. But then there are those who won't worship because they don't really like people to notice them. Let it go! Consider His worthiness to be worshiped. Consider His holiness. He created us to bring Him pleasure.

There are really only a few reasons I can think of as to why we hold back. Most of us, if not all of us, have been there at one time. We don't think He's worthy, really because we don't understand that He is holy. We don't like what He has done with our lives. We don't think He's done right by us. We aren't going to think these things in heaven. So, let's stop that thinking now.

Often when the trials of life seem overwhelming to me, I remind myself that God is on the throne and as long as He is on the throne, I'll be just fine. Now I realize that I should start my prayers by soaking in the fact that our God is on the throne AND that He is holy (perfect in all His ways). After acknowledging that He is in control—and He controls perfectly, whatever prayers follow have a new power and a new confidence—or at least they should. If they lack power and confidence, it's probably because I've forgotten either that He is on the throne or that He is holy.

As we can see from this first look into heaven, His pleasure and His will is to be worshiped. Eric Liddell, an Olympic runner made this statement: "When I run, I feel His pleasure."[30] He was doing what God created him to do. May you feel God's pleasure as you do what you were created to do—worship Him. Let's abandon ourselves and look at the One on the throne.

CLOSING THOUGHTS

Beginning with Revelation 4, many in our Jericho Road Christian Fellowship Women's Bible Study committed to an assignment. Here it is: after studying each chapter in Revelation, draw the events and characters described in the chapter. You may use stick figures or use your artistic gifts to their fullest, adding as much or as little detail as you'd like. It initially appeared to be time consuming, yet proved to be an awesome way to grasp and remember each chapter. Doing this exercise will help you both understand and remember what you've studied. It will be well worth the effort. Try it. You'll be glad you did!

REFLECTION QUESTIONS

(For more extensive study questions visit CathyDickinson.com)

1. How did John describe "the One on the throne"?

2. Who was around and before the throne?

3. Describe the response of the four creatures to "the One on the throne."

4. What was the response of the elders to "the One on the throne"?

5. Since the elders represent the believers, we know that one day we will worship "the One on the throne" with the same abandonment seen in this first look into heaven. What keeps you from doing it now?

6. From this chapter, list some things declared in heaven about God. (If you need more room to write, use the notes section on page 142.)

7. Thinking about Revelation 4:1 when John saw an open door to heaven, imagine what John saw beyond that door. Use this space to draw it.

Notes

Chapter Eleven

WORTHY IS THE LAMB: REVELATION 5

In Revelation 4, John saw the One sitting on the throne. Moving into chapter 5, John sees Jesus. We find John still in heaven, taking in the scene that is before and around God's throne. His focus will shift from the throne of God to the Lamb of God.

> And I saw in the right hand of Him who sat on the throne a scroll written inside and on the back, sealed with seven seals. 5:1

The shift begins when John sees something "in the right hand of Him who sat on the throne."

In chapter 4 we were reminded that God is Spirit, but here, He's got a hand. John didn't say, "I saw something *like* a hand." Essentially he said, "I saw His right hand had a scroll."

THE SCROLL

Scrolls were read horizontally, not vertically. The writing was in columns about three inches wide. The scroll was held in the left hand and unrolled with the right. As the reading went on, the previously read portion was re-rolled. A typical scroll of that day to contain the book of Revelation was about fifteen feet long. This scroll that is in God's hand is "written inside and on the back," indicating it's pretty full. Remember, we are warned in Revelation 22:18-19 not to add or take away from the words of this prophecy.

SEVEN SEALS

The scroll is sealed with seven seals, and as we will see later, after each of these seven seals is loosed, something happens. There is ample scriptural support that *seven* is the number of completion: (1) seven days of creation, (2) seven times around the city of Jericho to bring the walls down, (3) seven years of the tribulation, and the supreme example of all is (4) the seven Spirits of God (the Holy Spirit).

Culturally, Roman law required that a will, or testament, be sealed seven times. Each seal was located on the long edge of the scroll with a short description or title of what was on the inside, including the names of those authorized to open it. If it were indeed a will, the name of the testator, including the names of those who would inherit his property, would be written upon it. If it was a title deed, the names of the owners were written on it.

TITLE DEED

We believe that this scroll in God's hand is the title deed to the earth. As we see each seal loosed, that's certainly what it appears to be, as we once again use the Bible to interpret the Bible.

JEREMIAH 32

In Jeremiah 32, the Babylonians had laid siege upon Jerusalem. The city was surrounded; it was about to be overtaken and its inhabitants carried off to Babylon. But the word of the LORD came to Jeremiah and told him to buy his cousin's field, "for the right of redemption is yours to buy it" (Jeremiah 32:7). Jeremiah had the right to be what is known as the kinsman redeemer; the nearest relative that had first rights to the property.

This property was about three miles north of Jerusalem. Think about this offer. A couple of years prior to this time it might have been a good deal, but now it's about to come under Babylonian rule and Jeremiah had warned the people, prophesying their defeat and captivity for seventy years. He'd be dead by then. What possible good could this property be to Jeremiah? First of all, because the LORD told Jeremiah to. But the LORD told Jeremiah something else too. The LORD had promised that, "Houses and fields and vineyards shall be possessed again in this land" (Jeremiah 32:15). Jeremiah was to purchase this property as a witness to the people that the land would not always be in Babylonian captivity, and showing that he believed God.

After purchasing the title deed, he was to put it into an earthen vessel to preserve it until the title deed could be opened and the property reclaimed. Although Jeremiah owned the property, he could not take possession of it until after the Babylonians were gone. Jesus, as in this story of Jeremiah, has purchased the title deed to the earth, and will redeem the earth in His proper time.

The author of Hebrews wrote this referring to Jesus (quoting Psalm 40:7), "In the volume of the book it is written of Me" (Hebrews 10:7). Oh, how wonderful it is to see Jesus, our Redeemer, in this story of Jeremiah!

Pastor Chuck Smith wrote, "Most commentators see this scroll as the title deed to the earth, and I agree. God created the earth and gave it over to Adam. But when Adam and Eve sinned, they forfeited the earth over to the power of Satan. The cost of redeeming the earth was the blood of Jesus Christ. Jesus has already paid the price of redemption, but He hasn't yet taken possession of the earth. He will do so after the tribulation, and His judgments during the tribulation are the process by which He will take possession of those whom He redeemed with His blood." [31]

EZEKIEL 2:9-10

Here is another reference to this scroll. Ezekiel 2:9-10 says, "Now when I looked, there was a hand stretched out to me; and behold, a scroll of a book was in it. Then He spread it before me; and there was writing on the inside and on the outside, and written on it were lamentations and mourning and woe." In Revelation 6 we will begin our discovery of the "lamentations and mourning and woe."

DANIEL 12:4

Daniel is full of prophecies about the end times and is told to seal it up, roll it up, and set it aside for a future time. "But you, Daniel, shut up the words, and seal the book until the time of the end; many shall run to and fro, and knowledge shall increase" (Daniel 12:4).

Here in Revelation 5, we find John looking at that time. The time had come for the seals on the scroll to be loosed. What Ezekiel and Daniel only knew in part is about to be revealed to John and to us. We are going to see much more than they did as we study Revelation. This is information God saved for the church. Oh, how Ezekiel and Daniel would have loved to see what we can now see! The time has come for "the time of the end" to be revealed. One day, all who are in Christ will at the time of the rapture, actually see those seals loosed.

> Then I saw a strong angel proclaiming with a loud voice, "Who is worthy to open the scroll and to loose its seals?" And no one in heaven or on the earth or under the earth was able to open the scroll, or to look at it. 5:2-3

It seems that worship has stopped—as John's attention is drawn to this strong angel with a loud voice. As we go through Revelation, we will see that the things in heaven were always said loudly. This could mean either loud, as we understand the word, or great in power. We tend to associate loud with powerful. It was attention-grabbing. We can know that. What did the strong angel proclaim? "Who is worthy to open the scroll and to loose its seals?" No one was even able to "look at it"—no one.

> So I wept much, because no one was found worthy to open and read the scroll, or to look at it. 5:4

At that proclamation, John wept. John "wept much." The word *wept* in and of itself indicates a lot of crying, wailing, and lamenting; then he adds the word "much" to that. As long as we are in these earthly bodies, we are a sorry lot of people. Here John is, in heaven, seeing the glory of the throne, the holiness of God, angels and elders falling down and worshiping, and when he doesn't see anyone who can open the scroll, he falls apart. As much as we understand about the Lord, sometimes we still don't get it.

John has lost perspective (according to most commentators) thinking that Satan is going to keep running things on earth. And that would certainly be cause for weeping much, wouldn't it? John felt it even more intensely than we could, having seen the glories in heaven and seeing what it's really like when God is worshiped in His rightful place. Oh, how terribly, terribly evil the earth would look after seeing heaven. We would weep much too.

> But one of the elders said to me, "Do not weep. Behold, the Lion of the tribe of Judah, the Root of David, has prevailed to open the scroll and to loose its seven seals." 5:5

One of the elders comforts John. This is not an angel speaking to John, but just another redeemed man. It's as though he was saying to John, "No worries, John, we are just acknowledging that no angel and no man is worthy to open the scroll."

THE LION OF THE TRIBE OF JUDAH

The first title we hear of Jesus is "the Lion of the tribe of Judah." This goes all the way back to Genesis 49 when Jacob prophesied over his sons. He called Judah a lion. He prophesied that the scepter would not depart from Judah. And John would have been reminded of Isaiah 31:4.

> "For thus the LORD has spoken to me: 'As a lion roars, and a young lion over his prey (when a multitude of shepherds [or maybe kings] is summoned against him, he will not be afraid of their voice nor be disturbed by their noise), so the LORD of hosts will come down to fight for Mount Zion and for its hill.'"

THE ROOT OF DAVID

The second title is, "the Root of David." Paul, referring to Jesus in his letter to the Romans, quoted Isaiah 11:1.

> "There shall come forth a Rod from the stem of Jesse (David's father) and a Branch shall grow out of his roots."

Confirming once again that this refers to Jesus, look at the next verse in Isaiah:

> "The Spirit of the LORD shall rest upon Him, the Spirit of wisdom and understanding, the Spirit of counsel and might, the Spirit of knowledge and of the fear of the LORD." (Isaiah 11:2)

We have previously referred to Isaiah 11:2 in our study pointing to the sevenfold aspects of the Holy Spirit.

"Behold, the Lion of the tribe of Judah, the root of David has prevailed." John would have known that Jesus is the Lion of the tribe of Judah; Jesus is the Root of David. We can imagine John's memory triggered to the times he had walked with Him, eaten with Him, put his head on His shoulder, watched Him die, saw the empty tomb, saw his risen Lord, and watched Him ascend into heaven. JESUS, the Lion of the tribe of Judah, the Root of Jesse, is worthy to loose the seals.

> And I looked, and behold, in the midst of the throne and of the four living creatures, and in the midst of the elders, stood a Lamb as though it had been slain, having seven horns and seven eyes, which are the seven Spirits of God sent out into all the earth. 5:6

THE LAMB

John probably expected to see Jesus as a powerful Lion, but instead he saw a Lamb. Perhaps John's memories surfaced again, back to the day when John the Baptizer declared of Jesus, "Behold! The Lamb of God who takes away the sin of the world!" (John 1:29). Prior to that, the blood of lambs only covered sin. John the Baptist declared of Jesus, "Here is the Lamb of God and He will take away the sins of the world."

Jesus apparently likes to be seen as the Lamb. He is called "the Lamb" twenty-eight times in Revelation. John saw "a Lamb as though it had been slain," with marks of slaughter. What were those marks? Perhaps they were imprints from the crown crushed upon His head, slashes from the whippings, nail holes, or a gash from the spear thrust through His side. We don't know. We cannot help but wonder what it was like for John to see Jesus with all of those slaughter marks. What was it like for him to have his memories stirred of that absolutely awful day, when God's Lamb was sacrificed for John's sins and my sins and yours? John saw "the Lamb as though it had been slain," but NOT slain. Jesus is very alive, because John saw Him standing.

SEVEN HORNS AND SEVEN EYES

The Lamb John saw had seven horns. It is believed that horns represent power, and once again, we have the number seven, the number of completion. Therefore, seven horns would indicate complete power. The Lamb had seven eyes indicating all-seeing. Because Jesus sees all things perfectly as they are, this would be another way of saying He is all-knowing. So, in the seven horns and the seven eyes we have One who is completely powerful and completely knowing; omnipotent and omniscient. We are told that these eyes are "the seven Spirits of God sent out into all the earth." This fits so beautifully with Jesus' promise to send the Holy Spirit once He ascended to heaven.

> Then He came and took the scroll out of the right hand of Him who sat on the throne. 5:7

This is a picture of the Trinity in full agreement. The Father gives the scroll to Jesus and the Holy Spirit is upon Him.

> Now when He had taken the scroll, the four living creatures and the twenty-four elders fell down before the Lamb, each having a harp, and golden bowls full of incense, which are the prayers of the saints. 5:8

JESUS IS GOD

When Jesus took the scroll out of the Father's hand, worship turned to the Lamb as the four living creatures and the twenty-four elders fell down before the Lamb—the Lamb is God. This should remove all doubt.

We are told that they each had "a harp, and golden bowls full of incense, which are the prayers of the saints." It is hard to determine, but it looks like it was the elders who had the harps and the bowls of incense, though it's not clear. It is clear, however, that musical instruments accompany worship in heaven.

Each of them had "golden bowls full of incense, which are the prayers of the saints." Do the bowls contain every one of our prayers? We don't know. We do know that God keeps all of our tears in a bottle (Psalm 56:8). It is reasonable to accept that He keeps track of our prayers, our prayers provoked by those tears, as well as our prayers of praise and intercession. It may be that these bowls contain the prayers we have prayed for His kingdom to come, for suffering to be over, or for things to be made right, because those are the prayers that are about to be answered. He hasn't forgotten the pain and the wrongs; now He is going to make things right.

> And they sang a new song, saying: "You are worthy to take the scroll, and to open its seals; for You were slain, and have redeemed us to God by Your blood out of every tribe and tongue and people and nation, 5:9

WORTHY

They sang a new song. First, they sang of His worthiness to take the scroll and open its seals. Why was He worthy? He was worthy because He was slain and redeemed us to God by His blood.

THE REDEEMER

Secondly, they sang because He is our Redeemer. This is why we think the living creatures weren't singing this part of the song. Jesus did not redeem creatures or angels. He only redeemed men. Jesus, only Jesus, is worthy to open the scroll. Our Redeemer is now going to take possession of what is His. He is matchless. He is worthy of all. No one is really worthy of Him, yet He calls us His!

When Jesus our Redeemer died on the cross, was buried, and rose from the dead, He not only redeemed us from Satan's dominion, He redeemed this world.

Look at the parable of the hidden treasure in Matthew 13.

"Again, the kingdom of heaven is like treasure hidden in a field, which a man found and hid; and for joy over it he goes and sells all that he has and buys that field." In the parable right before this one, we are told that the field is the world (verse 38).

At the end of this age, "The Son of Man will send out His angels, and they will gather out of His kingdom all things that offend, and those who practice lawlessness, and cast them into the furnace of fire" (Matthew 13:41-42a).

Jesus redeemed (purchased) the world, in order to get the treasure—me! And you!

> "You have put all things in subjection under His feet. For in that He put all in subjection under Him, He left nothing that is not put under Him. But now we do not yet see all things put under Him." (Hebrews 2:8)

> "Ask of Me, and I will give You the nations for Your inheritance, and the ends of the earth for Your possession." (Psalm 2:8)

We see Jesus rising up to take possession of His purchase. It's the greatest close of escrow in all of history. He's going to establish His dominion just as He planned, just as He promised.

> And have made us kings and priests to our God; and we shall reign on the earth." 5:10

This is another reason why we believe the elders are men; angels were never promised kingships or priesthoods. This also reminds us of Jesus' description of Himself in Revelation 1.

> "...Jesus Christ, the faithful witness, the firstborn from the dead, and the ruler over the kings of the earth. To Him who loved us and washed us from our sins in His own blood, and has made us kings and priests to His God and Father, to Him *be* glory and dominion forever and ever. Amen" (vv. 5-6).

> Then I looked, and I heard the voice of many angels around the throne, the living creatures, and the elders; and the number of them was ten thousand times ten thousand, and thousands of thousands, 5:11

PERSONAL LOVE

Not only did John see the four living creatures and the twenty-four elders around the throne, now he saw angels; "the number of them was ten thousand times ten thousand, and thousands of thousands." Ten thousand times ten thousand (not including the thousands of thousands) is 100 million angels. That was innumerable to John!

When we think of there being so many, we might start to think that maybe the angels, and maybe we, will lose our individuality. The thought that God loves the whole world might make us think we are just part of a big redeemed lump of people. But that's bringing God down to our level, isn't it?

When I was on staff at Calvary Chapel of Costa Mesa, I counseled a lot of people. I didn't know most of them because the church was so big. One day a woman came in and said something about the fact that she had come in to see me before, but I couldn't remember her at all. Nothing she said triggered anything for me and we were far enough into our time together that I just couldn't admit that I didn't remember her. When our time ended, in great frustration I said to the Lord, *I can't do it. I can't keep track of just the few people You send my way. You keep track of everybody and You keep track of them all the time. How do You do it, Lord?* And He gently reminded me that His ways are way, way higher than mine, and His thoughts are much better than my own. He knows everything about everyone. And He doesn't stop at just knowing us; He loves all of His children individually.

Recently I made an appointment with the doctor because I was pretty certain that I had a sinus infection. The nurse asked me what my symptoms were and I told her, adding the comment that the only downside of having grandchildren is having their germs jump on me. She shared that she had a fourteen-month-old granddaughter and how precious she was. I told her I had six grandchildren and they are all very precious to me. She continued to fill out the information and all of a sudden she stopped and rolled her stool over to me and got right in my face. She said, "Can I ask you something personal?" My first thought was that she must have seen something on my chart that said I'm a Christian or a pastor's wife, so I shot up a quick prayer, *Lord, help me to share your gospel well.* This was her question: "Do you love each of your grandchildren equally?" That was a no-brainer. I told her, "Yes, I do." Then she said, "I just love my one granddaughter so much, I can't imagine having any more love in my heart for another." You that have more than one child or more than one grandchild know that somehow your heart stretches and you always have plenty. God's heart doesn't need to stretch. It's already more than big enough to individually love each one of us. Therefore, although there will be multitudes of us in heaven, He will know and love each of us individually.

> saying with a loud voice: "Worthy is the Lamb who was slain to receive power and riches and wisdom, and strength and honor and glory and blessing!" And every creature which is in heaven and on the earth and under the earth and such as are in the sea, and all that are in them, I heard saying: "Blessing and honor and glory and power be to Him who sits on the throne, and to the Lamb, forever and ever!" Then the four living creatures said, "Amen!" And the twenty-four elders fell down and worshiped Him who lives forever and ever. 5:12-14

PERSONAL WORSHIP

Chapter 5 concludes with an awesome scene of worship. What is the response of the angels, the living creatures, and the elders? The response to this finally happening provokes worship in heaven; worship of the Lamb who has not only redeemed us, but who also "made us kings and priests to our God."

In heaven we will be perfect—our worship will be perfect. What is perfect worship? Certainly it would include these things we have witnessed in Revelation 4 and 5; bowing down, falling down before Him, getting off our thrones (or in our case, getting off our seats) in some way. We don't know what perfect worship is as far as physical expression, but it seems that because we are all different, the way we express ourselves in worship would be different too.

Because we have John's eyewitness account, we do know that when the Lamb came forward, they physically and verbally worshiped Him; they responded.

Charles Spurgeon said this: "A seat in heaven shall one day be yours; but a chain in hell would have been yours if grace had not changed you." [32]

Most assuredly, had it not been for the Lamb, chains in hell would have been ours. Had it not been for the Lamb that was slain, the wrath and woes seen in the coming chapters of Revelation would have been ours. We are simply and only among the redeemed because of the Lamb. Therefore, He is worthy of a response.

REFLECTION QUESTIONS

(For more extensive study questions visit CathyDickinson.com)

1. What is the scroll in God's hand commonly believed to be?

The scroll is the title deed to the earth.

2. Jesus is called "the Lion of the tribe of Judah" in verse 5, yet how is He described in verse 6?

He is described as a lamb with seven horns and seven eyes, which is the seven spirits of God

3. In this chapter we see seven seals, seven horns, and seven eyes. What is the significance of the number seven? Horns represent power. Seven is the number of completion. Eyes represent seeing. There is complete power and vision with the Lord.

4. John saw the Lamb "having seven horns and seven eyes" (v. 6). What is the significance of these two characteristics? Jesus is omnipotent and omniscient - He is perfect. All seeing and all knowing

5. Look again at Revelation 5:6-7. How do we see the Trinity in these verses?

God the father is seated on the throne, Jesus is the risen lamb - the only one who can open the

6. We learned that the incense in the golden bowls "are the prayers of the saints" (v. 8). How does this minister to you regarding the importance of your prayers to God?

Our prayers are worth saving and they are placed in golden bowls - the prayers are considered valuable.

7. According to vv. 9 and 10, why was the Lamb the only one worthy to open the scroll?

Jesus was slain in order to redeem us to God by His blood.

8. Jesus redeemed (purchased) the entire world to get the treasure—you! Write a prayer of praise and thanksgiving to the Lamb who calls you His treasure.

Thank you all knowing perfect Lord. You are worthy forever and ever. Only you would love me in my sinful state and redeem me.

9. Read the words of praise in verses 12-14 and consider this scene of worship. How are you encouraged or challenged to respond to the Lamb? The Lamb is worthy of all power, riches, wisdom, strength, honor, glory and blessing. He sits on the throne forever and ever.

10. Use the space here to draw the scene in heaven as described by John in Revelation 5.

Notes

Chapter Twelve

WHO WILL BE ABLE TO STAND: REVELATION 6-7

As previously stated, we are approaching this study believing a pre-tribulation rapture. Therefore, if we have not experienced a natural death by this time, we who are in Christ will have been raptured and will not be partakers of this wrath to come. The judgments described in chapter 6 are just the beginning of sorrows. These judgments pale in comparison to what we see in the chapters that follow.

> Now I saw when the Lamb opened one of the seals; and I heard one of the four living creatures saying with a voice like thunder, "Come and see." 6:1

GOD'S WRATH BEGINS

John is still in heaven. He has watched the Lamb of God open the first seal when one of the four living creatures said to John, "Come and see." John probably had a choice. He could focus on the things of heaven or look back through the door, so to speak, and witness what would shortly take place on earth. We will see that John has to be told to refocus a few times in Revelation.

Let's review the words of Revelation 1:1. "The Revelation of Jesus Christ, which God gave Him to show His servants—things which must *shortly* take place. And He sent and signified it by His angel to His servant John." As I stated previously, this word *shortly* has the sense of happening quickly, in sudden succession, like one thing after another.

In Matthew 24, when Jesus is talking about these times, He calls them "the beginning of sorrows" or "birth pangs." Those who have given birth know just what Jesus was talking about. Real labor, once it starts, gets worse and worse. Once labor starts, there is no stopping it.

In Revelation 6, God's judgment is happening—quickly—in the span of seven years—one horrible thing after another.

WARNING BEFORE JUDGMENT

After studying "these things," we can certainly understand why John would rather keep his focus on heaven. But God, in His wisdom, wanted John to see His wrath so that John could write. So that John could warn. God always warns before He judges; this is the heart of God.

> "Say to them: 'As I live,' says the Lord GOD, 'I have no pleasure in the death of the wicked, but that the wicked turn from his way and live. Turn, turn from your evil ways! For why should you die, O house of Israel?'" (Ezekiel 33:11)

> "Turn at my rebuke; surely I will pour out my spirit on you; I will make my words known to you." (Proverbs 1:23)
>
> "For He does not afflict willingly...." (Lamentations 3:33)
>
> God "desires all men to be saved and to come to the knowledge of the truth." (1 Timothy 2:4)

It's important to God that you and I understand that He is holy, and therefore, He is good. God is one hundred percent good. He does the right thing one hundred percent of the time. As Pastor Chuck Smith so faithfully taught, "If you remember nothing else, remember that God is good."

So when we look at God's wrath to come, it is good. It's a time to bring evil to an end. It's a time to answer the prayers of the saints to make things right.

The first six seals are about to be opened, and the seventh seal will be opened in Revelation 8:1. As we study, we will see that from the seventh seal will come seven trumpets, and from the seven trumpets will come seven bowls, each ushering in greater devastation than the last. And God's goodness is in it all.

> And I looked, and behold, a white horse. He who sat on it had a bow; and a crown was given to him, and he went out conquering and to conquer. 6:2

THE FIRST SEAL: THE WHITE HORSEMAN

With the opening of the first four seals will come four horses. They have been called the four horses of the Apocalypse. With the first seal comes a white horse.

We have been saturated with the idea that the good guys wear white and the bad guys wear black. Therefore, we might think that the one on the first horse is a good guy, which is exactly what the Antichrist will want the people to think. Initially, we may think that since Jesus does come on a white horse in Revelation 19, this must be Jesus, but it can't be. It cannot be Jesus because of the horses that follow this white horse. What follows when Jesus comes is just the opposite of what follows this white horse in Revelation 6. But the rider on this white horse wants you to think he's a good guy. He's not.

At this point it is helpful to remember what Jesus told His disciples in Matthew 24 and Luke 21 when He answered the disciples' question, "What will be the sign of Your coming, and of the end of the age?" Jesus answered, "Take heed that no one deceives you. For many will come in My name, saying, 'I am the Christ,' and will deceive many" (Matthew 24:4-5).

> "Take heed that you not be deceived. For many will come in My name, saying, 'I am He,' and, 'The time has drawn near.' Therefore do not go after them." (Luke 21:8)

S. Mayfield

This first horseman will bring peace, a deceptive peace. We believe this because the second horseman to come will take away peace. Daniel 9:27 tells us that the tribulation will begin with the Antichrist making a covenant with Israel. Immediately following the rapture, there will surely be a lot of confusion. The Antichrist will step up and establish peace, albeit a deceptive and temporary one.

This horseman also has a crown, though not a crown of royalty; this is a crown of victory. He has a bow, but no arrows. Most commentators agree that the Antichrist will not have to fight to gain control.

> When He opened the second seal, I heard the second living creature saying, "Come and see." Another horse, fiery red, went out. And it was granted to the one who sat on it to take peace from the earth, and that people should kill one another; and there was given to him a great sword. 6:3-4

THE SECOND SEAL: THE RED HORSEMAN

John saw a fiery red horseman to take peace from the earth, or we believe—to make war. He was given a sword "that people should kill one another." Here's what Jesus said, "'But when you hear of wars and commotions, do not be terrified; for these things must come to pass first, but the end will not come immediately.' Then He said to them, 'Nation will rise against nation, and kingdom against kingdom'" (Luke 21:9-10).

According to Matthew 24:4-7 and Luke 21:8-10, war follows deception. This horseman is granted to take peace not only from some nations, but from the entire earth. There will be wars all over the place, devastating wars.

When I watch movies about World War II, some of the scariest scenes are planes flying over a city, like London, and indiscriminately dropping bombs. I just can't imagine what that would be like for a parent, knowing their children are in that kind of jeopardy all the time, never knowing when or where a bomb might drop. Today, the weapons of war are far more devastating, and the wars to come will be even worse.

> When He opened the third seal, I heard the third living creature say, "Come and see." So I looked, and behold, a black horse, and he who sat on it had a pair of scales in his hand. And I heard a voice in the midst of the four living creatures saying, "A quart of wheat for a denarius, and three quarts of barley for a denarius; and do not harm the oil and the wine." 6:5-6

THE THIRD SEAL: THE BLACK HORSEMAN

In John's time, a denarius was a day's wage. This means one would have to work all day just to buy a loaf of bread or one could work all day for three times that amount of barley. Barley was the cheap, less desirable grain that was fed to the animals. Those left behind will work all day, just for that day's bread.

As far as the instruction, "do not harm the oil or the wine," my personal theory is that the oil and the wine represent the finer things in life, indicating that the rich will continue to prosper, as they often do in times of famine. Famine follows war, as we see in Matthew 24:7. "For nation will rise against nation, and kingdom against kingdom. And there will be famines, pestilences, and earthquakes in various places."

> When He opened the fourth seal, I heard the voice of the fourth living creature saying, "Come and see." So I looked, and behold, a pale horse. And the name of him who sat on it was Death, and Hades followed with him. And power was given to them over a fourth of the earth, to kill with sword, with hunger, with death, and by the beasts of the earth. 6:7-8

THE FOURTH SEAL: THE PALE HORSEMAN

This is a pale yellowish color like grass that is dried up from the heat. We are told the rider's name is "Death." What follows famine? Death. We are told that Death is followed by Hades, which at this time, is the temporary place of the unsaved dead. Hades is riding alongside with Death to scoop up the souls of those who refused to trust the Lamb.

We don't know how many people will be left on the earth after the rapture, but just to get an idea of the enormity of the loss of life that will take place, let's use today's population numbers. The population of the earth right now is about seven billion. There are approximately two billion Christians, that leaves about five billion souls on earth after the rapture. One fourth of that is over one billion people. Over one billion people will die from the power given—notice *given*—to the fourth horseman.

None of these horsemen can go forward until they are released by God to do so; none of them have any power unless God gives it to them.

These first four seals occur in the first three-and-a-half years of the tribulation. The *peace* the first rider brought doesn't last very long as tragedies continue to accelerate.

> When He opened the fifth seal, I saw under the altar the souls of those who had been slain for the word of God and for the testimony which they held. 6:9

THE FIFTH SEAL: GOD'S GRACE

John sees the fifth seal opened. Matthew 24:9 falls right in line with this, but keep in mind, Jesus is talking to the Jewish believers here, not the church. "Then they will deliver you up to tribulation and kill you, and you will be hated by all nations for My name's sake."

The fifth seal doesn't reveal God's vengeance, but rather the prayers of those who died for their testimony of Jesus. It reveals God's grace even during judgment. Many people are going to be saved during the tribulation when they are martyred for their faith early in the tribulation, even before the command to take the mark of the beast (Revelation 13:16).

> And they cried with a loud voice, saying, "How long, O Lord, holy and true, until You judge and avenge our blood on those who dwell on the earth?" 6:10

Notice, these martyrs are in heaven; they are not sleeping in the ground. God has promised that when His people are harmed, in His perfect timing, He will make all things right. And then in verse 11 we see God's response to these martyrs.

> Then a white robe was given to each of them; and it was said to them that they should rest a little while longer, until both the number of their fellow servants and their brethren, who would be killed as they were, was completed. 6:11

There is still more persecution to come. Notice the phrase "until the number … was completed." God knows precisely how many will be martyred and who they are; He's going to allow it to happen. In the face of this we must remember—God is holy and God is good. Even those who are slain for their testimony of Him will declare this.

I'm sure a martyr's death is a terrible one. But once it happens, they are delivered from the tribulation, suffering, pestilence, hunger, and the horrendous results of cosmic disturbances. For all believers the difference between rapture and natural death is, for the most part, that period of time when we are dying, which for many can be very painful, but afterwards we will all bow before His throne.

Matt Redman says it well in his song, "10,000 Reasons."

> "And on that day when my strength is failing,
>
> the end draws near and my time has come;
>
> still my soul will sing Your praise unending,
>
> ten thousand years and then forevermore." [33]

I do not in any way want to lessen the price paid by martyrs; God certainly doesn't. He is their Avenger for what was done to them.

> I looked when He opened the sixth seal, and behold, there was a great earthquake; and the sun became black as sackcloth of hair, and the moon became like blood. And the stars of heaven fell to the earth, as a fig tree drops its late figs when it is shaken by a mighty wind. Then the sky receded as a scroll when it is rolled up, and every mountain and island was moved out of its place. 6:12-13

THE SIXTH SEAL: CATACLYSMIC EVENTS

Many will try to explain these events calling them natural disasters. But we will see, especially when we read about the two witnesses in chapter 11, that a lot of these things are similar to the plagues God let loose through Moses upon Egypt.

WALL STREET
Mall
NEW AGE
Adult Books
S. Mayfield

Take a moment to look at this list of cataclysmic events and consider how very awful each one will be.

A great earthquake

The sun became black

The moon became like blood

The stars fell to the earth

The sky receded as a scroll

Every mountain and island was moved out of its place

> And the kings of the earth, the great men, the rich men, the commanders, the mighty men, every slave and every free man, hid themselves in the caves and in the rocks of the mountains, and said to the mountains and rocks, "Fall on us and hide us from the face of Him who sits on the throne and from the wrath of the Lamb!" 6:15-16

THE RESPONSE

This is the response to those affected on earth and their response to these awful events. They hid themselves in the caves and in the rocks of the mountains from the wrath of the Lamb! No one is exempt here. Not even the rich have places of shelter as they, along with everyone else, hide.

Where did they learn these words, "Him who sits on the throne," and "the wrath of the Lamb," and "the great day of His wrath has come"? Who told them? How do they know? Maybe it was something you said or perhaps something you wrote or from the testimony of the martyrs. Somehow they will know and they won't credit natural disasters or global warming. They will know and they will acknowledge God's wrath being poured out upon them. But instead of crying out to Him, they will try to hide from Him.

This thinking goes all the way back to Adam and Eve (see Genesis 3). They made the same mistake when they tried to hide from the LORD in the garden. Man, in his sin, has changed very little over the ages. The unrighteous run to caves while the righteous run to the name of the LORD, to the character of the LORD.

> "The name of the LORD is a strong tower; the righteous run to it and are safe." (Proverbs 18:10)

This is a challenge to us. When life gets rough, where do we run; what do we run to? We see the vanity of running to caves, but isn't it equally vain to run to substances, people, shopping or anything rather than to God?

> "For the great day of His wrath has come, and who is able to stand?" 6:17

WHO IS ABLE TO STAND?

Consider all of the destruction and death that John was witnessing. No person in history ever has or ever will see all that John saw in such a short amount of time. Now in chapter 7, we temporarily pull away from the destruction of the earth to answer the question, "For the great day of His wrath has come, and who is able to stand?" Perhaps the Lord directed John's focus to scenes like those in chapter 7 to mercifully give him a little break.

> After these things I saw four angels standing at the four corners of the earth, holding the four winds of the earth, that the wind should not blow on the earth, on the sea, or on any tree. 7:1

The four corners can be likened to the four points of a compass, indicating the angels were holding back the wind from harming all of the earth.

> Then I saw another angel ascending from the east, having the seal of the living God. And he cried with a loud voice to the four angels to whom it was granted to harm the earth and the sea, saying, "Do not harm the earth, the sea, or the trees till we have sealed the servants of our God on their foreheads." And I heard the number of those who were sealed. One hundred and forty-four thousand of all the tribes of the children of Israel were sealed: of the tribe of Judah … Reuben … Gad … Asher … Naphtali … Manasseh … Simeon … Levi … Issachar … Zebulun … Joseph … Benjamin … twelve thousand [each] were sealed. 7:2-8

THE SEALED SERVANTS

Another angel came and cried out with a loud voice (remember, his voice is powerful as opposed to just loud), "Do not harm the earth, the sea, or the trees till we have sealed the servants of our God on their foreheads." Then John "heard the number of those who were sealed. One hundred and forty-four thousand." What is the answer to the question, "Who will be able to stand?" These one hundred and forty-four thousand. The Jehovah's Witnesses hope to be among the 144,000, but here's what the Bible says is the criteria from Revelation 7 and Revelation 14:3-5:

1. They will be from among the twelve tribes of Israel; twelve thousand from each tribe.
2. They will be virgin men, and therefore, single.
3. They will "follow the Lamb wherever He goes."
4. They will be among the "firstfruits to God and to the Lamb." It is believed they will be the first of the many Jews who will be saved. In the midst of all of this judgment, we see God's wonderful, loving intention to save Israel.
5. No deceit will be found in their mouth, meaning they will speak truth.
6. They will have the seal of God on their foreheads.

God's seal is that of His special protection and of His ownership. This isn't the first time God has placed His seal on those who are His. In the book of Ezekiel, the LORD gave this instruction commanding the destruction of the wicked at that time. "'Go after him through the city and kill; do not let your eye spare, nor have any pity. Utterly slay old and young men, maidens and little children and women; but do not come near anyone on whom is the mark; and begin at My sanctuary.' So they began with the elders who were before the temple" (Ezekiel 9:5-6).

But before this instruction, God gave another: "...and the LORD said to him, 'Go through the midst of the city, through the midst of Jerusalem, and put a mark on the foreheads of the men who sigh and cry over all the abominations that are done within it'" (Ezekiel 9:4).

We find another wonderful sealing in Ephesians 1:13-14. "In Him you also trusted, after you heard the word of truth, the gospel of your salvation; in whom also, having believed, you were sealed with the Holy Spirit of promise, who is the guarantee of our inheritance until the redemption of the purchased possession, to the praise of His glory."

That seal is God's promise that He will get us to heaven. We've been sealed and the enemy of our souls knows it. Satan loves to copy Jesus and it appears that this whole idea of sealing people with the mark of the beast, which we will look at when we get to chapter 13, is just his weak attempt to show God that he can mark people too. But rather than mark them for protection, he marks them for destruction.

> After these things I looked, and behold, a great multitude which no one could number, of all nations, tribes, peoples, and tongues, standing before the throne and before the Lamb, clothed with white robes, with palm branches in their hands, 7:9

A GREAT MULTITUDE

John saw another group of people standing. They were a great multitude of people of "all nations, tribes, peoples, and tongues." No one was excluded that came to the Lamb. John saw a great multitude—more than anyone could number. Although God in His righteousness must judge, God is intent on saving. We see here both the Jews and the Gentiles.

John saw them standing before the Lamb, clothed in white with palm branches in their hands. Palm branches represent triumph, celebration, a form of clapping, but much better.

> and crying out with a loud voice, saying, "Salvation belongs to our God who sits on the throne, and to the Lamb!" 7:10

Notice, this great multitude isn't complaining about their suffering on earth or asking why. They are worshiping. They no longer need answers.

> All the angels stood around the throne and the elders and the four living creatures, and fell on their faces before the throne and worshiped God, saying: "Amen! Blessing and glory and wisdom, thanksgiving and honor and power and might, be to our God forever and ever. Amen." 7:11-12

Heaven seems to be full of responders, and I can't wait until we will be singing new songs in heaven. We might sing some songs that we sing now, but some, we will definitely not be singing. We will not be singing songs with lyrics like, "Help me know You are near," or "Jesus, won't You show me just how far the east is from the west," or "I can't bear to see the man I've been rising up in me again." We will be singing, "I don't have to see the man I've been rising up in me again!" We will celebrate each of these things in detail when we get to chapters 21 and 22.

Everything that is good we will experience forever and anything bad we will never ever experience again.

> Then one of the elders answered, saying to me, "Who are these arrayed in white robes, and where did they come from?" And I said to him, "Sir, you know." 7:13-14

It appears that John had learned something since chapter 5, when he was bewildered by the question regarding who was worthy to open the scroll. He discovered then that he would be supplied with the answers to questions put before him. Now John understands, so he responds with, "Sir, you know." In verse 14 the elder gives John the answer.

> So he said to me, "These are the ones who come out of the great tribulation, and washed their robes and made them white in the blood of the Lamb." 7:14

Now blood doesn't make white. Blood stains. Yet when we are in Christ Jesus, we can bask in the promise of Isaiah 1:18. "'Come now, and let us reason together,' says the LORD, 'though your sins are like scarlet, they shall be as white as snow; though they are red like crimson, they shall be as wool.'"

Therefore, because they came to the Lamb to wash them, because they came to Jesus to forgive them, those who came through the tribulation and all who come to Him will be the beneficiaries of the things listed in verses 15-17.

> "Therefore they are before the throne of God, and serve Him day and night in His temple. And He who sits on the throne will dwell among them. They shall neither hunger anymore nor thirst anymore; the sun shall not strike them, nor any heat; for the Lamb who is in the midst of the throne will shepherd them and lead them to living fountains of waters. And God will wipe away every tear from their eyes." 7:15-17.

This great multitude gets to:

1. Be before the throne of God
2. Serve Him day and night in His temple
3. Have God dwell among them and,
4. They will be forever free from hunger, thirst, heat, and tears.

CLOSING THOUGHTS

I was watching a movie about the rapture and a pastor said, "I lost a quarter of my church." Three quarters of his congregation showed up on the Sunday after the rapture. They were the occasional attendees who showed up on Easter or after there had been a tragedy. Tragedies shake people up and awaken their need to get right with God, but for most, it doesn't stick. They don't have much of a relationship with Him, if they have one at all. I hope, I pray, that our church will be empty the Sunday after the rapture.

When I think about worshiping the Lord in heaven, I want to be there worshiping with my church family. Yet at the same time, I hope it will be full of people from this great multitude that comes forth from the great tribulation. People we've told—people that we've warned—of the coming wrath of God.

Raul Ries' son, Ryan, is part of a pretty radical Christian band and ministry. Ryan feels like much of his calling is to warn and equip people for the great tribulation. He is painfully aware that there are many who attend his concerts that will not respond to the gospel he preaches, but he hopes to plant seeds that the Lord can water after the rapture to bring to their remembrance the things they had heard.

What about you? What about me? If we are caught up in the rapture, what will people think happened to us? Will they believe the deceptive explanations that the unbelieving world will probably tell them or will it trigger thoughts of things we had said?

Until a month before my father went to be with Jesus, he would tell me he wanted nothing to do with God. But when my dad was facing death, he told my mom that he'd been thinking about the things Dale and I had told him. From my perspective, I would have told you that he hadn't heard one thing we had shared, but he did.

SHARING THE GOSPEL

Sharing the gospel can be a real challenge, but talking to people about a time when Jesus will come for believers and, in a millisecond, catch them up to take them to heaven takes that challenge to a new level. I don't think I've ever talked to an unbeliever about that. It seems that without knowing Jesus they just wouldn't get it, but then again, some do.

So what can we do to make a difference? Most of us have a written will. If not, this is a good time to consider one. Our will contains not only how we want our material things distributed, but it also contains our thoughts we want to share with those we love.

I remember the first time we went to Israel. I left an "in case the plane crashes or we get shot in Israel" letter on the desk for our two adult kids that were in rebellion at the time. I really didn't intend for them to read it unless we died. I didn't think either one of them would go into our house for any other reason, but our daughter did. She found the letter and she read it. It shook her up and got her thinking, almost to the point of turning back to the Lord right then.

If you are raptured, "somebody" is going to go through your important papers to find the pink slip of your car, or your insurance policy, or passwords to your bank accounts. Maybe it will be family or a neighbor, or someone looting your house, but somebody will look in that drawer or that box. I've decided that, whoever that is, they are going to find a letter that says something like, "In case of my disappearance." It will include a list of Bible verses that explain what happened to me and some verses that reveal what is about to happen to them. Finally, it will include the verses how they can know Jesus. I have included a sample letter after this chapter for you to copy in your own handwriting. And it might be nice to leave it with a copy of this book!

As we continue this study, we will see that lots and lots of people are going to get saved during the tribulation. I want to be among those who have a part in those salvations, don't you? The people who are left behind after the rapture will all go through terrible, terrible atrocities. Oh, how unimaginably terrible it will be if they manage to make it through the tribulation only to end up in hell for eternity.

REFLECTION QUESTIONS

(For more extensive study questions visit CathyDickinson.com)

1. Consider that God always warns before He brings judgment. What does this reveal about God's heart?

2. With the loosing of the first four seals come four horses. What color are they and what do the horsemen bring with them?

3. The fifth seal does not usher in more wrath, but rather God's grace as we hear the cry to God of those martyred for their faith in Jesus. What does this reveal to you about God's heart for His people—for you?

4. Proverbs 18:10 says, "The name of the Lord is a strong tower; the righteous run to it and are safe." List some of the attributes of the Lord that you "run to" in hard times.

5. Using this space, draw a scene as described by John in Revelation chapters 6-7.

In Case of My Disappearance

IF YOU ARE READING THIS LETTER, I don't know who you are, but please know this: I am in heaven. I am there either because my body has stopped functioning or I have been caught up in the rapture promised in the Bible to those who belong to Jesus. Either way, you can be assured that I am doing very well and have no desire to return to the earth—no desire at all.

If I have outlived the usefulness of my body, then I assume that family members are reading this. You all know very well the truths that will follow these words. My prayer, of course, is that you will not be reading this due to the rapture, as I long for us all to "go up" together.

But if you are reading this as a result of the disappearance of many people, then I would plead that you read on. Your eternal destiny depends on what you do with these truths.

The Bible spoke of a time when those who belong to Jesus will be caught up with Him. Here's what it says:

> "Behold, I tell you a mystery: We shall not all sleep (die), but we shall all be changed—in a moment, in the twinkling of an eye, at the last trumpet. For the trumpet will sound, and the dead will be raised incorruptible, and we shall be changed." (1 Corinthians 15:51-52)
>
> "For the Lord Himself will descend from heaven with a shout, with the voice of an archangel, and with the trumpet of God. And the dead in Christ will rise first. Then we who are alive and remain shall be caught up together with them in the clouds to meet the Lord in the air. And thus we shall always be with the Lord." (1 Thessalonians 4:16-17)

This is what has happened to so many others and me. We have been "caught up" to heaven to be with Jesus forever. In a way, since you are reading this in hindsight, you probably understand what happened more than I do as I am writing it. As I write, I believe this in faith. As you read this, you will know it to be fact.

The world is about to significantly change. Chapters 7 to 11 of the book of Daniel and chapters 4 to 22 of the book of Revelation predict many of these changes. They will occur over a period of seven years. The changes may be slow at first. They will increase dramatically and horrifically in three-and-a-half years. The first change you will probably see is a man who will step up and make a peace covenant with Israel. He will appear to be a great leader, but he is not. He will reveal himself to be the Antichrist, demanding that he be worshiped in three-and-a-half years. Until that time, he will deceive many. May you not be among the deceived.

HERE IS WHAT THE BIBLE SAYS ABOUT THIS MAN

> "Then he shall confirm a covenant with many for one week; but in the middle of the week he shall bring an end to sacrifice and offering." (Daniel 9:27)

(He shall make a covenant for one week [meaning seven years]. In the middle of the seven years, he will walk into the rebuilt temple and put an end to the sacrifices and offerings.)

> "He shall regard neither the God of his fathers nor the desire of women, nor regard any god; for he shall exalt himself above them all." (Daniel 11:37)

> "Let no one deceive you by any means; for that Day will not come unless the falling away comes first, and the man of sin is revealed, the son of perdition, who opposes and exalts himself above all that is called God or that is worshiped, so that he sits as God in the temple of God, showing himself that he is God." (2 Thessalonians 2:3-4)

> "The coming of the lawless one is according to the working of Satan, with all power, signs, and lying wonders, and with all unrighteous deception among those who perish, because they did not receive the love of the truth, that they might be saved. And for this reason God will send them strong delusion, that they should believe the lie, that they all may be condemned who did not believe the truth but had pleasure in unrighteousness." (2 Thessalonians 2:9-12)

People will believe his lies. But it is not God's desire that anyone perish (live an eternity in hell).

> "For God so loved the world that He gave His only begotten Son, that whoever believes in Him should not perish but have everlasting life. For God did not send His Son into the world to condemn the world, but that the world through Him might be saved." (John 3:16-17)

> "He causes all, both small and great, rich and poor, free and slave, to receive a mark on their right hand or on their foreheads, and that no one may buy or sell except one who has the mark or the name of the beast, or the number of his name." (Revelation 13:16-17)

For those who take this mark, Revelation 14:9 essentially warns if anyone worships the beast and his image, and receives *his* mark on their forehead or on their hand, that person will receive God's wrath.

This world, and the people in it, is about to suffer great cataclysmic disasters. These disasters are the judgments of a righteous God upon those who have rejected Him. They are also His warnings—His attempts to get man to repent. Yet if you read the book of Revelation, you will see that many will not repent (turn from their sins and turn to Jesus). Instead, they will blame God and continue in their ways.

I am writing this letter because it is my prayer that you, who read it, will understand that just as the first coming of Jesus was promised in the Bible, and just as the rapture was promised in the Bible, both have occurred—just as God declared. The predictions in the Bible about the next seven years are just as accurate and dependable. May you not harden your heart to God's love for you. May you not be deceived into believing He is not good and caring and would not do anything to save you.

Jesus declared in John 14:6, "I am the way, the truth, and the life. No one comes to the Father except through Me."

During these next seven years, you will either be following the Antichrist and sealing your eternal fate in hell, or following Jesus and sealing your eternal life in heaven. There is no middle path.

I am with Jesus, experiencing complete and total joy. When I gave my life to Him, my life was forever changed. I am forever grateful that Jesus loves me that much, enough to come and die on the cross so that He could forgive me of my sins and I could live with Him forever.

If you are reading this letter, and are witness to the disappearance of multitudes, you are not saved. You need Jesus. My heart's cry for you is that you would bow your head right now and admit to Jesus that you have failed Him in so many ways and ask Him to forgive you and save you. If you sincerely ask Him, He will be faithful to make you His.

May I see you in heaven. With the love of Jesus I write this, Cathy

On a separate sheet of paper, in your own handwriting, write your letter to those who are left behind after the rapture and file it with your important papers, or make a copy of this one and sign your name.

Notes

Chapter Thirteen

BECAUSE YOU PRAYED: REVELATION 8-9

In chapters 8 and 9 of Revelation, we see the opening of the seventh seal from which come the events of the seven trumpets. Six of the seven trumpets will be covered in these chapters. The sounding of the seventh trumpet is in the last part of chapter 11.

> When He opened the seventh seal, there was silence in heaven for about half an hour. 8:1

SILENCE

When Jesus opens the seventh seal, the first thing John noticed was not a cataclysmic event; it was silence. For the most part, as we have been looking at the first seven chapters of Revelation, John has been describing a lot of sounds—trumpets, voices, thunderings, proclamations, worship—holy sounds—incredible sounds—sounds unlike any he had ever heard on earth—sounds that you and I have yet to hear.

We too will hear the angels speak, thunder boom, living creatures, angels, and the redeemed exclaiming, "Holy, holy, holy…" and proclaiming the worthiness of the Father and the Son to receive glory and power and dominion forever and ever. We will hear the souls of the martyred crying out, "How long?" These are all holy sounds. In contrast, the earth will be filled with the noise of earthquakes, the sound of stars falling, and the unredeemed crying out in terror. This has been just about non-stop sound until now, the opening of the seventh seal.

THIRTY MINUTES

A half hour of silence is really not very long, especially in terms of eternity. The sense of its length is about perspective. Sadly, some of our longest half hours are on Sunday mornings when we have lost our spiritual perspective and can't wait for the pastor to stop preaching. It seems strange that John refers to this time in minutes. It's so earthly, yet nothing else is time specific.

We were not told the length of the worship or the duration of the songs. If I were a worship leader, I'd want to know, "How long did they sing?" It's good that John didn't tell us, because too many worship leaders would make a doctrine out of it and expect all songs to be that length.

What did John mean that this silence in heaven was about half an hour? Did he time it? We don't know, but we do know that as an orchestra falls silent at the lifting of the conductor's baton, so heaven hushed when the Lamb opened the seventh seal. Every song ceased. The living creatures that did not rest day or night in their worship, hushed. Every being in heaven hushed.

Remember that as believers, we will be there. For some of us silence is okay, but for others, it's nerve-wracking. Silence caused Peter to blurt out some pretty dumb things on the Mount of Transfiguration. I had a friend whose neck would get blotchy when there was silence during Bible study group time. Then she would blurt out some of the strangest things—anything to break the silence. She won't do that during this half hour. And it will probably be a reminder to her of one of the many ways God has changed her.

I feel like I get a little taste of this when I come into the sanctuary to teach our women's Bible study. When I enter the sanctuary, there are lots of voices and conversations going on, but as soon as I walk up to the podium, right at the half-hour point, the time to start the message, there is silence. It so blesses me that the ladies are ready to study God's Word. It is time and they put aside their conversations to listen, to take in. So much more was this silence and this anticipation in heaven.

Max Lucado, who really inspired a lot of my thoughts about this silence, wrote "A sudden stillness fell like a curtain." [34]

As the first six seals revealed how God acts, the seventh seal revealed how God listens. After thirty minutes, the silence breaks.

> And I saw the seven angels who stand before God, and to them were given seven trumpets. Then another angel, having a golden censer, came and stood at the altar. He was given much incense, that he should offer it with the prayers of all the saints upon the golden altar which was before the throne. And the smoke of the incense, with the prayers of the saints, ascended before God from the angel's hand. 8:2-4

PRAYERS OF ALL THE SAINTS

Why did the worship stop? Maybe because someone was praying. Heaven paused—heaven paused to acknowledge the prayers of all the saints.

I've always assumed that God kept our written prayers, but maybe, in a sense, there is an invisible recording of each one of them. Perhaps it was the sound of our words that rose with the incense. This incense along with the prayers of the saints is offered to God. Look at just a few phrases from the heart of God encouraging us to pray.

> "Blessed be God, who has not turned away my prayer, nor His mercy from me!" (Psalm 66:20)

> "He shall call upon Me, and I will answer him; I will be with him in trouble; I will deliver him and honor him." (Psalm 91:15)

> "He will fulfill the desire of those who fear Him; He also will hear their cry and save them." (Psalm 145:19)
>
> "Call to Me, and I will answer you, and show you great and mighty things, which you do not know." (Jeremiah 33:3)
>
> "Ask, and it will be given to you; seek, and you will find; knock, and it will be opened to you." (Matthew 7:7)
>
> "Whatever things you ask in prayer, believing, you will receive." (Matthew 21:22)
>
> "For everyone who asks receives, and he who seeks finds, and to him who knocks it will be opened." (Luke 11:10)
>
> "If you then, being evil, know how to give good gifts to your children, how much more will your heavenly Father give the Holy Spirit to those who ask Him!" (Luke 11:13)
>
> "… men always ought to pray and not lose heart." (Luke 18:1)
>
> "If any of you lacks wisdom, let him ask of God, who gives to all liberally and without reproach, and it will be given to him." (James 1:5)

If it's good for you and you pray, you've got it—in God's way and in God's time—which is always for your best. There are many more verses, but the point is summarized with this passage in Isaiah. King Hezekiah had been threatened with war and was shaken. Isaiah 37:14-15 tells us that when Hezekiah received the letter threatening war, he went up to the house of the Lord, and spread it before Him and persisted in prayer to defend Jerusalem. Then we have these absolutely glorious words from the Lord to Isaiah in verse 21: "Because you have prayed to Me."

BECAUSE YOU PRAYED

I don't know why our prayers affect God. I don't know why anything about us affects Him. Who am I? Who are you? But certainly God has made it very clear that our lives matter so much to Him that Jesus died for us. Wouldn't it go without saying that our prayers matter?

I read a poem written by a friend that spoke of how important our prayers are to God. It spoke of angels waiting, swords in hand, to execute God's will. I picture this scene in heaven like that—the angels standing, ready to go, waiting for the Lamb to say, "Now!" Waiting for Him to break open the seal. Waiting for the silence to end. But the Lord in essence told them, "Wait, not yet, I'm waiting for the prayers of the saints." Here we see the angel offering the sweet-smelling incense with the prayers of ALL the saints. It seems reasonable that the word *all* would include you and me. And this aroma ascended before God.

Looking at this scene, Max Lucado wrote these inspiring words: "You are the someone of God's kingdom. You have access to God's furnace. Your prayers move God to change the world. You may not understand the mystery of prayer. You don't need to. But this much is clear: Actions in heaven begin when someone prays on earth. What an amazing thought! When you speak, Jesus hears. And when Jesus hears, thunder falls. And when thunder falls, the world is changed. All because someone prayed." [35]

Our prayers seem to activate God's action of avenging the evil done to His children and at the same time calling anyone who would repent to join us. Then it all broke lose.

> Then the angel took the censer, filled it with fire from the altar, and threw it to the earth. And there were noises, thunderings, lightnings, and an earthquake. So the seven angels who had the seven trumpets prepared themselves to sound. 8:5-6

GOD'S PURPOSE: REPENTANCE

Hebrews 1:3 tells us that Jesus upholds "all things by the word of His power." This word *upholds* not only means that Jesus is holding it all together, but there is also a sense of carrying it along. Jesus is holding it all together as He is carrying it all along to His purposed end. Here we see Him begin to let go. But once again we will witness God's grace as we study the effects of the first four trumpets. Even though He could, not all of mankind is taken out at once.

As a parent, I can identify a little bit with what God is doing. My goal would be to help my children see the error of their ways, repent (really be sorry), and change. My purpose would not be to make them suffer, but to repent. Oftentimes, I would start out with a discipline that was not severe.

My sister is four years younger than I, and although I am very independent, I've never really been rebellious. When we were young, for some reason, my sister just loved to rile my mom. My mom would then exact some sort of punishment and my sister would take great efforts to let my mom know it had no effect. I remember one time my mom grabbed a coat hanger and spanked her. Afterwards, my sister looked at her and said, "Do you feel better now?" This, of course, resulted in my mother becoming more determined to break her. I used to watch in amazement and wonder why my sister would harden herself the way she did.

As we study Revelation, we see the unsaved doing the same sort of thing. Rather than softening to God and running to Him in repentance, they seem to harden to Him and run from Him. He responds by turning up the heat, but not because He loves to see people suffer. In the last chapter, we looked at a few verses that show us very clearly that God takes absolutely no pleasure in all of the suffering the unsaved endure during the tribulation.

> The first angel sounded: And hail and fire followed, mingled with blood, and they were thrown to the earth. And a third of the trees were burned up, and all green grass was burned up. 8:7

S. Mayfield
4/23/15

THE FIRST TRUMPET: VEGETATION IS STRUCK

The first four trumpets focus on the environment—the thing man once took for granted and many placed in importance above God.

In Romans 1:20, God declares that man is without excuse because He has revealed Himself in His creation. Then He laments because of man's lack of thankfulness. We just assume trees will stay green, oceans will stay blue, and stars will stay up in the sky.

> Then the second angel sounded: And something like a great mountain burning with fire was thrown into the sea, and a third of the sea became blood. And a third of the living creatures in the sea died, and a third of the ships were destroyed. 8:8-9

THE SECOND TRUMPET: THE SEAS ARE STRUCK

The best guess on this side of heaven is perhaps an asteroid. Guessing is really much of what we are doing when we try to identify things in Revelation. We are taking our best guess, which is to compare it to something of our time that we understand.

One problem many people have in understanding Revelation is that they try to make sense of it by relating the things in Revelation to what they understand or have knowledge of today. When really, we should be focusing on what happens in Revelation. Even more so, we should be focusing on God's character revealed through it all. We would be wise to apply the acronym F.O.T.O.—Focus On The Obvious.

> As a result of this *mountain* falling into the sea, we have the following devastating results:
>
> A third of the sea became blood (possibly from all that the mountain killed when it fell)
>
> A third of the living creatures in the sea died, and
>
> A third of the ships were destroyed.

Maybe you have walked along the shore of the beach where a dead seal has washed up. As you read about this devastation, one of your first thoughts might be how really bad it smells. Well, a whole lot of sea creatures are going to die and be washed up to shore. That stench is going to be pretty raunchy, not to mention the effects to the food supply and the ecological imbalance. Add to that the destruction of a third of the ships. Thousands of cargo carriers ply the world's seas and oceans, handling the bulk of international trade. Commerce will be crippled! Despite this devastation, God is in control of every aspect of these events that take place.

> Then the third angel sounded: And a great star fell from heaven, burning like a torch, and it fell on a third of the rivers and on the springs of water. The name of the star is Wormwood. A third of the waters became wormwood, and many men died from the water, because it was made bitter. 8:10-11

THE THIRD TRUMPET: THE WATERS ARE STRUCK

Psalm 147:4 tells us, "He counts the number of the stars; He calls them all by name." This star was named *Wormwood*, which means "bitter." As a result, a third of the waters became bitter and many men died.

> Then the fourth angel sounded: And a third of the sun was struck, a third of the moon, and a third of the stars, so that a third of them were darkened. A third of the day did not shine, and likewise the night. And I looked, and I heard an angel flying through the midst of heaven, saying with a loud voice, "Woe, woe, woe to the inhabitants of the earth, because of the remaining blasts of the trumpet of the three angels who are about to sound!" 8:12-13

THE FOURTH TRUMPET: THE HEAVENS ARE STRUCK

A third of the sun was struck

A third of the moon was struck

A third of the stars were struck so that a third of them were darkened

A third of the day did not shine and a third of the night did not shine.

This is some awful stuff. Three more trumpets, each with a woe, remain to be sounded. I would have proclaimed, "Woe! Woe! Woe!" a long time before this, but these angels know what is about to happen and it is far worse than what has happened so far.

There are some 600 warnings from God in the Bible. People have heeded few of them. We have, at least, as believers heeded the most important, but many of us ignore some of them, don't we? If you were driving down a road and there were 600 warning signs posted along the way, "Warning! Road washed out ahead" and you kept driving and drove into a ditch, just whose fault would that be?

We looked at this verse in the last chapter, but it's worthy of repeating: "Say to them: 'As I live,' says the Lord GOD, 'I have no pleasure in the death of the wicked, but that the wicked turn from his way and live. Turn, turn from your evil ways! For why should you die, O house of Israel?'" (Ezekiel 33:11).

In chapter 8, the sounding of the first four trumpets caused devastation to fall on the earth. The sounding of the next three trumpets will cause devastation to fall on mankind. We will see two of them in chapter 9.

> Then the fifth angel sounded: And I saw a star fallen from heaven to the earth. To him was given the key to the bottomless pit. And he opened the bottomless pit, and smoke arose out of the pit like the smoke of a great furnace. So the sun and the air were darkened because of the smoke of the pit. 9:1-2

THE FIFTH TRUMPET: TORMENTING LOCUSTS

John saw "a star fallen from heaven to earth," literally, a star which had *already* fallen from heaven. This star is a person because John refers to the star with the personal pronoun *him*. "To him was given the key to the bottomless pit."

> Then out of the smoke locusts came upon the earth. And to them was given power, as the scorpions of the earth have power. They were commanded not to harm the grass of the earth, or any green thing, or any tree, but only those men who do not have the seal of God on their foreheads. And they were not given authority to kill them, but to torment them for five months. Their torment was like the torment of a scorpion when it strikes a man. 9:3-5

Not locusts as we know them. These creatures were nothing like John had ever seen since they come up from the bottomless pit. Maybe 2,000 years later we might liken them to something else, but we would probably still fall very short in our description, because it's doubtful that we have seen anything like them.

So, what or who are these "locusts" that come up from the bottomless pit?

Consider these two verses:

> "For if God did not spare the angels who sinned, but cast them down to hell and delivered them into chains of darkness, to be reserved for judgment." (2 Peter 2:4)

> "And the angels who did not keep their proper domain, but left their own abode, He has reserved in everlasting chains under darkness for the judgment of the great day." (Jude 1:6)

God releases these locusts and God gives them power—power to harm men who do not have the seal of God on their foreheads—power to harm all but the 144,000 sealed Jews. They are given power to torment for five months, but not power to kill. Remember that God gave Satan power to cause great harm in Job's life, but God did not give him power to take Job's life, even though Job's misery was so bad that he wanted to die.

> In those days men will seek death and will not find it; they will desire to die, and death will flee from them. The shape of the locusts was like horses prepared for battle. On their heads were crowns of something like gold, and their faces were like the faces of men. They had hair like women's hair, and their teeth were like lions' teeth. And they had breastplates like breastplates of iron, and the sound of their wings was like the sound of chariots with many horses running into battle. They had tails like scorpions, and there were stings in their tails. Their power was to hurt men five months. 9:6-10

WHY CAN'T THEY DIE?

The misery of those afflicted by these locusts will be so bad that they will want to die. Have you ever been in that much pain? I have. Death would have been a welcome relief.

You just don't want to live anymore when you hurt that badly, but the idea of death as an escape is a demonic deception. Somehow these people can't die. Though they will seek it, death will elude them. God will intercede in some way. He's keeping them alive. Why? So they might repent and escape hell. They want to escape five months of pain; God wants to keep them from eternal pain, because if these scorpion-type locusts are demons, they won't stop their destructive ways in hell. In hell, death will not be an option; its sufferings are forever and ever. This is just a taste.

> And they had as king over them the angel of the bottomless pit, whose name in Hebrew is Abaddon, but in Greek he has the name Apollyon. One woe is past; two more woes to come. 9:11-12

THE LOCUSTS' KING

Proverbs 30:27 tells us, "The locusts have no king, yet they all advance in ranks." But these locusts have a king. His name is *Abaddon* in Hebrew, which means "Destruction," but in Greek he has the name *Apollyon*, "The Destroyer."

One woe is past. Behold, still two more woes are coming after these things.

> Then the sixth angel sounded: And I heard a voice from the four horns of the golden altar which is before God, saying to the sixth angel who had the trumpet, "Release the four angels who are bound at the great river Euphrates." 9:13-14

THE SIXTH TRUMPET: EUPHRATES' FOUR DEMONS

When the sixth angel sounded, the four angels who are bound at the great river Euphrates were released. Now remember, demons were once angels. There would be no reason to bind good angels. They were obedient—always obedient. God wouldn't have to tie them up. Either way, as we have seen, even the forces of evil are subject to God.

> So the four angels, who had been prepared for the hour and day and month and year, were released to kill a third of mankind. 9:15

We read here that they have been prepared for this time, this exact time. God is in control. They were prepared and God released them to kill a third of mankind.

> Now the number of the army of the horsemen was two hundred million; I heard the number of them. And thus I saw the horses in the vision: those who sat on them had breastplates of fiery red, hyacinth blue, and sulfur yellow; and the heads of the horses were like the heads of lions; and out of their mouths came fire, smoke, and brimstone. By these three plagues a third of mankind was killed—by the fire and the smoke and the brimstone which came out of their mouths. For their power is in their mouth and in their tails; for their tails are like serpents, having heads; and with them they do harm. 9:16-19

There was this huge army of horsemen, two hundred million of them to be exact. What is interesting is that mankind was not killed by the power of the horsemen, but by the *horses*. It sounds like the horses could actually be weaponry of some sort. At this point, about half of mankind has been killed as a result of the seven seals.

As you read the last two verses of chapter 9, keep in mind God's heart. The heart that "so loved the world that He gave His only begotten Son, that whoever believes in Him should not perish but have everlasting life" (John 3:16). John had watched Jesus suffer so very much for the salvation of others. Allow yourself to feel just a little bit of what it must have been like for John to write these words.

> But the rest of mankind, who were not killed by these plagues, did not repent of the works of their hands, that they should not worship demons, and idols of gold, silver, brass, stone, and wood, which can neither see nor hear nor walk. And they did not repent of their murders or their sorceries or their sexual immorality or their thefts. 9:20-21

WHY DON'T THEY REPENT?

After all of this suffering, what could these people have been thinking? Why was repentance so hard for them? Why? Because they loved the things of their world more than they loved the things of God.

I have counseled a lot of Christian women. It is an exceptionally rare thing for a woman to make an appointment to tell me how well she is doing, how God is blessing her. Women come to me when life is hard. And life is hard! In this world we have been promised tribulations, but some tribulations are a result of our own choices.

Often when people find themselves under the heavy hand of God due to sin in their life, they are well aware that if they would give up the sin, God would take His hand of chastising off of them. Remember, "For He does not afflict willingly, nor grieve the children of men" (Lamentations 3:33). He does not afflict willingly, but He does afflict.

For those who are His children, for believers, He afflicts to get us to wake up and come back to Him. He doesn't afflict to punish us. He's out to save us—not to punish us. We know this because Jesus died so we wouldn't have to suffer punishment for our sins.

Yet sadly, a believer who knows God is afflicting them will often say to me, "I know, I know, if I would give this up, He'd stop and I will. I know I will." When I press them with the question, "When?" all too often the answer is, "Soon."

ONE MORE NIGHT

When Moses came before Pharaoh and told him that God said, "Let my people go," Pharaoh refused. Then Moses would call a plague upon Egypt and Pharaoh would back off. Moses would stop the plague and then Pharaoh would go back on his word and not let the people go. Moses would then call another plague upon the people of Egypt.

When it came to the plague of the frogs, "the LORD spoke to Moses, 'Say to Aaron, "Stretch out your hand with your rod over the streams, over the rivers, and over the ponds, and cause frogs to come up on the land of Egypt"'" (Exodus 8:5). Frogs are kind of cute, but I wouldn't want to find one in my bed or in my food cupboards.

> "Then Pharaoh called for Moses and Aaron, and said, 'Entreat the LORD that He may take away the frogs from me and from my people; and I will let the people go.'" (Exodus 8:8)

Moses asked, "When?" Do you know what Pharaoh replied? He said, "Tomorrow."

I heard a message about this many years ago titled, "One More Night with the Frogs." Why is it that people just want one more night with the frogs—one more night with the things that are so bad for them when God has so much good?

CLOSING THOUGHTS

Is there something in your life that you know should go? Or something you know you should do and you don't? Are you deceiving yourself into thinking, *One day; one day I'll deal with it. One day I'll do what I'm supposed to do.* Maybe it's that you need to forgive someone. I say that because the sin of not forgiving really hangs us up. How heavy do you want God's hand to get? God doesn't let us get away with ignoring Him.

Repentance is agreeing with God—not the attitude of *I know, I know*. Repentance is sincerely believing He is right. If you really believe that He knows best, you will walk away from anything He tells you to walk away from and you will put into your life anything He tells you to.

Oh, how very sad, if God is saying about you right now, "But (your name) did not repent. I showed her my love, then I brought repercussions into her life—and still, still she did not repent."

We read about the rebellious, faithless Israelites in the Old Testament and think, *How terrible. After all God did for them, how could they be so faithless?* Possibly, as you read in Revelation of those remaining on the earth still not repenting, you are thinking, *How could they not repent?* As Pastor Dale says, "When you point a finger at someone, there's often three fingers pointing back at you."

Are there fingers pointing back at you today? Fingers calling you to have more faith in the power of your prayers? Fingers calling you to repent—to agree with God, by obeying God about something in your life? Or maybe fingers pointing at you telling you that you have given God a bad rap when life closes in on you. Have you failed to see His heart of love in it all, His goodness? Have you been viewing God differently than He actually is?

In the midst of reading about the falling mountains, falling stars, and tormenting locusts, I was touched greatly as I studied. It is my prayer that God has touched you too.

REFLECTION QUESTIONS

(For more extensive study questions visit CathyDickinson.com)

1. Consider the phrase, "because you prayed." Record a time when the Lord acted because you prayed. Thank and praise Him as you write. Lord you have blessed me in prayer time so often. Thank you for allowing me to pray for others in my church, at school and my family. Thank you for providing my chemo on time and for letting me a part of VBS. Please heal Rose.

2. The locust creatures will be given power by God to inflict pain on the unsaved. What will they not have the power to do? How is God's mercy demonstrated through this?

The locusts may not harm the earth – grass, green things and trees and those with God's seal. God cares for His things and people – He has mercy on those who acknowledge and come to Him. Unsave can be tormented but not killed.

3. All of the horror is a mere sampling of what eternity holds for the ones who "did not repent." Make a list of those you know who are yet unsaved. Commit to praying for them and ask the Lord how He would use you to demonstrate His love and mercy.

Lord, I pray for my sister, dad and other family members, my unsaved students and people in this cancer treatment room. Pray and share in love and be merciful in love and deed.

4. Consider the phrase, "one more night with the frogs." Is there something in your life that you know should go? Or you know you should do but have been putting it off?

More Bible Study and practiced prayer. I want to discipline my body to receive prayer as I get closer to the Lord.

5. A lack of saving faith in Jesus will cost the unsaved eternity in heaven. Consider the saying, "When you point a finger at someone, there's often three fingers pointing back at you." As a believer, heaven is yours, yet your areas of little faith still cost you. Ask the Lord to reveal these areas to you. God has multiple gifts for me and he is not finished with me – pray, trust and believe that he who started a good work in me will faithfully complete it.

6. Find Scripture to support the joy, peace, and satisfaction that awaits you when you choose to believe Him in the areas you listed in Question 5.

7. Using the space below, draw a scene as described by John in Revelation chapter 8.

8. Using this area draw a scene as described by John in Revelation chapter 9.

Chapter Fourteen

GOD'S INSTRUMENTS: REVELATION 10–11:14

As we look at the first few verses of Revelation 10, we see John apparently back on earth. Before the sounding of the seventh trumpet (in Revelation 11:15), from which will come seven bowls, is an interlude.

I love these interludes or breaks that God gives us. They give us an opportunity to regain perspective. In the midst of all these terrible judgments and calamities, we are reminded of God's heart, ever calling men to repent of their ways and to come to Him. We are reminded that the fate of those who refuse Him is not the fate of those who come to Him. Although evil seems so powerful—greater, far greater is our God. Although evil seems to be winning, it is not, and God is carrying things along just as He promised.

> I saw still another mighty angel 10:1

ANOTHER MIGHTY ANGEL

What do we know about this extraordinary, mighty angel? First, the word *another* is significant. In English, we have one word for *another*. In Greek, there are two different words: "another of the same kind" and "another of a different kind."

My grandson, Gabe, plays both baseball and basketball. An example of another of the same kind would be: "I'm going to one baseball game on Saturday morning and another on Saturday afternoon." Another of a different kind would be: "I'm going to a (baseball) game in the morning and another game (basketball) in the afternoon." This angel is another of the same kind—the same kind of angel like the ones who have been sounding the trumpets.

Some believe this mighty angel is Jesus. Although this angel has some attributes that are like Jesus, he is not. When John sees Jesus in Revelation, he lets us know that it is Jesus. John tells us here, "I saw a mighty angel." I'm going to take it just as John said.

There are three instances of an angel being referred to as a *mighty* or *strong* angel in Revelation (same Greek word). One you've seen before in Revelation 5:2 when the *strong* angel asked, "Who is worthy to open the scroll?" Clearly we can see he is not Jesus. John saw Jesus separately as the Lamb of God and identified Him as such. The other reference is in Revelation 18:21 when "a *mighty* angel took up a stone like a great millstone and threw it into the sea."

> coming down from heaven, clothed with a cloud. And a rainbow was on his head, his face was like the sun, and his feet like pillars of fire. 10:1

I love this! In the last chapter we saw locust-like demons coming *up* from the bottomless pit. Now, in our interlude, God shows John (and us) a mighty angel coming *down* from heaven clothed in a pretty heavenly description.

A rainbow was on his head, his face was like the sun, and his feet like pillars of fire. Now, that sounds like Jesus. Certainly, if this mighty angel is not Jesus, he is fully representing Him. In the coming chapters we will be introduced to the Antichrist. He was fully empowered by the devil. This angel could be a reminder that God empowers too as we'll see Him empower the two witnesses in Revelation 11.

A RAINBOW ON HIS HEAD

We saw a rainbow around the throne in Revelation 4:3, didn't we? But this rainbow is not emerald in color. The rainbow has never represented God. It represents His promised covenant with us. This mighty angel is reminding us, and the believers who are going through the tribulation, that God keeps His promises.

HIS FACE LIKE THE SUN

In Exodus 34, after Moses beheld the glory of God, his face shone so much that he had to put a veil over it. This angel came from heaven where the whole place is full of God's glory.

FEET LIKE PILLARS OF FIRE

Fire represents judgment and that is what this mighty angel was about to proclaim. Ezekiel described the feet of the four living creatures much the same way. They were some sort of angelic beings, but certainly not Jesus.

> He had a little book open in his hand. And he set his right foot on the sea and his left foot on the land, 10:2

The idea here is authority. God's angel has his right foot on the sea and his left foot on the land. We will see very soon that the beast is going to come out of the sea with great authority.

> and cried with a loud voice, as when a lion roars. When he cried out, seven thunders uttered their voices. Now when the seven thunders uttered their voices, I was about to write; but I heard a voice from heaven saying to me, "Seal up the things which the seven thunders uttered, and do not write them." 10:3-4

OBEDIENCE TO WHAT WE KNOW

This mighty angel is speaking for Jesus. There are verses that refer to the king's wrath being like that of a lion. So combining thunders and the roar of a lion, I think we can assume that whatever was said, was judgment. It must have been intelligible, because John was going to write what he heard. What did they say? We don't know. Only John knew what was thundered and he likely didn't even understand it.

As Job pointed out long before, "Indeed these are the mere edges of His ways, and how small a whisper we hear of Him! But the thunder of His power who can understand?" (Job 26:14).

Maybe in the world today we see the mere edges of the judgment to come. I think you will agree, we don't want to see more. We don't know what was said in those thunders, as they have not yet been revealed to us; it is only those things that are revealed that we are responsible for. They are revealed so that we might obey Him.

> "The secret things belong to the Lord our God, but those things which are revealed belong to us and to our children forever, that we may do all the words of this law." (Deuteronomy 29:29)

Are you obedient to the things you know?

> The angel whom I saw standing on the sea and on the land raised up his hand to heaven and swore by Him who lives forever and ever, who created heaven and the things that are in it, the earth and the things that are in it, and the sea and the things that are in it, that there should be delay no longer, 10:5-6

NO MORE DELAY

In these verses, we also see further support that this mighty angel is not Jesus. If this mighty angel were Jesus, He would not be swearing by Himself, would He? When Jesus walked this earth, people were amazed at the way He spoke with such authority. He said words like, "I say," and needed no support for them. This mighty angel seems to be speaking for God. Jesus is God. What was the angel's message? "There should be delay no longer."

In Revelation 6:9-11 we heard the cry of the martyrs who had been slain for the word of God and for their testimony, "How long, O Lord, holy and true, until You judge and avenge our blood on those who dwell on the earth?" Here we have a response to the martyrs' question, "There should be delay no longer."

> but in the days of the sounding of the seventh angel, when he is about to sound, the mystery of God would be finished, as He declared to His servants the prophets. 10:7

When we get to the sounding of the seventh trumpet in Revelation 11:15, we'll see the time has indeed come. Again, Jesus declared these things to the prophets and He declared them here to the seventh angel.

THE MYSTERY IS FINISHED

A mystery is the revelation of a truth that has not yet been revealed. What is the "mystery of God" that would be finished? Some say it's the answer to the question, *Why doesn't God do something about all of the evil?* The events of the seventh trumpet surely will answer that one. Maybe it's the answer to every question you and I have ever had, because at the end of all of this, all our questions will be answered.

S. Mayfield
11/5/14

Paul encourages us, "For now we see in a mirror, dimly, but then face to face. Now I know in part, but then I shall know just as I also am known" (1 Corinthians 13:12). He reminds us that when it's all over, there will be no more mysteries, no more questions. And when we get to Revelation 15, we'll see that we will like all of the answers.

> Then the voice which I heard from heaven spoke to me again and said, "Go, take the little book which is open in the hand of the angel who stands on the sea and on the earth." So I went to the angel and said to him, "Give me the little book." 10:8-9

THE LITTLE BOOK

As we continue to look at this angel and what is said about him, we close in on the conclusion that he is, as John said, a mighty angel. It seems inconsistent that a voice from heaven would identify Jesus as an angel. Also, when we see John saying to the angel, "Give me the little book," it sounds demanding, doesn't it? But John is just obeying the voice from heaven that told him to take it.

What is the little book? In Revelation 5:7, we read that Jesus took the *scroll*. This is the same word meaning as this word, *book*, except it's described as *little*; therefore, it cannot be the same book—it's a smaller one. Could it contain only the part revealed by the opening of the seventh seal? It certainly is possible. We don't know. We do know God wrote it, so we know it is God's Word.

> And he said to me, "Take and eat it; and it will make your stomach bitter, but it will be as sweet as honey in your mouth." 10:9

SWEET AND BITTER

Eating this little book indicates taking it in or assimilating it. John is told what to expect when he eats the book, much like the warnings that accompany medications when they are advertised. They first tell us how great the medications are and then warn us of all the possible side effects such as heart attacks, strokes, etc. What would you put on a warning label of God's Word? You know it to be sweet, but as we study Revelation we taste some bitterness.

The Bible says of itself that it is sweet, sweeter than honey; that it shows us wonderful things; that it gives understanding; that it's better than thousands of coins of gold and silver; that it can thoroughly equip us for every good work and make us wise for salvation. But once we take it in—and notice it's not until we take it in and really start understanding it—we discover its bitter side. There is a bitterness of sorts in the way it sheds light on our sins that we've tried to hide or ignore.

I love this quote: "Men do not reject the Bible because it contradicts itself but because it contradicts them."[36]

This contradiction, this revealing of what we are really like makes us sorrowfully bitter if we first receive it as honey. Its warnings and judgments for others should also produce a bitterness in us—not a bitterness like unforgiveness or hardness—but bitter to swallow or taste, like Ezekiel, when he was told to lament with bitterness and a breaking heart as he saw the future of God's rebellious people.

Surely, if this little book was about the times to come, it would be sweet like honey as John anticipated all God has for His people who come to Him. Yet John would have also tasted the bitterness of sorrow as he watched the torment that men would be subjected to in these final days. The only way God can establish His wonderful kingdom is to also render judgment; both are sweet and bitter.

> Then I took the little book out of the angel's hand and ate it, and it was as sweet as honey in my mouth. But when I had eaten it, my stomach became bitter. And he said to me, "You must prophesy again about many peoples, nations, tongues, and kings." 10:10-11

EAT FIRST THEN SPEAK

There was more that God wanted John to say and I like that God had John eat the book first. Truly you and I have nothing to say and no power to say it until we have first taken in God's Word.

There is a parallel passage in Ezekiel 2 and 3. Ezekiel was told to speak to a rebellious people. He was told to eat a book that had "writing on the inside and on the outside, and written on it were lamentations and mourning and woe" (Ezekiel 2:10). Ezekiel ate it, and it was in his mouth "like honey in sweetness" (Ezekiel 3:3). Ezekiel was told that he was to speak God's words, but that the people wouldn't listen to him. Then Ezekiel said, "So the Spirit lifted me up and took me away, and I went in bitterness, in the heat of my spirit; but the hand of the Lord was strong upon me" (Ezekiel 3:14).

Ezekiel's experience was sweet, yet bitter. We experience such a gamut of emotions when we serve the Lord too. I was talking to someone recently who said of her ministry, "I feel so much pressure." And I said, "Yes, but you love it, don't you?"

I was just reading last week about the women who came to Jesus' empty grave. It said they hurried away from the tomb afraid, yet filled with joy. Our walk with the Lord is often like that too.

Chapter 10 is a vivid reminder that no matter how many demons run all over the earth, no matter how much demonic power is released resulting in havoc and devastation around the world, God is still in charge. Jesus is still coming. He is coming to set things right and absolutely nothing and no one can stop Him.

> Then I was given a reed like a measuring rod. And the angel stood, saying, "Rise and measure the temple of God, the altar, and those who worship there. 11:1

THE TEMPLE

In chapter 10 John was given a little book. In chapter 11 John was given a measuring rod. In John's time, the temple had been totally destroyed by the Romans—not one stone had been left upon another. This is another temple on earth and John was to measure it.

The temple was man's way of trying to be righteous before God. There are several examples of God having things measured, which is most commonly believed to be a sign of His protection. The altar was in the holy of holies—the place where only the high priest could go once a year. The worshipers were the Jews—the people God was pursuing to save during this time.

There is going to be a temple again. Daniel tells us that the temple sacrifices are going to be reestablished. There is no temple today. Many people believe there can never be a temple again without a full-on war with the Muslims, because they believe the temple has to go where the Dome of the Rock currently stands. However, without going into too much detail, archaeologists have dug under the Eastern Gate and many now believe that to be the actual location of the temple. Therefore to rebuild the temple, it would not need to be built where the Dome is, but next to it at the Eastern Gate.

THE REBUILT TEMPLE

If you go to Israel today, there is a place called the Temple Institute, an organization focusing on the endeavor of establishing the Third Temple. They have some of the temple instruments ready to go, like the menorah, which is large and pure gold; other temple instruments are yet to be made. This is a significant financial undertaking, so they are going to need help.

According to Daniel 9:27, it is believed that at the beginning of the tribulation, when the Antichrist makes the seven-year covenant with the Jews, he will help them reestablish the sacrifices and offerings in the temple, only to desecrate the temple three-and-one-half years later, in the middle of the tribulation, bringing an end to the sacrifices once again. Daniel spoke of the Antichrist in the temple (Daniel 11-12). In Matthew 24:15, Jesus spoke of the "abomination of desolation … standing in the holy place."

If you ask a Jew what they are looking for in the Messiah, most will tell you that they aren't looking for the Messiah to be the Son of God; they are looking for a savior and liberator of the Jewish people, a great man who will help them to rebuild their temple. The scene is all set up and ready to go.

Jesus said, "I have come in My Father's name, and you do not receive Me; if another comes in his own name, him you will receive" (John 5:43).

> But leave out the court which is outside the temple, and do not measure it, for it has been given to the Gentiles. And they will tread the holy city underfoot for forty-two months. 11:2

OUTSIDE THE TEMPLE

John was told not to measure outside the temple. Outside the temple was the court of the Gentiles. There was a wall—a partition between the temple and the Gentiles. Ephesians 2 tells us that the wall of separation between Jew and Gentile was broken down by Jesus' death and resurrection. "For He Himself is our peace, who has made both one" (Ephesians 2:14). However, at this point, the wall is back up. Perhaps this is a confirmation that the church isn't around; we're in heaven.

> And I will give power to my two witnesses, and they will prophesy one thousand two hundred and sixty days, clothed in sackcloth." 11:3

TWO WITNESSES

Revelation 11:3-13 tells of the two witnesses God will raise up and He will protect them for 1,260 days (three-and-one-half years). Is this the first three-and-one-half years or the second? We aren't told. Who are these two witnesses? Verse 4 tells us.

> These are the two olive trees and the two lampstands standing before the God of the earth. 11:4

ANOINTED AND EMPOWERED

The angel speaks to John as though he knows the meaning. Outside of Revelation, we have the same access to God's Word that John did. The only thing similar to this is found in Zechariah 4. Zechariah saw "a lampstand of solid gold with a bowl on top of it, and on the stand seven lamps with seven pipes to the seven lamps. Two olive trees are by it, one at the right of the bowl and the other at its left" (Zechariah 4:2).

The angel asked Zechariah if he knew what they were. He didn't. So the angel answered, "This is the word of the LORD to Zerubbabel, 'not by might nor by power, but by My Spirit' says the LORD of hosts'" (Zechariah 4:6).

Zerubbabel led in the rebuilding of the temple in the face of much opposition. Zechariah asked specifically about the two olive trees and was told, "These are the two anointed ones, who stand beside the Lord of the whole earth" (Zechariah 4:14).

What we can conclude is that the two witnesses are anointed and will be completely empowered and equipped by the Holy Spirit. They will be continually filled with the Holy Spirit and do mighty miracles.

> And if anyone wants to harm them, fire proceeds from their mouth and devours their enemies. And if anyone wants to harm them, he must be killed in this manner. These have power to shut heaven, so that no rain falls in the days of their prophecy; and they have power over waters to turn them to blood, and to strike the earth with all plagues, as often as they desire. 11:5-6

As believers, the Holy Spirit empowers us to do something out of the ordinary every once in a while, but the gist here is that these two witnesses will be super-powered all of the time.

WHO ARE THEY?

We are not told who they are, but most commentators have narrowed it down to three people. The first, almost all agree, is probably Elijah.

"Behold, I will send you Elijah the prophet before the coming of the great and dreadful day of the LORD" (Malachi 4:5). Elijah had called for God to withhold rain and He did. Elijah called down fire and consumed those who were out to get him. Elijah never experienced death. And Elijah was with Jesus on the Mount of Transfiguration.

The second possibility is Enoch because he also did not experience death. But it's more likely to be Moses, who is known for turning water into blood and striking the earth with plagues. And like Elijah, Moses was with Jesus on the Mount of Transfiguration.

In this book, you are being presented with what we think may be the case along with what we know today. We don't conclusively know who the mighty angel was and we don't know for certain who the two witnesses will be. What is most important is that God's character is accurately represented. What we absolutely must understand is that through all of this judgment, God is merciful. God is reaching out to anyone who will come to Him. In spite of all the power of the evil one, God is so much more powerful. God will accomplish all He has set out to accomplish. Satan can't even come close to making that claim. That's a fact, not a guess or a hope.

> When they finish their testimony, the beast that ascends out of the bottomless pit will make war against them, overcome them, and kill them. 11:7

THE BEAST

This is the first mention of the beast and it won't be the last. He will be one of the main characters for a while, but then he'll be gone—banished to hell forever. The beast is Revelation's favorite description of the Antichrist, but the unbelieving world does not see him as a beast. They see him as a hero. No one was able to touch these two witnesses, yet the beast rises up and kills them. He puts an end to these guys who were tormenting all the people of the world.

> And their dead bodies will lie in the street of the great city which spiritually is called Sodom and Egypt, where also our Lord was crucified. Then those from the peoples, tribes, tongues, and nations will see their dead bodies three-and-a-half days, and not allow their dead bodies to be put into graves. And those who dwell on the earth will rejoice over them, make merry, and send gifts to one another, because these two prophets tormented those who dwell on the earth. 11:8-10

THE PEOPLE'S RESPONSE

In their apparent relief from the torment, the people partied. They celebrated and gave gifts to one another.

Their hatred for these two witnesses reminds me of Stephen in the book of Acts. He was filled with the Holy Spirit and the Jews hated him. They despised him so much they stoned him to death. And he said to them, "You stiff-necked people! You are just like your fathers: you always resist the Holy Spirit!" (Acts 7:51 NIV).

The bodies of the two witnesses were just left lying in the street for three-and-a-half days. Culturally, this is the ultimate sign of disgrace. People from every part of the world saw this. Until recent years, it would have been impossible for everyone in the world to see what was happening in one place. People all over the globe will be viewing the two dead bodies of God's witnesses who spoke until their testimony was finished. You and I also have a testimony, or calling, and we too will be here until it's finished.

> Now after the three-and-a-half days the breath of life from God entered them, and they stood on their feet, and great fear fell on those who saw them. 11:11

GOD'S RESPONSE

God changes everything. The partying is over. Imagine seeing that on the news. That's a sight that will be seared in the minds of all of the partiers, drunk or not. Maybe God will have them at parties so they would be with other people when they saw it.

> And they heard a loud voice from heaven saying to them, "Come up here." And they ascended to heaven in a cloud, and their enemies saw them. 11:12

We are not called down to the grave. We are called UP to heaven! "And their enemies saw them," which is literally just about everybody in the world. In due time, every believer will hear that voice—the voice of our Lord Jesus calling us home to Him, whether it be in rapture or death.

Put yourself in their place for just a few seconds. These people may have heard about Jesus coming back to life from death and then caught up into heaven, but they certainly had heard the rumors about all those who disappeared, maybe three-and-one-half years ago. Perhaps they had reasoned it away somehow, but now things are beginning to add up. 2+2=4.

They all had seen and heard these witnesses who definitely told them about Jesus, and likely told them about the believers who had been called into heaven. These witnesses, after lying dead in the street for three-and-a-half days, stood on their feet and then went up out of their sight.

> In the same hour there was a great earthquake, and a tenth of the city fell. In the earthquake seven thousand people were killed, and the rest were afraid and gave glory to the God of heaven. 11:13

To add to their shock, there was a great earthquake strong enough to kill 7,000 people. "And the rest were afraid…." The rest? Who are the rest? I don't know. It would seem to be everyone, because the sense of the word is "a remnant, everyone that was left."

What did they do? They were afraid and "gave glory to the God of heaven." It appears that all those from the tribes, tongues, and nations who were rejoicing in the death of the two witnesses were afraid after seeing their hated enemies come to life, stand up, and rise up to heaven. You bet they were afraid when these events were punctuated by an earthquake that killed thousands. And they gave God glory, or more accurately, they gave Him the credit due for what was happening.

> The second woe is past. Behold, the third woe is coming quickly. 11:14

CLOSING THOUGHTS

The third woe is the worst and will bring it all to an end. But before God reveals the pouring out of His wrath in the seven bowls, He has reminded us of five things:

1. "The Son of God came to seek and to save the lost" (Luke 19:10).
2. His goal has never changed.
3. God is in charge! He always has been in charge, but now He is taking over what is rightfully His.
4. Things are going to be done His way, and
5. His way is always best. He wants us to know that we can count on it.

REFLECTION QUESTIONS

(For more extensive study questions visit CathyDickinson.com)

1. When John ate the *little book*, he was warned it would make his stomach bitter and taste sweet as honey in his mouth. How have you found the assimilation of God's Word into your life to be sweet?

2. What bitter effects have you experienced?

3. Most Jews today have placed their hope in the Messiah to come and rebuild the temple. How will the Antichrist use this misguided hope to gain favor with the Jews early in the tribulation?

4. What act will reveal that their hope was misplaced?

5. Misplaced hope leaves us vulnerable to the enemy. Ask the Lord to reveal to you any misplaced hope that you are holding on to and write it down. Next to it write one or more Scriptural truths to serve as an anchor for your soul.

6. There are many things we do not know conclusively about the events to come in Revelation, but we can know absolutely about the attributes and character of our God that are revealed even in the midst of His judgment. List the attributes that have been revealed or magnified to you through this study.

7. This study concluded with five things the Lord wants us to know (be reminded of) that we can count on before His final wrath is poured out. Fill in the blanks:

The Son of God came to __________ and to __________ the __________. (Luke 19:10)

His goal has never ______________.

God is in ______________!

Things will be done His ______________.

His way is always ______________!

8. Which one of these is the most challenging for you to count on? What Scriptures come to mind to lend support? Write them here.

9. Using this space, draw a scene as described by John in Revelation 10-11:14.

Romans 11:33 O the depths of the riches both of the wisdom and knowledge of God! How unsearchable are His judgments and His ways past finding out!

Psalm 103:11 For as high as the heavens are above the earth, so great is His loving devotion for those who fear him.

Chapter Fifteen

THE MAIN CHARACTERS: REVELATION 11:15–12:17

Revelation 11:14 tells us the second woe is past; now we move into the events of the third and final woe.

A RECAP

In Revelation 8, seven seals are opened and there is the sounding of six trumpets. John heard and saw an angel flying through the midst of heaven, saying with a loud voice, "Woe, woe, woe to the inhabitants of the earth" (Revelation 8:13). These three woes directed to "the inhabitants of the earth" are directed to unbelievers, earth dwellers—those who belong to the earth. Believers are not earth dwellers; we are pilgrims.

At the sounding of the fifth trumpet, locusts are released from the bottomless pit to torment men to death—but no one can die (Revelation 9:3). With the sounding of the sixth trumpet, the second woe comes, and four demonic angels cause death to a third of mankind (Revelation 9:14).

As we look at the sounding of the seventh trumpet in verse 15, we see something has significantly changed.

GOD'S KINGDOM PROCLAIMED

> Then the seventh angel sounded: And there were loud voices in heaven, saying, "The kingdoms of this world have become the kingdoms of our Lord and of His Christ, and He shall reign forever and ever!" 11:15

This sounding of the seventh trumpet, this time of Jesus reclaiming the earth, takes us all the way into Revelation 20. It will include God's final wrath, the judgment of the dead, and the reward of the saints.

Out of the seventh trumpet will come seven bowls—then Jesus will wrap it all up. Keep in mind the bitter sweetness of these woes. Sweet for the believer—oh, how we long for Jesus to take His rightful place—but we also grieve for those who reject Him.

> And the twenty-four elders who sat before God on their thrones fell on their faces and worshiped God, saying: "We give You thanks, O Lord God Almighty, the One who is and who was and who is to come, because You have taken Your great power and reigned. 11:16-17

How glorious to see heaven's reaction when Jesus takes His rightful place. That's the sweet part. Then we see the reaction of the earth dwellers.

> "The nations were angry, and Your wrath has come, and the time of the dead, that they should be judged, 11:18

The dead unbelievers, that is. To gain a better understanding, look at Psalm 2.

> "Why do the nations rage, and the people plot a vain thing? The kings of the earth set themselves, and the rulers take counsel together, against the LORD and against His Anointed, saying, 'Let us break Their bonds in pieces and cast away Their cords from us.' He who sits in the heavens shall laugh; the Lord shall hold them in derision. Then He shall speak to them in His wrath, and distress them in His deep displeasure: 'Yet I have set My King on My holy hill of Zion. I will declare the decree: the LORD has said to Me, "You are My Son, today I have begotten You. Ask of Me, and I will give You the nations for Your inheritance, and the ends of the earth for Your possession. You shall break them with a rod of iron; You shall dash them to pieces like a potter's vessel."' Now therefore, be wise, O kings; be instructed, you judges of the earth. Serve the LORD with fear, and rejoice with trembling. Kiss the Son, lest He be angry, and you perish in the way, when His wrath is kindled but a little. Blessed are all those who put their trust in Him" (Psalm 2:1-12).

Look at the phrase in verse 1, "the nations rage," and in verse 2, "the kings set themselves against the LORD." Yet look at what the LORD has to say to them: "Kiss the Son, lest He be angry, and you perish in the way." The passage concludes with, "Blessed are all those who put their trust in Him" (v. 12).

It's still not too late! God is still calling out to the earth dwellers.

> "And that You should reward Your servants the prophets and the saints, and those who fear Your name, small and great, and should destroy those who destroy the earth." 11:18

"The saints" encompasses all believers. All those who come to Him as Savior will be rewarded, while all those who deny Christ will be judged. God again is warning—judgment or reward—the choice is ours.

> Then the temple of God was opened in heaven, and the ark of His covenant was seen in His temple. And there were lightnings, noises, thunderings, an earthquake, and great hail. 11:19

THE TEMPLE OF GOD

The ark represents the presence of God and it contained the law—God's Ten Commandments. Man can take the Ten Commandments out of government buildings, but he can't take them out of heaven. When God's law comes in contact with sin and rebellion, it must result in judgment. While judgment is never God's choice, it is God's *must* reaction to sin that is not covered by the blood of His Son.

The lightnings, thunderings, and hail indicate that a terrible storm is about to hit the earth.

God has stepped up His judgment, as man has stepped up his rejection. Remember in chapter 6, men hid in caves and cried out in terror, "hide us from … the wrath of the Lamb!" (v. 16). At this point men are no longer in terror or fear; they are enraged at God and plotting against Him.

THE WAR ROOM

We've been looking at the war. But now in chapter 12, God pulls back the curtain and shows us the war room and what's been going on back stage. Much of this chapter does not reveal what happened after the blowing of the seventh trumpet, instead it shows us a behind-the-scenes view. We see the main characters of history as God sees them: a woman, her Child, and a dragon, as well as the angels, and those who are the offspring of the woman.

> Now a great sign appeared in heaven: 12:1

This clarifies John is seeing signs. They are representative of the characters being revealed.

> A woman clothed with the sun, with the moon under her feet, and on her head a garland of twelve stars. Then being with child, she cried out in labor and in pain to give birth. 12:1-2

ISRAEL

The first of the characters is a pregnant woman. Some have identified the woman as Mary. You may have seen pictures of Mary with a halo of twelve stars over her head. The problem is, as we look at this woman later in this chapter, when she flees to the wilderness, Mary did not and will not "flee to the wilderness."

Some have said this woman is the church, but the church has always been depicted as the bride of Christ waiting for her wedding day. Paul wrote, "For I am jealous for you with godly jealousy. For I have betrothed you to one husband, that I may present you as a chaste virgin to Christ" (2 Corinthians 11:2). This woman is pregnant; therefore, she cannot represent the church.

Using the Old Testament to give us understanding, look at Joseph's dream in Genesis 37. He dreamed of the sun, the moon, and eleven stars bowing down. Jacob (Joseph's father) identified them: Jacob the sun, his wife the moon, and Joseph's eleven brothers the stars. These twelve sons of Jacob (whom the Lord renamed Israel) make up the twelve tribes that we have come to know as the nation of Israel. As we continue to read the chapter, this seems to fit best. The woman represents Israel.

> And another sign appeared in heaven: behold, a great, fiery red dragon having seven heads and ten horns, and seven diadems on his heads. 12:3

SATAN

Verse 9 identifies this dragon for us, "that serpent of old, called the Devil and Satan."

Satan's desire from the very beginning is to thwart God's plan to save all of mankind. This is what the Bible tells us about him.

1. MURDERER

"You are of your father the devil, and the desires of your father you want to do. He was a murderer from the beginning." (John 8:44)

2. LIAR

"And does not stand in the truth, because there is no truth in him. When he speaks a lie, he speaks from his own resources, for he is a liar and the father of it." (John 8:44)

"But Peter said, 'Ananias, why has Satan filled your heart to lie to the Holy Spirit and keep back part of the price of the land for yourself?'" (Acts 5:3)

3. OPPOSES RIGHTEOUSNESS

"Who opposes and exalts himself above all that is called God or that is worshiped, so that he sits as God in the temple of God, showing himself that he is God." (2 Thessalonians 2:4) This speaks of the Antichrist who is empowered by Satan.

4. SCHEMER

"Put on the whole armor of God, that you may be able to stand against the wiles (schemes) of the devil." (Ephesians 6:11)

5. TEMPTER

"Now when the tempter (Satan) came to Him, he said, 'If You are the Son of God, command that these stones become bread.'" (Matthew 4:3)

6. HINDERS

"Therefore we wanted to come to you—even I, Paul, time and again—but Satan hindered us." (1 Thessalonians 2:18)

7. ENSNARES

"... that they may come to their senses and escape the snare of the devil, having been taken captive by him to do his will." (2 Timothy 2:26)

8. A DEVOURING LION

"Be sober, be vigilant; because your adversary the devil walks about like a roaring lion, seeking whom he may devour." (1 Peter 5:8)

His tail drew a third of the stars of heaven and threw them to the earth. 12:4

A THIRD OF THE ANGELS

The Bible refers to angels as stars and Satan took a third of them with him.

In Hebrews 2:16 we are told that, "He (God) does not give aid to the angels, but He does give aid to the seed of Abraham (which is all believers)."

This word *aid* has the sense of "to take hold of." God did not *take hold of* those angels that rebelled; He did nothing to keep them. He just let them go. But you and me—He gives aid to us. He devised a means to take hold of us and bring us to Himself.

One third of the angels left. That leaves two-thirds that stayed with the Lord. Remember that the next time you think about powerful demons roaming the earth, looking for ways to devour you. There are twice as many angels in the Lord's service watching over you. Ultimately, the choice of who gets our attention is ours.

> And the dragon stood before the woman who was ready to give birth, to devour her Child as soon as it was born. 12:4

ANTI-SEMITISM

Satan has made many attempts throughout history to wipe out the Jews; first, because Jesus would come from their line; and secondly, because God calls them His chosen people. Satan's desire was to kill "the woman" (Israel, the Jewish nation) before she could have "the Child."

Satan almost achieved his goal in 2 Chronicles 22. It tells us of a woman named Athaliah who sought to kill all the royal heirs of the house of Judah. But Jehoshabeath, the daughter of the king, took Joash, one of the king's sons and hid him for six years. The line of Jesus was down to one person, yet God protected him.

That didn't work. So, next—kill the Child. Satan ultimately tried to destroy Jesus Himself.

After Jesus was born, Herod the king was troubled and put to death all the male children who were in Bethlehem, from two years old and under. But an angel of the Lord appeared to Joseph in a dream, saying, "Arise, take the young Child and His mother, flee to Egypt, and stay there until I bring you word; for Herod will seek the young Child to destroy Him" (Matthew 2:13).

Curses! Foiled again! Throughout history, Satan would have said that many, many times. Satan is a villain; he is the villain of villains and he loves attention. He loves for us to talk about him, even negatively, but he hates the name of Jesus.

I make it a practice to never talk about Satan unless I talk about Jesus. So in direct opposition to the character of Satan, let's look at our Lord Jesus.

> She bore a male Child who was to rule all nations with a rod of iron. And her Child was caught up to God and His throne. 12:5

JESUS

Who is the Child? Jesus, the Son of God. He is God's plan to save all of mankind. God promised that the Messiah would come through Israel, from the tribe of Judah to the line of David, a Jew.

"Therefore the Lord Himself will give you a sign: Behold, the virgin shall conceive and bear a Son, and shall call His name Immanuel" (Isaiah 7:14). *Immanuel*, "God with us."

> "'Though you are little among the thousands of Judah, yet out of you shall come forth to Me the One to be Ruler in Israel, whose goings forth are from of old, from everlasting.' Therefore He shall give them up, until the time that she who is in labor has given birth; then the remnant of His brethren shall return to the children of Israel." (Micah 5:2-3)
>
> "And He Himself will rule them with a rod of iron … And He has on His robe and on His thigh a name written: KING OF KINGS AND LORD OF LORDS." (Revelation 19:15, 16)
>
> "So then, after the Lord had spoken to them, He was received up into heaven, and sat down at the right hand of God." (Mark 16:19)

Look at the attributes of Jesus as compared with the Antichrist:

1. LIFE GIVER

> "The thief does not come except to steal, and to kill, and to destroy. I have come that they may have life, and that they may have it more abundantly." (John 10:10)

2. THE TRUTH

> "But because I tell the truth, you do not believe Me. Which of you convicts Me of sin? And if I tell the truth, why do you not believe Me?" (John 8:45-46)
>
> "Jesus said to him, 'I am the way, the truth, and the life. No one comes to the Father except through Me.'" (John 14:6)

3. RIGHTEOUS

> "And if anyone sins, we have an Advocate with the Father, Jesus Christ the righteous." (1 John 2:1)
>
> "Because He has appointed a day on which He will judge the world in righteousness." (Acts 17:31a)

4. SAVIOR

> "For the Son of Man has come to save that which was lost." (Matthew 18:11)
>
> "Therefore He is also able to save to the uttermost those who come to God through Him, since He always lives to make intercession for them." (Hebrews 7:25)

5. SINLESS

"And you know that He was manifested to take away our sins, and in Him there is no sin." (1 John 3:5)

6. HELPER

"So we may boldly say: 'The Lord is my helper; I will not fear. What can man do to me?'" (John 13:6)

7. SETS FREE

"Therefore if the Son makes you free, you shall be free indeed." (John 8:36)

8. A PREVAILING LION

"Behold, the Lion of the tribe of Judah, the Root of David, has prevailed to open the scroll and to loose its seven seals." (Revelation 5:5)

"You are my hiding place; You shall preserve me from trouble; You shall surround me with songs of deliverance." (Psalm 32:7)

"And the Lord will deliver me from every evil work and preserve me for His heavenly kingdom. To Him be glory forever and ever. Amen!" (2 Timothy 4:18)

Oh, how Satan tried to defeat Jesus—to the point of His death, but Jesus rose from the dead to forever live to intercede for us, and one day take His rightful place as King of kings and Lord of lords.

Then the woman fled into the wilderness, where she has a place prepared by God, that they should feed her there one thousand two hundred and sixty days. 12:6

We'll look at this more later in verse 14. "One thousand two hundred and sixty days" is three-and-a-half years.

And war broke out in heaven: Michael and his angels fought with the dragon; and the dragon and his angels fought, but they did not prevail, nor was a place found for them in heaven any longer. 12:7-8

HEAVEN'S WAR: MICHAEL VS. SATAN

What did that battle look like? We are only told that Satan and his angels "did not prevail." I love this. The Greek word for *prevail* here indicates that Satan didn't have the strength; he didn't have the power.

This war was between Michael the archangel and the dragon. We don't find the word archangels (plural) in the Bible. The word *archangel* means "chief angel." Michael is the counterpart of Satan. Satan is a created being; Jesus is not. Jesus is Mighty God.

When the prince of Persia withstood Michael in Daniel 10:13, Michael is called one of the chief princes. (Michael won by the way).

In Daniel's prophecy, we are told that in the time of trouble (the great tribulation) "Michael shall stand up, the great prince who stands watch" over Israel (Daniel 12:1).

In the book of Jude we discover that Michael disputed with the devil about the body of Moses. Michael is a powerful being, yet as powerful as Michael is, look what Jude wrote about him: "Yet Michael the archangel, in contending with the devil, when he disputed about the body of Moses, dared not bring against him a reviling accusation, but said, 'The Lord rebuke you!'" (Jude 1:9). May we learn from this example and always call upon the Lord to do the rebuking of satanic powers.

So the great dragon was cast out, that serpent of old, called the Devil and Satan, 12:9

SATAN'S HISTORY

This "serpent of old" takes us right back to the beginning when he deceived Eve. He is called the Devil. His name is Satan.

He started out well. Ezekiel 28 says of him: "You were the seal of perfection, full of wisdom and perfect in beauty. You were in Eden, the garden of God; every precious stone was your covering: the sardius, topaz, and diamond, beryl, onyx, and jasper, sapphire, turquoise, and emerald with gold. The workmanship of your timbrels and pipes was prepared for you on the day you were created. You were the anointed cherub who covers; I established you; you were on the holy mountain of God; you walked back and forth in the midst of fiery stones. You were perfect in your ways from the day you were created, till iniquity was found in you" (Ezekiel 28:12-15).

What happened? "Your heart was lifted up because of your beauty; you corrupted your wisdom for the sake of your splendor" (Ezekiel 28:17a).

Isaiah 14:13-14 tells us a little bit more about Satan when he asserts five "I will" statements: "For you have said in your heart:

1. I will ascend into heaven.
2. I will exalt my throne above the stars of God.
3. I will also sit on the mount of the congregation on the farthest sides of the north.
4. I will ascend above the heights of the clouds.
5. I will be like the Most High.

But God's response is clear in the following two verses, "Yet you shall be brought down to Sheol, to the lowest depths of the Pit. Those who see you will gaze at you, and consider you, saying: 'Is this the man who made the earth tremble, who shook kingdoms?'" (Isaiah 14:15-16).

Even so, from the time Satan rebelled to the time that he will be brought down to hell, he has and will continue to wreak havoc on the earth. How does he do that?

who deceives the whole world; 12:9

HE DECEIVES

I was watching a documentary about a cult leader named Jim Jones who had quite a following during the 70s. That was a time when my generation was searching. We didn't like the choices our parents had made and we wanted something different and new that we could pour ourselves into, to make sense of life. I praise God that I found Jesus, but some were deceived. Some were deceived into following Jim Jones, who ultimately convinced his more than 900 followers to drink cyanide that resulted in their death. Three hundred of them were children.

How could something like that happen? How could people be duped like that? When they interviewed someone who had been a part of his cult, but who did not go to Guyana where the suicides took place, he said something like this, "You don't understand. He (Jim Jones) could get into your head and know what you want. Then he would promise it to you. Once you gave in, he had you. And it was really hard to get out."

Oh, how true that is of the devil, isn't it? Satan deceives the whole world. In contrast, Matthew 22:16 tells us, "Teacher, we know that You are true, and teach the way of God in truth." (Matthew 22:16)

BELIEVERS

We have a choice. We can either follow the voice of the deceiver who is out to devour us or obey the voice of the Savior who is out to set us free, because as believers:

1. WE ARE NOT IGNORANT OF HIS DEVICES

"Lest Satan should take advantage of us; for we are not ignorant of his devices." (2 Corinthians 2:11)

2. WE CAN STAND AGAINST HIM

"Put on the whole armor of God, that you may be able to stand against the wiles of the devil." (Ephesians 6:11)

3. RESIST HIM

"Therefore submit to God. Resist the devil and he will flee from you." (James 4:7)

Satan is powerful. Against you and me, we are no match for him. But against Jesus, Satan is no match. If Jesus is in you and you look to Him and believe His truths rather than Satan's lies, you will find yourself standing and Satan fleeing.

> he was cast to the earth, and his angels were cast out with him. 12:9

This is the fruition of God's response to this war. Satan and his angels were cast out of heaven. This is written in the past tense as John is seeing it, but for us, it's still in the future.

> Then I heard a loud voice saying in heaven, "Now salvation, and strength, and the kingdom of our God, and the power of His Christ have come for the accuser of our brethren, who accused them before our God day and night, has been cast down." 12:10

THE ACCUSER OF BRETHREN

The casting out of Satan set some things in motion. For now, Satan is still going back and forth from heaven to earth. He is still accusing the brethren before the throne of God.

We only have three times in the Bible where Satan is recorded.

1. The first time was in the garden of Eden when Satan accused God before man when he said to Eve, "Has God indeed said …?" (Genesis 3:1).
2. We hear it again in the book of Job, when Satan accuses Job for obeying God only because God blessed Job.
3. The next time we hear Satan is when he tempted Jesus in the wilderness and tried to get Him, who could not sin, to sin.

That pretty much sums up Satan's bag of tricks.

SATAN'S GOALS ARE:

1. DOUBT GOD

To bring questions into our lives to get us to doubt God.

2. CURSE GOD

To bring trials into our lives to get us to curse God (that includes thinking or speaking of Him in ways that are untrue).

3. DISOBEY GOD

To bring temptations into our lives to get us to disobey God.

Look at how Satan is described in Revelation 12:9, "who deceives the whole world." Satan is still successful in deceiving you and me, even as believers. Oh, for the day that you and I will never hear his voice again. Won't that be glorious? How can you and I recognize that voice? We can be watchful for his motives—to get us to doubt God, curse God, or disobey God.

Let's pause here for a minute and appreciate this. Satan has been cast down, the one who accuses the brethren (you and me) before our God continually day and night.

Just imagine how many times he's approached the throne and brought something we've done before the Lord. But Jesus has taken care of those accusations. He washed away everything Satan said about us!

> "And they overcame him by the blood of the Lamb and by the word of their testimony, and they did not love their lives to the death." 12:11

THE OVERCOMERS

Verse 11 tells us that we have overcome Satan. We saw this over and over again in Jesus' letters to the churches in the first chapters of Revelation; we are overcomers. As believers, we can overcome by:

1. THE BLOOD OF THE LAMB

We are saved only through the blood of Jesus.

> "knowing that you were not redeemed with corruptible things, like silver or gold … but with the precious blood of Christ." (1 Peter 1:18-19)

2. THE WORD OF OUR TESTIMONY

> "I have written to you, young men, because you are strong, and the word of God abides in you, and you have overcome the wicked one." (1 John 2:14)

3. NOT LOVING OUR LIVES UNTO DEATH

Isaiah gives us the key to overcoming Satan's attempt to keep us from victory and the key to continually overcoming his lies designed to keep us from experiencing the joy and peace of heaven now. "You will keep him in perfect peace, whose mind is stayed on You, because he trusts in You." (Isaiah 26:3)

We must remember to look to the power of Jesus' cleansing blood, to testify of Him (proclaim Him and praise Him), and not love our lives.

> "Therefore rejoice, O heavens, and you who dwell in them! Woe to the inhabitants of the earth and the sea! For the devil has come down to you, having great wrath, because he knows that he has a short time." 12:12

This gives us a taste of both sweetness and bitterness. Rejoicing for the heaven dwellers—that's the sweetness. Knowing the woe coming to the earth dwellers—that's the bitterness. I don't know how much wrath Satan has had over the millennia, but he has "great wrath" at this point. And his first act of wrath is to go after Israel.

> Now when the dragon saw that he had been cast to the earth, he persecuted the woman who gave birth to the male Child. But the woman was given two wings of a great eagle, that she might fly into the wilderness to her place, where she is nourished for a time and times and half a time, from the presence of the serpent. 12:13-14

A PLACE PREPARED BY GOD

What are "the two wings of an eagle?" Here is where people love to speculate. Some think these will be huge cargo planes. They had better be huge or there had better be a lot of them, because there are going to be a whole lot of Jews escaping.

Since Scripture says that God is preparing the place, here's a thought: "You have seen what I did to the Egyptians, and how I bore you on eagles' wings and brought you to Myself" (Exodus 19:4).

Part of a song that Moses wrote about the LORD's care for Israel says this: "He found him in a desert land and in the wasteland, a howling wilderness; He encircled him, He instructed him, He kept him as the apple of His eye. As an eagle stirs up its nest, hovers over its young, spreading out its wings, taking them up, carrying them on its wings" (Deuteronomy 32:10-11).

We can safely conclude that whatever carries her, ultimately it's the Lord. She is then nourished, taken care of, and fed for three-and-a-half years. Just as God took care of the Israelites for forty years, keeping their shoes from wearing out and their stomachs full of manna, He is certainly able to take care of them again for three-and-a-half years.

> So the serpent spewed water out of his mouth like a flood after the woman, that he might cause her to be carried away by the flood. 12:15

That's powerful! You and I couldn't do that. He spewed out so much water that its power can carry away an entire nation of people. That's really powerful! The serpent, being full of great wrath, is determined to destroy this woman; determined to destroy God's people.

> But the earth helped the woman, and the earth opened its mouth and swallowed up the flood which the dragon had spewed out of his mouth. 12:16

JESUS IS GREATER

I love the use of the contrasting word "but" in this chapter as the Lord triumphs over Satan again and again. Michael and his angels fought Satan and his angels, BUT they did not prevail (vv. 7-8). Satan persecuted the woman (Israel), BUT the woman was given two wings (vv. 13-14).

Satan spewed out enough water to cause a flood that could carry away Israel, BUT the earth swallowed up the flood (vv. 15, 16).

Satan is a copycat, an imitator. He desperately wants to be like God, but he's just not. God caused water to flood the entire earth. Satan spewed out enough to flood a nation, but God just used the earth to swallow up Satan's efforts. "He who is in you is greater than he who is in the world" (1 John 4:4b). Jesus is much, much greater. Ephesians 2 says this to believers:

> "And you He made alive, who were dead in trespasses and sins, in which you once walked according to the course of this world, according to the prince of the power of the air, the spirit who now works in the sons of disobedience, among whom also we all once conducted ourselves in the lusts of our flesh, fulfilling the desires of the flesh and of the mind, and were by nature children of wrath, just as the others." (Ephesians 2:1-3)

STANDING STRONG IN THE LORD

To one degree or another, every one of us has lived according to our own ways. We have made choices according to what we have figured out works best for us—just as others! Then there is this absolutely glorious statement:

> "But God, who is rich in mercy, because of His great love with which He loved us, even when we were dead in trespasses, made us alive together with Christ." (Ephesians 2:4-5)

You see, all too often, you and I take a truth of God and we say, "yeah, but ..." to Him, challenging what God has declared. What we should be doing is taking the lies of Satan, and by using God's truth declare, "yeah, but ..." to Satan's lies. Try it—you will find yourself standing strong in the Lord.

> And the dragon was enraged with the woman, and he went to make war with the rest of her offspring, who keep the commandments of God and have the testimony of Jesus Christ. 12:17

ISRAEL'S OFFSPRING

Who are her offspring? Those "who keep the commandments of God and have the testimony of Jesus Christ."

Oh, what good news this chapter will be to those believers living on the earth during the tribulation. What a very good reminder to us, a reminder worth celebrating. Satan is a defeated foe. At this point, he's starting to get that. He knows he has a short time.

PRIDE, THE GREAT DECEIVER

So why is Satan so foolish? He can read the Bible. He knows who God is, how powerful He is, and that not one thing that God determines will come to naught. But the great deceiver is himself deceived. Pride did that to him. That's why God hates pride so very much. That's why God resists the proud. Pride makes us blind to others and to ourselves. Pride might be one of the toughest things for God to break through, because it's so deceiving.

Just as one definition of humility is not just thinking lowly of yourself, but to not think of yourself at all; pride is not only thinking highly of yourself, it's thinking of yourself and factoring in just you, and what's best for you.

When we choose ourselves above others or above God, that's pride. When you know God is telling you to do something and you don't, that's pride.

CLOSING THOUGHTS

I was reading in Galatians where Paul recounted his testimony to the saints in Jerusalem. They knew how he had persecuted believers and was now preaching the gospel. Paul concluded with, "And they praised God because of me" (Galatians 1:24 NIV). I encourage you to let that thought sink in. Pride does not cooperate with God. Humility cooperates with God and causes others to praise Him. Oh, that you and I would have this goal: to live in such a way that people praise God because of us.

This chapter reveals the enemy. He is a dragon; he is your accuser; he is a liar and a deceiver, but he is also a loser. He is a loser deceived by his own pride into thinking he can be like God. For the believer, his power is broken. He cannot latch on to you. He cannot spiritually hurt you any longer. He will soon realize that his time is short and he will unleash his wrath upon those who dwell on the earth like never before. You and I are going to be above it all—literally! We will be joining the twenty-four elders worshiping the One who has defeated our foe. We will be praising Jesus because of Jesus. We should be doing it now. As long as we are on the earth we have this calling: to live in such a way that people praise God because of us. If there is pride in us, that won't happen.

REFLECTION QUESTIONS

(For more extensive study questions visit CathyDickinson.com)

1. Who do the three main characters likely represent?

The Woman: ________________

The Child: ________________

The Dragon: ________________

2. List the descriptions of the devil and next to them write Jesus' attributes.

Satan	Jesus

3. Ponder that God did nothing to give aid to (hold onto) one third of the angels that chose rebellion; yet, though we are sinners, He devised a means to take hold of us and bring us to Himself. Respond to Him by writing a prayer of thanksgiving and awe-filled praise.

Thank you Lord for knowing my weaknesses, and being rich in Mercy, you come to my aid. You literally take hold of me and bring me to you. You preserve me and you are my hiding place (Psalm 32:7) You are my deliverer (2 Tim 4:18). Praise your Holy and precious name!

4. Satan essentially has three goals for us. The ability to recognize them is key to avoiding their snare. List them below: Satan is our accuser and he wants to deceive us. His goals are to get us to: 1) doubt God, 2) curse God, and 3) disobey God. But we are overcomers because of who God is

5. One of the enemy's goals is to get you to curse God, which includes speaking (or even thinking) of Him in ways that are untrue. The best protection against this is to be steeped in the truth of who He is. List the attributes, truths, and promises of God that most directly speak to your life's trials today. The Lord gives life and He alone is righteous, He saves me and promises to walk with me through my trials. Jesus is my advocate and protects me from the accuser

6. We learned from Revelation 12:11 that believers overcome by three things. List them below and what each means to you practically. As a believer I can overcome because: 1) I am not ignorant of his (Satan's) devices, 2) I can stand against him (Eph 6:11), and 3) I can submit to God and resist my enemy and he will flee. (James 4:7). 2 Cor 2:11

7. Based on what you learned in this chapter, why does the Lord hate pride so much?

Pride is a great deceiver - it causes us to think of ourselves as more important - we become blind to others and to ourselves. We only think about what is best for ourselves - there is no room for the Lord. We become self-absorbed and self seeking

8. This chapter closed with an exhortation to live in such a way that people praise God because of you. Take some time to ask the Lord to reveal any areas in your attitude where pride is keeping people from praising God. (If you need more room to write, use the notes section on page 218.) I need to praise Him more, pray more and be about His business - Lord please help me in my weakness and please give me the words to speak.

9. Draw a scene that comes to mind as you think about what you learned in Revelation 11:15-12:17.

→ We overcome by
1) The blood of the Lamb of God—Christ (1 Peter 1:18-19)
2) The word of our testimony (1 John 2:14)
3) Not loving our lives unto death (Isaiah 26:3)
Keep my mind "stayed" on Him.

Notes

Chapter Sixteen

SATAN'S INSTRUMENTS: REVELATION 13

Many have thought Revelation is all about the revealing of the Antichrist. But John called him the Antichrist in his epistles, describing him as a deceiver and one who denies the Father and the Son. His epistles had already been written before he wrote Revelation, so this wasn't news to believers. John wrote to them in 1 John 2:18, "Little children, it is the last hour; and as you have heard that the Antichrist is coming …."

People will be deceived into thinking he is a good guy, a great guy, out for their good, until he is revealed for who he is at the midway point of the tribulation. If we are correct in our position about the rapture preceding the tribulation, we who belong to Jesus will be looking at the events of Revelation 13 from heaven; we will not be experiencing them. But there is much for us to consider in this portion of Revelation as far as personal application—this one caught me by surprise.

THE UNHOLY TRINITY

In chapter 12, Satan had been thrown from heaven and was enraged. Now in chapter 13, we find two men attempting to fulfill Satan's tactics in destroying God's plan to bring Israel into the millennium. We have, in a sense, an unholy trinity: Satan, the father of both beasts; the Antichrist, the first beast; and the False Prophet, the second beast, who points to the Antichrist to give him the glory—just as the Holy Spirit points us to Jesus to worship Him.

> Then I stood on the sand of the sea. And I saw a beast rising up out of the sea, 13:1

THE ANTICHRIST

The first eight verses introduce the Antichrist to us. This word *Antichrist* does not indicate that he is against Christ (which, of course, he is) but rather that he is a counterfeit Christ. As we discussed in the last chapter, Satan attempts to copy what God does because he wants to be like God.

Paul called him the man of sin, the son of perdition, the lawless one "who opposes and exalts himself above all that is called God or that is worshiped, so that he sits as God in the temple of God, showing himself that he is God" (2 Thessalonians 2:4).

> having seven heads and ten horns, and on his horns ten crowns, and on his heads a blasphemous name. 13:1

SEVEN HEADS AND TEN HORNS

Looking back at Revelation 12:3, it tells us that Satan had "seven heads and ten horns, and seven diadems on his heads." This beast in chapter 13 is very similar to Satan, but he is not because we learn in verse 2 that Satan gave this beast his power.

The Bible is our best commentary and Revelation 17 helps us to identify his heads and horns.

"Here is the mind which has wisdom: The seven heads are seven mountains on which the woman sits" (Revelation 17:9). The woman represents a false religious system.

> "There are also seven kings. Five have fallen, one is, and the other has not yet come. And when he comes, he must continue a short time. The beast that was, and is not, is himself also the eighth, and is of the seven, and is going to perdition. The ten horns which you saw are ten kings who have received no kingdom as yet, but they receive authority for one hour as kings with the beast." (Revelation 17:10-12)

> "Now the beast which I saw was like a leopard, his feet were like the feet of a bear, and his mouth like the mouth of a lion." 13:2

To clarify here, the four living creatures in heaven discussed in earlier chapters are described as four living beasts in some translations. This is a different word than that used to describe these two beasts in Revelation 13. This word describes a wild beast—particularly one that is venomous in nature.

DANIEL'S VISION

In the book of Daniel we learn about the leopard, bear, and lion characteristics.

> "Those great beasts, which are four, are four kings which arise out of the earth" (Daniel 7:17).

The fourth beast is different. "After this I saw in the night visions, and behold, a fourth beast, dreadful and terrible, exceedingly strong. It had huge iron teeth; it was devouring, breaking in pieces, and trampling the residue with its feet. It was different from all the beasts that were before it, and it had ten horns" (Daniel 7:7).

> "I was considering the horns, and there was another horn, a little one, coming up among them, before whom three of the first horns were plucked out by the roots. And there, in this horn, were eyes like the eyes of a man, and a mouth speaking pompous words" (Daniel 7:8).

> "Then I wished to know the truth about the fourth beast, which was different from all the others, exceedingly dreadful, with its teeth of iron and its nails of bronze, which devoured, broke in pieces, and trampled the residue with its feet; and the ten horns that were on its head, and the other horn which came up, before which three fell, namely, that horn which had eyes and a mouth which spoke pompous words,

> whose appearance was greater than his fellows. I was watching; and the same horn was making war against the saints, and prevailing against them" (Daniel 7:19-21).
>
> "Thus he said: 'The fourth beast shall be a fourth kingdom on earth, which shall be different from all other kingdoms, and shall devour the whole earth, trample it and break it in pieces. The ten horns are ten kings who shall arise from this kingdom. And another shall rise after them; he shall be different from the first ones, and shall subdue three kings. He shall speak pompous words against the Most High, shall persecute the saints of the Most High, and shall intend to change times and law. Then the saints shall be given into his hand for a time and times and half a time'" (Daniel 7:23-25).

Did you notice some verses were skipped? They are very important because they pull us back to see our Lord and His part in all of this. Let's read them next.

UNTIL THE ANCIENT OF DAYS CAME

> "I watched till thrones were put in place, and the Ancient of Days was seated; His garment was white as snow, and the hair of His head was like pure wool. His throne was a fiery flame, its wheels a burning fire; a fiery stream issued and came forth from before Him. A thousand thousands ministered to Him; ten thousand times ten thousand stood before Him. The court was seated, and the books were opened" (Daniel 7:9-10).
>
> "I was watching; and the same horn was making war against the saints, and prevailing against them, until the Ancient of Days came, and a judgment was made in favor of the saints of the Most High, and the time came for the saints to possess the kingdom" (Daniel 7:21-22).
>
> "Then the kingdom and dominion, and the greatness of the kingdoms under the whole heaven, shall be given to the people, the saints of the Most High. His kingdom is an everlasting kingdom, and all dominions shall serve and obey Him" (Daniel 7:27).

Keep this in mind as we look at these terrible, evil men who will have great powers and will execute those powers against God's people. God wins!

A MAN OF TERROR

People won't know that the Antichrist, this beast, is a really bad guy. At first he will look like a man of peace. He will make a covenant with Israel in the first three-and-a-half years of the tribulation, but then the Jews will see that he is evil. But the rest of the unsaved world will not see how terrible he is and they will worship him.

To summarize, he's a man that will come out of the nations, and according to Daniel 7, he's a man who is:

1. Exceedingly strong
2. Different from the other rulers

3. Pompous and speaks against the Most High God
4. Evil and makes war against and persecutes the saints
5. Powerful and prevails against the saints for three-and-a-half years
6. Dreadful, terrible, and devours the whole earth

The dragon gave him his power, his throne, and great authority. 13:2

A GREAT POLITICAL LEADER

The dragon, Satan, gave the beast "(1) his power, (2) his throne, and (3) great authority." Remember when Satan tried to tempt Jesus in the wilderness? He promised those same things. Jesus refused. The Antichrist will take Satan up on his offer, even though he will have no power in or of himself. All his power and authority will come from Satan. Compare this to our Lord Jesus in John 5:30.

> "I can of Myself do nothing. As I hear, I judge; and My judgment is righteous, because I do not seek My own will but the will of the Father who sent Me."

Yet again, we can see how the Antichrist is just a phony imitator getting his power from his father, the devil.

> And I saw one of his heads as if it had been mortally wounded, and his deadly wound was healed. And all the world marveled and followed the beast. 13:3

Is this another attempt of Satan to copy Jesus' resurrection? Or even to copy God when He brought back to life the two witnesses that the beast had killed? Did the Antichrist actually die? Good question. If he did, it would seem that God would have had to bring him back to life, as it is doubtful Satan has the power to do that one.

> So they worshiped the dragon who gave authority to the beast; and they worshiped the beast, saying, "Who is like the beast? Who is able to make war with him?" 13:4

WRONG QUESTION

The world marveled, followed the beast (Antichrist), and worshiped the dragon (Satan). Was it flat out Satan worship? Maybe it was, but maybe not. Through the ages, there have been many ways that people worshiped things or people other than God, not realizing that Satan was behind it all.

As we see in their worship, they were declaring praise of the Antichrist, saying, "Who is like the beast? Who is able to make war with him?" Wrong. The right question is, "Who is like our God?"

> "Who is like You, O Lord, among the gods? Who is like You, glorious in holiness, fearful in praises, doing wonders?" (Exodus 15:11). "No one is holy like the Lord, for there is none besides You, nor is there any rock like our God" (1 Samuel 2:2).

The right question is, "Who is able to make war with the Lord our God?"

"These will make war with the Lamb, and the Lamb will overcome them, for He is Lord of lords and King of kings; and those who are with Him are called, chosen, and faithful" (Revelation 17:14). Jesus is not only able to make war, He will overcome those who make war with Him!

> And he was given a mouth speaking great things and blasphemies, and he was given authority to continue for forty-two months. Then he opened his mouth in blasphemy against God, to blaspheme His name, His tabernacle, and those who dwell in heaven. It was granted to him to make war with the saints and to overcome them. And authority was given him over every tribe, tongue, and nation. 13:5-7

The first beast was given or granted:

1. A mouth speaking great things and blasphemies
2. Authority to continue for forty-two months
3. To make war with the saints and to overcome them
4. Authority over every tribe, tongue, and nation

In verses 14-15, we see that the second beast was given or granted:

5. To deceive those who dwell on the earth with signs
6. Power to give breath to the image of the beast

The power came from the dragon, but the dragon's power is limited by God. Satan certainly would not have limited the reign of the Antichrist to forty-two months.

> All who dwell on the earth will worship him, whose names have not been written in the Book of Life of the Lamb slain from the foundation of the world. 13:8

The earth dwellers worship the beast. In other words, those who are saved and alive during this time won't worship the Antichrist. I love that. I love God's keeping power. The sealing of the Holy Spirit, the mark of God on His own just won't let a believer worship the Antichrist or take the beast's mark.

Ephesians tells us, "In Him you also trusted, after you heard the word of truth, the gospel of your salvation; in whom also, having believed, you were sealed with the Holy Spirit of promise, who is the guarantee of our inheritance until the redemption of the purchased possession, to the praise of His glory" (Ephesians 1:13-14). But that doesn't mean it won't be hard for believers on the earth.

> If anyone has an ear, let him hear. He who leads into captivity shall go into captivity; he who kills with the sword must be killed with the sword. Here is the patience and the faith of the saints. 13:9-10

THE SAINTS' PATIENCE AND FAITH

During the tribulation, those who have "an ear to hear" and respond with believing faith can know they will be subject to great suffering, but their suffering will have an end. You and I can endure far more if we know there's going to be an end to it.

It is important that the believers during the tribulation know this and it's important for us too. As the saying goes, "For Christians, this present life is the closest they will come to hell. For unbelievers, it is the closest they will come to heaven." [37]

This is what patience and faith will look like in those times. Those years are going to be really tough for believers. They will be overcome physically, but not spiritually.

You see, these two beasts and many who follow them will be taking believers into captivity and killing them with the sword. Matthew warned, "And do not fear those who kill the body but cannot kill the soul. But rather fear Him who is able to destroy both soul and body in hell" (Matthew 10:28).

Prior to this, we have the examples of Jesus when he looked down from the cross, "Father, forgive them, for they do not know what they do" (Luke 23:34), and Stephen who petitioned on behalf of those who were killing him: "Lord, do not charge them with this sin" (Acts 7:60). At this point however, the period of grace is over. Forgiveness will no longer be extended. God's judgment has begun. While there will be salvation during this time, there will be no hope for those who worship the beast.

For those who cause suffering, their suffering will be beyond description, beyond all measure of time. Their suffering will be eternal. God promises to take those who persecute His saints and who reject Him into a captivity that is eternal, much worse than physical death.

HOW THE SAINTS WILL LIVE

The believers who come to the Lord during the tribulation are going to endure incredible hardships, not only losing the ability to buy and sell for themselves, but for their children too. We may be able to endure hunger somewhat, but to watch our children or grandchildren suffer in any way is heartbreaking. And the saints may ask, "Where is God in that? Where is the protection we thought we could trust in?" These are questions we ask, not only as we read about the suffering of the tribulation saints, but we have asked them about ourselves, as we have seen God lift His hand and grant Satan the power to harm us. Where is the holiness in that?

Consider the numerous times in the Bible that Satan prevailed over God's people.

Job. Godly, God-fearing Job lost his wealth, his property, his health, and his children—all of them!

Joseph. Doing nothing to deserve such cruelty, was sold by his brothers into years of slavery.

Paul. Not only did he suffer with a thorn in the flesh that greatly debilitated him, he went through shipwrecks, beatings, starving, rejections, and nakedness.

Hebrews 11 Saints. Consider those who suffered mockings, scourgings, chains, and imprisonment. Others were stoned, sawn in two, and slain with the sword.

Martyrs today. Many suffer presently around the world for their faith in Jesus.

Jesus. Finally, there is God's Son who endured the cross and despised the shame for you and for me.

GIVEN INTO SATAN'S HAND

The Antichrist will prevail over God's people for three-and-a-half years just as he prevailed over Job and just as he prevailed over many of the saints through the ages. He has prevailed in our lives at times—some of us more than others. Look again at what Daniel 7:25 says: "Then the saints shall be given into his hand for a time and times and half a time."

Notice the phrase, "given into his hand."

We see it again in Job. "And the LORD said to Satan, 'Behold, he is in your hand, but spare his life'" (Job 2:6).

God allows His saints to be given into Satan's hand. I don't get that. I don't even agree with that! Why does God allow suffering? I don't know the answer to that any better than you do, but I do know that He is God—I'm not. He is perfect—I'm not. He is always right—I'm not. It's very clear, God is still in charge. He limits what Satan can do and how long he can do it.

GOD'S PROTECTION

We probably all have stories of how God has protected us from something or someone. We even have stories of times God protected us from ourselves by stopping us from making some really dumb decisions. But we also have stories where God seemingly didn't protect, where it sure seemed like He gave us over to Satan's hand.

We are so temporal in our thinking and, all too often, our goal is immediate relief from pain and protection from physical harm. God often does that for us, but that's not what He has promised us. He has promised to use all suffering for good and that good is to make us more like Jesus. He has promised to keep and protect our soul.

Why aren't we just over the top thankful for that? What if He saved you and then left it up to you to keep yourself worthy of that salvation. And if you failed, He dropped you—not just into Satan's hand, but into Satan's realm and destination? He has promised to get you to heaven. He has promised that one day all this pain, sorrow, and grief will be over.

This is "the patience and the faith of the saints." Believing this is what will keep the tribulation saints from losing their minds. It is what will keep you and me from losing ours.

> Then I saw another beast coming up out of the earth, and he had two horns like a lamb and spoke like a dragon. 13:11

THE FALSE PROPHET

Verse 11 introduces us to the second beast, the one who is primarily referred to as the False Prophet. The first beast, the Antichrist, will be the great political leader. The second beast, the False Prophet, will be a great religious leader. He will be a leader of a false religion. The Antichrist and the False Prophet are Satan's instruments.

> And he exercises all the authority of the first beast in his presence, and causes the earth and those who dwell in it to worship the first beast, whose deadly wound was healed. He performs great signs, so that he even makes fire come down from heaven on the earth in the sight of men. 13:12-13

THE GREAT RELIGIOUS LEADER

This beast, the False Prophet, has two horns like a lamb. He will look like the real thing. He will appear to be gentle and harmless, but he'll speak like the dragon. His words and his miracles will be those of Satan. Satan can perform signs and miracles too. We must be careful not to think that only God can perform miracles, though it's easy to tell the difference—pay attention to who gets the glory. The False Prophet's call to worship will be focused on the Antichrist, or the image of the Antichrist.

> And he deceives those who dwell on the earth by those signs which he was granted to do in the sight of the beast, telling those who dwell on the earth to make an image to the beast who was wounded by the sword and lived. He was granted power to give breath to the image of the beast, that the image of the beast should both speak and cause as many as would not worship the image of the beast to be killed. 13:14-15

TO WORSHIP SATAN

The False Prophet will deceive the unsaved earth dwellers to make an image of the first beast, the Antichrist, and he will be "granted power to give breath (or life) to the image of the beast." It won't be like any idol the Bible has ever talked about. This image can speak and it can cause those who refuse to worship it to be killed. The unsaved worship the beast; the saved and those who would be saved, especially the Jews, will not.

This is a big move for the Antichrist. Many of the Jews may not have become believers yet, but they know enough not to worship idols. This setting up of the image of the beast unites the Jews who will believe and the Christians, dividing them from everyone else.

> He causes all, both small and great, rich and poor, free and slave, to receive a mark on their right hand or on their foreheads, and that no one may buy or sell except one who has the mark or the name of the beast, or the number of his name. 13:16-17

THE MARK TO FOLLOW THE BEAST

The mark of the beast, or the lack of it, will unmistakably separate believing Jews and Christians from the unbelievers.

This technology already exists and most of us are aware of it and even microchip our pets. In some other countries, governments are much more invasive than the United States. Americans still fight for their right to privacy, but others around the world have accepted that their government know the whereabouts and activities of the people and give in to being microchipped.

The technology is here, but even having a microchip or an ID mark is not the mark of the beast. This mark will represent the choice to follow the beast. It will mark that a person's eternity is doomed to hell. It's not the taking of the mark that dooms them, but in the taking of the mark, they have chosen to align themselves with the beast who blasphemes God, the Father and Jesus Christ, the Son.

> Here is wisdom. Let him who has understanding calculate the number of the beast, for it is the number of a man: His number is 666. 13:18

THE NUMBER OF THE BEAST

Both the Hebrew and Greek alphabets assign numbers to each letter making it easy to come up with names that add up to 666. I really don't care. He might be alive right now, I don't know. When he appears on the scene, the wise and the understanding will be able to figure out that it's him. That knowledge will be very helpful to them. It's not helpful to us. We are to be looking for Jesus, not for the Antichrist.

It will be granted to these two evil men, the Antichrist and the False Prophet, to persecute believers and kill them. These will be horrible times for those who belong to the Sovereign God, the One who rules over all, the Most High God. So, where is God's sovereignty?

GOD'S SOVEREIGNTY

I found myself indirectly asking that question when I was praying for someone. I reminded myself that God is on the throne. He rules. He is not only El Elyon, the sovereign Most High God, He is also Jehovah Sabaoth, the Lord of Hosts who rules and reigns over all powers and all principalities. And He is holy. He does everything right.

I thought, *I can believe that for me, but what about those I love who are not saved?* Or what about those who are saved, but are making choices outside of God's will? I'm flat out scared for them. God's judgment is a very scary thing. I found myself weeping. I wanted relief and I began to pray for relief—relief for me. I didn't want to be troubled about their lives anymore and I wanted the hurt to go away.

Then it hit me. God wants that hurt to go away too when people, saved or unsaved, choose other than Him. He knows the judgment or consequences they will face if they don't turn to Him. God gives us just a piece of what it's like for Him and puts just a little piece of His hurt in us. That's all you and I can handle—just a piece. But He does that to provoke us to pray, because if we didn't hurt, we wouldn't pray nearly as much.

SO—JUST WHAT DO WE PRAY?

Pray God's will be done. John told us, "… that if we ask anything according to His will, He hears us. And if we know that He hears us, whatever we ask, we know that we have the petitions that we have asked of Him." (1 John 5:14-15)

But God will not overrule our freedom of choice. There are times we may wish He would, but He won't. So in light of that, how do we pray for our loved ones? Pray that their eyes would be opened.

> "To open their eyes, in order to turn them from darkness to light, and from the power of Satan to God, that they may receive forgiveness of sins and an inheritance among those who are sanctified by faith in Me." (Acts 26:18)

He will open their eyes. Then He leaves the choice to them. God is sovereign, but He has chosen not to be sovereign over our choices.

When people we love make stupid choices, it hurts—it's just going to hurt. May our pain lead us to pray for them. It's a pain that Christians feel at a greater depth than non-Christians feel because God shares His pain with us. He knows the pain. He is grieving too. As believers, when you and I pray we can get a sense of being in this thing together with God. We are not only in it together with Him, but He intercedes for us by helping us to pray according to His will. Paul talked about this in his letter to the Roman church.

> "Likewise the Spirit also helps in our weaknesses. For we do not know what we should pray for as we ought, but the Spirit Himself makes intercession for us with groanings which cannot be uttered. Now He who searches the hearts knows what the mind of the Spirit is, because He makes intercession for the saints according to the will of God." (Romans 8:26-27)

CLOSING THOUGHTS

A friend of mine emailed me yesterday. It was just after I had spent time with the Lord seeking Him about this portion of Revelation. I told her I was undone. I had this ache, but it felt like an anointed ache. "Anointed ache?" she asked. I shared that God had shown me what it's like for Him when people reject His Son.

Afterwards, while I was worshiping that day I was truly undone. I was overwhelmed. I was on my face. I was reminded in such an awesome way that yes, this world is full of tribulation, but in it all He holds us. When what is sacred and important is torn from us, He holds us. He will hold these tribulation saints even when the Antichrist is prevailing over them. And He will hold you. David said, "Even there Your hand shall lead me, and Your right hand shall hold me" (Psalm 139:10).

"Even there" speaks volumes. We each have our own "even there." Wherever it is, He will lead you and He will hold you. That is the patience and the faith of the saints.

Don't allow the enemy to cause you to dwell on the hard times, but rather dwell on how God holds you "even there."

REFLECTION QUESTIONS

(For more extensive study questions visit CathyDickinson.com)

1. The Antichrist is revealed in Revelation 13. Write a few points that describe him and the source of his power (vv. 1-8).

2. The second beast is also revealed in Revelation 13. Write a few things that describe him and his apparent purpose (vv. 11-17).

3. During the tribulation, these beasts will physically prevail over God's people (those who believe in Him after the rapture). These saints will not be able to buy food and many will be taken into captivity and killed. List some truths about God that you cling to at times when it appears that God is not sovereign (in control). Use Scripture to support your list.

a.

b.

c.

d.

e.

4. There is one area that God has chosen NOT to be sovereign over. What is it?

5. God sometimes allows us, or those we love, to be "in Satan's hand" like Job and these tribulation saints. Our goal is often temporal relief from emotional pain or physical harm. What is God's goal—what has He promised?

6. Draw a scene from Revelation 13 in the space provided.

Chapter Seventeen

GOD'S PROCLAMATION: REVELATION 14

In Revelation 12 and 13, John zooms in on the events taking place primarily during the first three-and-a-half years of the tribulation, while chapter 14 focuses more on the end of the tribulation.

There are no chapter divisions in John's account. For John, the revelation of God's power in what we call chapter 14 was God's response to the questions asked in Revelation 13:4. "Who is like the Beast? Who is able to make war with him?"

> Then I looked, and behold, a Lamb standing on Mount Zion, and with Him 144,000, having His Father's name written on their foreheads. 14:1

THE LAMB

John saw two beasts in Revelation 13. In Revelation 14, John saw the Lamb.

Mount Zion is the hill just outside the old city walls of Jerusalem. It's also known as Mount Moriah, the place where Abraham took Isaac in obedience to God's command to offer him as a burnt offering (Genesis 22).

This sight of the Lamb on Mount Zion was foretold in Psalm 2, a messianic psalm. "Yet I have set My King on My holy hill of Zion" (v. 6).

144,000

These 144,000 men, 12,000 from each of the twelve tribes of Israel, were introduced to us in Revelation 7. Each one had the seal of God on their foreheads. Revelation 13 tells us about those who took the seal of the Beast on their hand or forehead. Now we see those who were sealed on their forehead with the seal of God.

> And I heard a voice from heaven, like the voice of many waters, and like the voice of loud thunder. 14:2

John not only saw—he heard. Scripture is pretty clear that this is the voice of God. Revelation 1:15 tells us it is the voice of Jesus.

> And I heard the sound of harpists playing their harps. 14:2

Yes, this is where they get it—all those pictures of saints sitting on clouds having nothing to do but play a harp. We'll see as we get to the end of this book that we will be doing much more than that.

John heard the sounds of harpists playing. I wonder if the music was coming from the earth and heaven was joining them. Or maybe it was coming from heaven and those on earth were joining in. It's not clear. It was a song that no one could learn but the 144,000.

> They sang as it were a new song before the throne, before the four living creatures, and the elders; and no one could learn that song except the hundred and forty-four thousand who were redeemed from the earth. 14:3

A NEW SONG

The word *learn* here has the sense of having full knowledge—actually experiencing the words of the song. Verse 1 tells us they are standing on Mount Zion with the Lamb. Their song is rising up to the throne, the four living creatures, and the twenty-four elders. Every once in a while I will say to a worship leader before they start leading worship, "Okay, take us before the throne." And here, we are reminded that our worship can do that—rise up to God's throne! May you and I be aware of this when we sing.

What did they sing? They sang a new song. I found nine references in the Bible about singing a new song. Here are just two:

> "Oh, sing to the LORD a new song! Sing to the LORD, all the earth. Sing to the LORD, bless His name; proclaim the good news of His salvation from day to day." (Psalm 96:1-2)

> "Praise the LORD! Sing to the LORD a new song, and His praise in the assembly of saints." (Psalm 149:1)

These 144,000 sang a new song. We don't know exactly what that means other than it was new—it hadn't been sung before. I found this quote by Jamieson-Faussett-Brown:

> "The song is that of victory after conflict with the dragon, beast, and false prophet: never sung before*;* for such a conflict had never been fought before; therefore new: till now the kingdom of Christ on earth had been usurped; they sing the new song in anticipation of His blood-bought kingdom with His saints." [38]

We don't know what they sang, but they knew it—personally knew it. This song, that only the 144,000 could learn or understand, was their story. It was their story of what Jesus had done for them. It was their story of how He had protected and redeemed them. It was their song. You may sing one that is especially yours too! What will you sing? What do you sing now?

I bet you and I will have a lot of new songs to sing when we stand with Jesus. We are to sing new songs now, continually coming up with new ways to praise Him. I love praising Him alphabetically. I am always trying to come up with new words. As long as I've been praising Him, He still gives me new words. It makes me smile inside when a new word about the LORD pops into my mind.

> These are the ones who were not defiled with women, for they are virgins. These are the ones who follow the Lamb wherever He goes. These were redeemed from among men, being firstfruits to God and to the Lamb. 14:4

VIRGINS

Paul wrote of the benefits of not marrying in 1 Corinthians 7. Marriage can be a distraction, as we spend a lot of our time on another person. These 144,000 were able to be completely dedicated to doing nothing else but following the Lamb.

This by no means gives the married an excuse. We are to follow the Lamb where He takes us. He fully understands the commitments we have on this earth and expects us to honor them. We are each accountable to the callings on our individual lives—to allow the Lord to use us as He has individually equipped us and called us.

These 144,000 stand in stark contrast to those who took the mark of the Beast. They remained sexually pure (something that certainly would reveal their commitment to the Lord and His keeping power), while those who followed the Beast certainly did not.

> And in their mouth was found no deceit, for they are without fault before the throne of God. 14:5

PROTECTED

Chapter 13 revealed that the Antichrist had a mouth that spoke blasphemous things; he and his False Prophet are deceivers. Most significantly, those who took the mark of the Beast worshiped the Beast, while the 144,000 followed the Lamb.

Our best guess is that this is at the end of the tribulation reminding us that the Beast (Antichrist) had three-and-a-half years, but now his time is going to end. Notice how many are with Jesus. They started out with 144,000. Although the Beast would overcome the saints, these Jews had been protected with God's seal—every single one of them survived. We who are saved are also sealed by the Holy Spirit for the purpose of protection, but our promise of protection is the protection of our souls—to get our souls to heaven.

THE PROCLAMATION OF THE THREE ANGELS

The rest of chapter 14 is about the proclamations of three angels all anticipating the judgment of the seventh trumpet. Again, these are little vignettes that John is showing us. They do not necessarily follow in chronological order after the first verses of chapter 14, or even after what John wrote about the two beasts.

In fact, when we read about the proclamation of the third angel, my guess is, he flew around the earth with this message the moment the False Prophet demanded that people take the mark of the Beast, ensuring that everyone would have been warned.

> Then I saw another angel flying in the midst of heaven, having the everlasting gospel to preach to those who dwell on the earth—to every nation, tribe, tongue, and people—14:6

THE FIRST ANGEL

John saw him in the midst of heaven, or literally middle heaven, the sky. The people who live during the tribulation will hear the witness of the 144,000. They will hear the testimony of the two witnesses. Now they will hear another witness—this angel preaching the everlasting gospel. This is clearly talking about the good news of the redemption available through Jesus Christ.

> saying with a loud voice, "Fear God and give glory to Him, for the hour of His judgment has come; and worship Him who made heaven and earth, the sea and springs of water." 14:7

Oh, what a warning to those about to take the mark. Don't fear the Beast. Fear God. Don't worship the Beast. Worship God.

Jesus, in telling His disciples about the tribulation times said, "And this gospel of the kingdom will be preached in all the world as a witness to all the nations, and **then the end will come**" (Matthew 24:14). People have interpreted this to mean that the gospel will go out to all corners of the earth and be preached by men. Of course we have many means by which to do this now via satellite, radio, and the Internet. And of course that's a very good thing, as He clearly has commanded that we "go into all the world and preach the gospel" (Mark 16:15). But in context, Jesus could have been referring to this verse in Revelation when the angel preaches the gospel to all the world—then the end will come.

> And another angel followed, saying, "Babylon is fallen, is fallen, that great city, because she has made all nations drink of the wine of the wrath of her fornication." 14:8

THE SECOND ANGEL

Sadly, this is an implication that there remains those who rejected the first angel's message. We understand the word *fornication* to refer to sexual sin. Certainly there was a lot of that happening. But it also refers to the forsaking of the true God to worship idols.

Prophetically, Babylon sometimes refers to the city, sometimes to a religious system, and sometimes to a political system—all stemming from the evil character of historic Babylon. At this point, the worldwide kingdom of the Antichrist is about to fall. But this is not a warning—it's a proclamation! This is bad news to the unbelievers, but it is an announcement of glorious news to the believers still on the earth.

> Then a third angel followed them, saying with a loud voice, "If anyone worships the beast and his image, and receives his mark on his forehead or on his hand, 14:9

THE THIRD ANGEL

Angel number one proclaimed the gospel. Angel number two proclaimed the judgment. Angel number three proclaimed the damnation. Each one reinforces the previous one and takes the inhabitants of the earth closer to the end.

Essentially, this angel is crying out, "Don't do it! Don't worship the Beast! Don't take the mark! If you do, some very horrible judgments will come upon you!" Here is what those who take the mark of the Beast can expect:

> he himself shall also drink of the wine of the wrath of God, which is poured out full strength into the cup of His indignation. 14:10

GOD'S WRATH

God's wrath upon them will be full strength—unmixed with water, unmixed with mercy—just wrath, 100% pure wrath.

> "For in the hand of the LORD there is a cup, and the wine is red; it is fully mixed, and He pours it out; surely its dregs shall all the wicked of the earth drain and drink down." (Psalm 75:8)

The Bible often uses the analogy of the cup. The "cup of His wrath" is mentioned many times, but there are other cups. There was the cup that Jesus shared with His disciples the night He was betrayed. The cup they took and we take, remembering His blood shed and body broken for us; the price He paid so that we could be His. And then the cup He spoke of in the garden of Gethsemane; that cup He so dreaded. Yet He drank that cup filled with God's wrath toward all the sins of this world, your sins and mine—Jesus drank it so we wouldn't have to.

> He shall be tormented with fire and brimstone in the presence of the holy angels and in the presence of the Lamb. And the smoke of their torment ascends forever and ever; and they have no rest day or night, who worship the beast and his image, and whoever receives the mark of his name." 14:10-11

Three things stand out:

1. Torment
2. No rest, and
3. Forever and ever.

For the tribulation saints, the ones who refuse the mark, they will have at the most three-and-a-half years of very rough stuff. They'll probably call it torment, until they know the fate of those who worshiped the Beast and took the mark. Their torment will not be for three-and-a-half years, but forever and ever, without **any** rest.

One commentary says of the phrase *forever and ever*: "Literally 'into the ages of ages,' the strongest expression of eternity of which the Greek is capable." [39]

> Here is the patience of the saints; here are those who keep the commandments of God and the faith of Jesus. Then I heard a voice from heaven saying to me, "Write: 'Blessed are the dead who die in the Lord from now on.'" 14:12-13

BLESSING FOR THE SAINTS

I love this! It's as if God said, "John, write this so the saints will be encouraged."

Blessed are those who die from this point in the tribulation. What a contrast. The previous verses spoke of damnation for those who refused Jesus. These verses speak of blessing to those who receive Him. There is no in-between. Either people will take the mark and be damned or they will keep the commandments of God and the faith of Jesus and be blessed.

> "Yes," says the Spirit, "that they may rest from their labors, 14:13

REST FOR THE SAINTS

"Yes," says the Spirit. When the Holy Spirit says yes, there's an affirmation in our hearts. While those who take the mark will get no rest ever, those who refuse the mark will get rest—rest from the moment they die and it will last forever and ever and ever.

Those who take the mark are able to buy food and clothing for three-and-a-half years, then damnation—nothing, absolutely nothing good for all of eternity. For those who refuse the mark, no clothing, no food, awful days for three-and-a-half years—then rest—blessed rest with Jesus for all eternity.

> and their works follow them." 14:13

REWARDS FOR THE SAINTS

These works represent the tribulation saints' service to the Lord. The author of Hebrews reminds us, "For God is not unjust to forget your work and labor of love which you have shown toward His name, in that you have ministered to the saints, and do minister" (Hebrews 6:10).

There are most certainly blessings here and now for the works we do for Him, but there will be rewards for these works that will follow us right into heaven. Our works will follow us—not our stuff and not our self-motivated achievements.

So why do we spend so much time, effort, and worry on stuff and self-gratification? Paul made it clear in his letter to the Colossians where we should focus our time and efforts.

> "If then you were raised with Christ, seek those things which are above, where Christ is, sitting at the right hand of God. Set your mind on things above, not on things on the earth. For you died, and your life is hidden with Christ in God. When Christ who is our life appears, then you also will appear with Him in glory." (Colossians 3:1-4)

WHAT GOOD WORKS?

This promise of Revelation 14:13 is not just for the tribulation saints—it's for us. One day we will enter glorious, forever rest and stand before the Lord with our works right there with us. Will you be standing there surrounded by the times you chose Jesus? Oh, that we would not only comprehend but apprehend this truth!

It's not only the time you led someone to the Lord or when you went on a mission trip that will follow you. It's those times when you were tempted to do other than He would have you do, or to say other than He would have you say—and you didn't fall, but rather, you chose to minster and serve or bless. Each and every one of those works, done in His name, will follow you.

Ephesians 2:8-9 reminds us that we have been saved, not by works, but by grace through faith. Paul followed that statement with, "For we are His workmanship, created in Christ Jesus for good works, which God prepared beforehand that we should walk in them" (Ephesians 2:10).

God has prepared good works for you and me to walk in. There are different good works for each of us. You don't have to do mine and I don't have to do yours, but when we do those works God has chosen for us, they will follow us—right into heaven.

> Then I looked, and behold, a white cloud, and on the cloud sat One like the Son of Man, 14:14

JESUS

The One like the Son of Man is Jesus. He liked to call Himself that. John would have heard Him say it many times. John saw the One like the Son of Man in Revelation 1:13:

> "and in the midst of the seven lampstands One like the Son of Man, clothed with a garment down to the feet and girded about the chest with a golden band."
>
> John clearly identified Him as Jesus, "the First and the Last," the One "who lives and was dead" and behold, is "alive forevermore" (Revelation 1:17-18).

> having on His head a golden crown, 14:14

John saw Jesus sitting on a cloud with a golden crown on His head. This is not a crown of royalty, which Jesus does wear, but this is a crown of victory.

> and in His hand a sharp sickle. 14:14

We are not accustomed to this view of Jesus. The first time Jesus came to earth, He came as the sower; next time He will come as the reaper.

> And another angel came out of the temple, crying with a loud voice to Him [Jesus] who sat on the cloud, "Thrust in Your sickle and reap, for the time has come for You to reap, for the harvest of the earth is ripe." So He who sat on the cloud thrust in His sickle on the earth, and the earth was reaped. 14:15-16

S. MayField
2/10/16

OVERRIPE

The angel proclaimed that the harvest of the earth was ripe—ready for the harvest. The Greek word here is *overripe*. When something is overripe it turns mushy and brown. When something is overripe, it's useless. So, what do you do with it? You throw it out. At this point, it looks like no one wants grace. And without grace, only justice remains. It's time to throw out the bad. So Jesus thrust His sickle on the earth.

> Then another angel came out of the temple which is in heaven, he also having a sharp sickle. And another angel came out from the altar, who had power over fire, and he cried with a loud cry to him who had the sharp sickle, saying, "Thrust in your sharp sickle and gather the clusters of the vine of the earth, for her grapes are fully ripe." 14:17-18

Two angels came from the temple, representing the will of God, and one came from the altar, representing the prayers of the saints. John saw "under the altar the souls of those who had been slain for the word of God and for the testimony which they held. And they cried with a loud voice, saying, 'How long, O Lord, holy and true, until You judge and avenge our blood on those who dwell on the earth?'" (Revelation 6:9-10). Well, the time has come for things to be made right. And when the prayers of the saints align with the will of God, we have that which we have prayed for.

> So the angel thrust his sickle into the earth and gathered the vine of the earth, and threw it into the great winepress of the wrath of God. 14:19

THE WINEPRESS

The winepress is a large carved-out piece of stone. Just below it would rest another hewn stone that would catch the juice. A trough ran from the upper stone to the lower one and the grapes were thrown in and trampled. Workers would stamp and crush the grapes causing the juice to burst forth and flow downward through the trough into the second basin.

THE GRAPES OF WRATH

During the Civil War in 1861, Julia Ward Howe toured a Union Army camp. She overheard soldiers singing a song to John Brown who had been hanged for attempting to lead an insurrection of slaves at Harper's Ferry.

The words of the song were,

> "John Brown's body lies a-mouldering in the grave,
>
> His soul's marching on.
>
> He's gone to be a soldier in the army of the Lord,
>
> His soul's marching on."

Julia Ward Howe thought the music was great, but the words needed some improvement. So she wrote the following words to what we know to be "The Battle Hymn of the Republic."

> "Mine eyes have seen the glory of the coming of the Lord;
>
> He is trampling out the vintage where the grapes of wrath are stored;
>
> He hath loosed the fateful lightning of His terrible swift sword;
>
> His truth is marching on." [40]

> And the winepress was trampled outside the city, and blood came out of the winepress, up to the horses' bridles, for one thousand six hundred furlongs. 14:20

The blood was four feet deep (the height of a horse's bridle), or as the blood came out of the winepress it would splatter up to four feet high. For almost 200 miles there was blood up to four feet high. Either way, it's a lot of blood. As we will see in the final battle, the battle of Armageddon, that much blood will be spilled.

CLOSING THOUGHTS

When Jesus comes again, it will be very different. Consider the contrasts between His first and second comings.

Jesus' First Coming	**Jesus' Second Coming**
1. Servant (Matthew 20:28)	1. King (Revelation 17:14, 19:16)
2. Obeying (John 4:34, Phil. 2:8)	2. Commanding (Rev. 2:27, 19:15)
3. Alone (Luke 2:7)	3. With His angels & us (Matt 16:27)
4. Take on the earth (John 1:29, 3:16-17)	4. Take over the earth (Rev 6:2; 19:11)
5. In humility (Philippians 2:5-8)	5. In majesty & splendor (Matt 24:30)
6. To seek & save the lost (Luke 19:10)	6. To judge & sentence the lost (2 Tim 4:1)
7. In grace (John 1:14)	7. In wrath (Revelation 6:16,17; 14:19)
8. As the sower (Mark 4:14-20; John 6:63)	8. As the reaper (Revelation 14:6)

REFLECTION QUESTIONS

(For more extensive study questions visit CathyDickinson.com)

1. The 144,000 Jews will be sealed by God to protect them from the wrath Jesus pours out. You too are sealed with the Holy Spirit. What protection does this guarantee for you?

This seal of the Holy Spirit guarantees the protection of my soul.
No tribulation, borders for our lives, never separated from Christ.

2. The 144,000 Jews stood on Mount Zion singing a new song to the Lord about their own story of what Jesus had done for them. What is your story of what Jesus has done for you, understood only by the Lord and you? Take time to write it. Jesus saved me in my uncertainty and sinful life. During my backsliding and self-centered path He again rescued me and from certain hopelessness and provided a family of believers. He will yet again move through healing my body and helping me with my husband and children.

3. As a believer, you are promised rest from your labors in eternity. You are also promised a rest of sorts here on earth. How would you describe this rest? Support your answer with Scripture. (1) Matt 11:28 He gives rest to the weary and burdened (2) Ps 62:1 My soul is at rest because of His plan of salvation (3) Ps 4:8 I can sleep peacefully because he allows me to dwell in His safety (4) Jer. 6:16 Walking in His path gives rest for the soul (5) Ps 91:1-2 He is my shelter - I rest in His shadow - a refuge and fortress (6) Matt 11:29-30. He is gentle and humble - his yoke easy and light

Rest in his Word and prayer presence

4. The wrath described in Revelation is real, and therefore should cause us to take seriously the need to pray for those who don't know Jesus as Savior. Make a list of those you know who need Jesus and commit to praying for them on a regular basis.

1. John
2. Dad
3. Chris
4. Steve
5. Ben, Nate, Ella
6. Aunty and Ron
7. Cathleen and Bill
8. Les
9.

5. Draw a scene from Revelation 14.

Chapter Eighteen

THE HEART OF GOD: REVELATION 15-16

It appears that Revelation chapters 12-15 consist of different events which could be happening simultaneously. In Revelation 15 we find John looking into heaven once again.

> Then I saw another sign in heaven, great and marvelous: seven angels having the seven last plagues, for in them the wrath of God is complete. 15:1

Seven, the number of completion, indicates there will be no more plagues after these for in these "the wrath of God is complete."

> And I saw something like a sea of glass mingled with fire, and those who have the victory over the beast, over his image and over his mark and over the number of his name, standing on the sea of glass, having harps of God. 15:2

VICTORS OVER THE BEAST

John's attention moves to "something *like* a sea of glass." Revelation 4:6 told us that before the throne of God "was a sea of glass, like crystal." This could be the same one. This time John sees it "mingled with fire," and he sees "those who have the victory over the beast" standing on it with harps. For these people who came to know Jesus during the tribulation, suffering is over. From the viewpoint of the earth, they had lost and the Antichrist had won. They didn't bow to him, so he took their lives, but alas, he could not take their souls. Here they stand not in defeat, but in victory—eternal victory. The Antichrist and his followers will live in eternal defeat.

Although we will not have to face the prevailing powers of the Antichrist, we still face the powers of the one who empowered him—the devil and his demons. He is right now, as Peter declared, "seeking whom he may devour."

"Be sober, be vigilant; because your adversary the devil walks about like a roaring lion, seeking whom he may devour." (1 Peter 5:8)

The same devil who will seek to devour God's people during the tribulation is seeking to devour God's people now. The word *devour* means "to swallow up." Interestingly, that is literally what the devil will attempt to do with Israel—swallow them up in a flood, as we read in Revelation 12. He uses different means, but his goal is the same—to swallow us up. He is looking for a weakness, some vulnerable area, any way to get to us, but he can never have our soul.

Think about how very good it's going to be when we are on the other side of all of this. Like these tribulation saints, one day we too will stand in victory before the throne.

Those tribulation saints standing on the sea of glass each had a harp of God. Heaven is going to be full of music. God must love music. I heard someone recently say, and I can surely relate to this, "I'm a prison singer. I'm behind a few bars and I can't find the key." In heaven, we will have been set free and that includes our voices.

They sing the song of Moses, the servant of God, and the song of the Lamb, 15:3

Possibly these are two separate songs or maybe only one. This reminds me of how we combine worship songs into a medley and how sweetly they go together.

There are two other songs of Moses recorded in the Bible. We find one in Exodus 15 written right after the Israelites crossed the Red Sea—then God *swallowed up* their enemies.

SONG OF MOSES 1

In Exodus 15, Moses wrote phrases like,

"I will sing to the LORD, for He has triumphed gloriously!" (v. 1).

"The LORD is my strength and song, and He has become my salvation; He is my God, and I will praise Him" (v. 2).

"The LORD is a man of war; the LORD is His name" (v. 3).

"Your right hand, O LORD, has become glorious in power; Your right hand, O LORD, has dashed the enemy in pieces. And in the greatness of Your excellence You have overthrown those who rose against You; You sent forth Your wrath; it consumed them like stubble" (vv. 6-7).

"Who is like you, O LORD, among the gods? Who is like You, glorious in holiness, fearful in praises, doing wonders?" (v. 11).

"The LORD shall reign forever and ever" (v. 18).

SONG OF MOSES 2

The other song of Moses is in Deuteronomy 32. He uses phrases like,

"For I proclaim the name of the LORD" (v. 3).

"He is the Rock, His work is perfect; for all His ways are justice, a God of truth and without injustice; righteous and upright is He" (v. 4).

"Rejoice, O Gentiles, with His people; for He will avenge the blood of His servants, and render vengeance to His adversaries; He will provide atonement for His land and His people" (v. 43).

PRELUDE SINGING BEFORE THE BOWLS

Just before the pouring out of the seven bowls, which came from the seventh trumpet, from the opening of the seventh seal—they sang "the song of Moses" and "the song of the Lamb." We don't know what else they sang, but we know they sang these words:

> saying: "Great and marvelous are Your works, Lord God Almighty! Just and true are Your ways, O King of the saints! Who shall not fear You, O Lord, and glorify Your name? For You alone are holy. For all nations shall come and worship before You, for Your judgments have been manifested." 15:3-4

You might have noticed that Moses wrote a lot of phrases similar to these. This is how I want to be found worshiping—totally free from my analytical brain.

HOW TO SING NOW

You and I are going to sing those words when we are in heaven. You and I are going to boldly declare everything He has done, everything He allowed in our lives—that they are great and marvelous, just and true. We are going to realize that He knew what He was doing and all He did was perfect.

God allows evil. He limits it, but He allows it. You and I don't comprehend why a loving, powerful God with a protective Father's heart would allow evil. We don't comprehend why He allows the things that happen to you and me, but one day we are going to understand. Right now, you and I are to believe Him in faith. He is worthy of our trust. He is worthy of us declaring these truths with our voices and with our lives.

We are reminded that "at the name of Jesus every knee should bow … and that every tongue should confess that Jesus Christ is Lord" (Philippians 2:10-11). One day every knee will bow and every tongue will confess that Jesus is Lord. It would be sad indeed if that final day were our first time to declare it.

Since you and I are going to sing of our own free will and acknowledgment, "Great and marvelous are Your works, Lord God Almighty! Just and true are Your ways, O King of saints!" let's sing it now. Let's declare it now with our lives and our attitudes. When you and I fret or grumble about something in our lives, when we choose a way or a path other than what God has for us, we are declaring the opposite of these truths. We are declaring that His ways are not just or true or great or marvelous. While we may not always *feel* like His ways are just and marvelous, our feelings don't alter the truth.

James wrote that God does not change. "Every good gift and every perfect gift is from above, and comes down from the Father of lights, with whom there is no variation or shadow of turning" (James 1:17), or as the NIV translates it, "who does not change like shifting shadows." God just can't do anything wrong, it's impossible.

Paul put it this way: "If we are faithless, He remains faithful; He cannot deny Himself" (2 Timothy 2:13). Just and true, great and marvelous is who He is. He simply cannot act in opposition to Himself.

Our choices reveal whether we believe it or not. Let's sing these things now, because it seems like God really enjoys songs like this in heaven. I imagine He enjoys it, maybe even more, when we sing them now, because we are singing them in faith—and faith pleases Him. It pleases Him a lot.

After these things, 15:5

AFTER THE SEVENTH TRUMPET

This worship, this song of Moses and of the Lamb, brings us right back to the scene in Revelation 11 when John saw the temple of God opened in heaven and the ark of His covenant was seen. John saw right into the Holy of Holies. He saw when the seventh angel sounded, saying, "The kingdoms of this world have become the kingdoms of our Lord and of His Christ, and He shall reign forever and ever! And there were lightnings, noises, thunderings, an earthquake, and great hail" (Revelation 11:15, 19).

At this point, Revelation 15:5 continues where we left off in chapter 11.

I (John) looked, and behold, the temple of the tabernacle of the testimony in heaven was opened. And out of the temple came the seven angels having the seven plagues, clothed in pure bright linen, and having their chests girded with golden bands. Then one of the four living creatures gave to the seven angels seven golden bowls full of the wrath of God who lives forever and ever. 15:5-7

This probably marks the beginning of the final three-and-a-half years of the tribulation. The word *bowls* here indicates they are shallow. It's like they just have to be tilted for the plagues to spill out.

The temple was filled with smoke from the glory of God and from His power, and no one was able to enter the temple till the seven plagues of the seven angels were completed. 15:8

GOD'S PRESENCE ALONE

Throughout the Old Testament, when the temple was filled with smoke or a cloud from God, it represented God's presence and His presence alone. In other words, no one else was in the temple. That's precisely what this verse says. "No one was able to enter the temple until the seven plagues of the seven angels were completed." From this, we can surmise that no one was able to enter the presence of God for three-and-a-half years.

We aren't told of any songs being sung during this time, not that they couldn't be. But to me, and I emphasize *to me*, this verse reveals God's heart toward mankind. He takes "no pleasure in the death of the wicked" (Ezekiel 33:11). I believe this will be a rough time for Him. I imagine He loved that song acknowledging that He does everything right just prior to Him releasing these final bowls of wrath. God doesn't need reassurance. He knows perfectly well that He does everything right, but Scripture is abundantly clear that He loves it when we acknowledge who He is and what He does. For His people to acknowledge this right before the bowls of His wrath are poured out will likely be a very sweet fragrance to Him.

It appears that for three-and-a-half years God was alone in the temple. Some commentators say He was grieving, grieving over the calamities occurring on the earth below. God hates sin. Habakkuk put it this way, "You are of purer eyes than to behold evil, and cannot look on wickedness" (Habakkuk 1:13). We know from Matthew 27:46 that He turned away from Jesus when Jesus took all of our sins upon Himself.

WHAT EMOTIONS DOES GOD FEEL?

Zephaniah 3:17 tells us He sings over us; He rejoices over us. We know He experiences joy. He can be pleased. He feels compassion. Since the Holy Spirit is God and the Holy Spirit can be grieved (Ephesians 4:30), we know God experiences grief. Psalm 2:4 tells us He laughs. He also weeps. Jesus wept over Jerusalem when He cried, "O Jerusalem, Jerusalem … How often I wanted to gather your children together, as a hen gathers her chicks under her wings, but you were not willing!" (Matthew 23:37).

He will feel the same emotions when those on the earth reject Him during the tribulation. He doesn't experience emotions like guilt or depression. He can't. His emotions are primarily because of someone else, people like you and me. What we do affects Him and what is done to us does too, because He is love. Love cares about people. God so loved people that He did not spare His own Son, but freely gave Him up for us.

God will have absolutely no pleasure in the wrath that is poured out of the seven bowls upon mankind, even though they have utterly rejected Him.

> Then I heard a loud voice from the temple saying to the seven angels, "Go and pour out the bowls of the wrath of God on the earth." So the first went and poured out his bowl upon the earth, and a foul and loathsome sore came upon the men who had the mark of the beast and those who worshiped his image. 16:1-2

THE FIRST BOWL

The tables are quickly turned as God's wrath is poured out upon those who refused to worship Him. Those who chose God and did not take the mark are still facing death, but not the loathsome sores. God is separating His people from His wrath.

Notice, as we look at these plagues, that many of them were also sent by God upon those in Egypt who rejected the LORD at the time of Moses.

> Then the second angel poured out his bowl on the sea, and it became blood as of a dead man; and every living creature in the sea died. 16:3

THE SECOND BOWL

In Revelation 8, with the blast of the second trumpet, only a third of the sea creatures died. God is escalating things here because every living creature in the sea died.

S. Mayfield
2/24/15

> Then the third angel poured out his bowl on the rivers and springs of water, and they became blood. And I heard the angel of the waters saying: "You are righteous, O Lord, the One who is and who was and who is to be, because You have judged these things." 16:4-5

THE THIRD BOWL

"These things"—these evil things that man had been doing could not be ignored. They must be judged or God is not righteous. God cannot doubt Himself, because He is not capable of making a mistake, yet there must be something about these affirmations that is pleasing to Him.

The angel continues saying,

> "For they have shed the blood of saints and prophets, and You have given them blood to drink. For it is their just due." And I heard another from the altar saying, "Even so, Lord God Almighty, true and righteous are Your judgments." 16:6-7

It's the right thing. We learned that under the altar were "the souls of those who had been slain for the word of God and for the testimony which they held" (Revelation 6:9) and on the altar were the prayers of the saints. Certainly those slain for their testimony have the right to declare that these judgments are the right thing.

God is pouring out sores on those who worship the beast, turning the seas and rivers to blood and ALL of it is the right thing to do. It's not too much. It's not too harsh. And it's not because He doesn't care; it's because they don't care. They haven't cared about Him and they haven't cared about His people.

> Then the fourth angel poured out his bowl on the sun, and power was given to him to scorch men with fire. And men were scorched with great heat, and they blasphemed the name of God who has power over these plagues; and they did not repent and give Him glory. 16:8-9

THE FOURTH BOWL

Men were scorched. Not sunburned—scorched. That's got to be very painful. There will be no refuge from the heat, no SPF that will protect their skin. This sounds like a little taste of hell. When Pharaoh was faced with the plagues of Egypt, he was smart enough to give in, at least until Moses took the plague away. But these guys blasphemed God's name. They declared things about Him that were contrary to who He is. Essentially, that is blasphemy, saying something about God that isn't true.

They did not repent because they did not regret what they had done. They were not sorry for taking the mark, they were not sorry for worshiping the Beast, or for any other sins they had committed. They did not give God glory. They did not acknowledge Him for who He is. They knew these awful plagues were coming from God. They knew it was because of what they had done; yet they continued to blaspheme His name and deny Him. They could still repent, but they would not.

Did something happen to them when they took the mark? Did they become possessed? We don't know. There are some pretty stubborn, strong-willed people out there. It's as if these people were shouting out, "You can't make me!" Well, God could make them, but He won't, and like many strong-willed people, they'd rather die than give in.

But one day, they WILL bow their knee to Jesus and declare that He is Lord. It would be contrary to God's character to say that He will make them do it. They will acknowledge it one day, of their own choice, but it will be too late for their salvation.

> Then the fifth angel poured out his bowl on the throne of the beast, and his kingdom became full of darkness; 16:10

THE FIFTH BOWL

We must assume that even the power went out. Try to imagine fumbling and stumbling around and finding no flicker of light anywhere. Total darkness would be paralyzing. There is no light at the end of their tunnel during this plague or into eternity.

> and they gnawed their tongues because of the pain. They blasphemed the God of heaven because of their pains and their sores, and did not repent of their deeds. 16:10-11

Have you ever had something hurt so badly that you bit your tongue to distract yourself from the pain? That seems like what was happening. What a horrifying sight that must have been, to see these scorched people gnaw their tongues as they blasphemed God because of their pain. Still they did not repent. We find one such warning from Jesus in Matthew 25. "And cast the unprofitable servant into the outer darkness. There will be weeping and gnashing of teeth" (Matthew 25:30).

This is just a preview of what they will experience for all of eternity because they would not heed God's many warnings. God always warns before He judges.

OPPORTUNITY FOR REPENTANCE

In the Old Testament, over and over again the Lord pleaded with the people to repent. He warned of His judgment before He executed it, always giving an opportunity for repentance.

In the absence of repentance, His judgments happened just as He said they would, and they are happening in these tribulation days. They did not choose to repent. Therefore, their just and final judgment will be hell.

Because it doesn't say, "they could not repent," we can conclude that it was still possible to repent—to turn to Jesus—to receive the everlasting gospel that the angel preached to them. They chose not to repent.

> Then the sixth angel poured out his bowl on the great river Euphrates, and its water was dried up, so that the way of the kings from the east might be prepared. And I saw three unclean spirits like frogs [demons] coming out of the mouth of the dragon [Satan], out of the mouth of the beast [the Antichrist], and out of the mouth of the false prophet. For they are spirits of demons, performing signs, which go out to the kings of the earth and of the whole world, to gather them to the battle of that great day of God Almighty. 16:12-14

THE SIXTH BOWL

From Satan's perspective, he is sending out demons to gather kings for a great battle.

> "Behold, I am coming as a thief. Blessed is he who watches, and keeps his garments, lest he walk naked and they see his shame." 16:15

COMING AS A THIEF

First, it's a warning to those who are not believers. Jesus is "coming as a thief," meaning they won't know when. His coming will be sudden and unexpected. They may say, "I'll turn to Him just before He comes," but it's impossible to know the time of His arrival. He's coming as a thief and He's coming to take them out.

Second, it's a blessing to those who are believers. Oh, how the tribulation saints will need to hear these words. "Blessed is he who watches, and keeps his garments, lest he walk naked and they see his shame." Watch—keep waiting. Jesus is coming.

WARNING FOR BELIEVERS

This speaks of His second coming as a blessing, as well as a bit of warning, specifically for those believers to remain faithful so they can be confident and not ashamed at His coming. This is not referring to their salvation, but to the condition of their faith when He arrives.

This also applies to you and to me. John wrote this instruction to believers: "And now, little children, abide in Him, that when He appears, we may have confidence and not be ashamed before Him at His coming" (1 John 2:28).

One day Jesus is coming for us. If we are not abiding in Him, that time will find us ashamed. We will be sorry, so sorry. We will feel sorry that we chose other than Him, not for salvation, but for so many other things.

After studying this chapter, I really don't want Him to find me complaining because that speaks poorly and wrongly about Him, it's blasphemy. How much sweeter it will be if, when He comes, He finds us abiding in Him, so that we can look up at Him with the sweetness that only a healthy relationship experiences. When we behold Him face to face, don't we want the first words out of our mouths to be praises, not apologies?

> And they gathered them together to the place called in Hebrew, Armageddon. 16:16

Throughout history over 200 wars have been fought in this valley. It has been the site of some major Israelite victories, such as in the book of Judges when Deborah led an attack against the forces of Jabin king of Canaan, and also Gideon who reluctantly fought the Midianites. It's an incredible valley. Just as God planned to save us long, long ago, He also planned this battle for a very long time.

God confirmed this when He spoke these words to Job: "Have you entered the treasury of snow, or have you seen the treasury of hail, which I have reserved for the time of trouble, for the day of battle and war?" (Job 38:22-23).

> Then the seventh angel poured out his bowl into the air, and a loud voice came out of the temple of heaven, from the throne, saying, "It is done!" 16:17

THE SEVENTH BOWL

Remember, no one was in the temple but God. The angels had spoken, the saints had spoken, now God had something to say, "It is done!" This implies a change of state, condition, or the passing from one state to another. It is done! God's wrath is complete, finished. A new condition of life is about to begin. All of these calamities had to happen for that to take place. It is done! God has declared it.

> And there were noises and thunderings and lightnings; and there was a great earthquake, such a mighty and great earthquake as had not occurred since men were on the earth. Now the great city was divided into three parts, and the cities of the nations fell. And great Babylon was remembered before God, to give her the cup of the wine of the fierceness of His wrath. Then every island fled away, and the mountains were not found. And great hail from heaven fell upon men, each hailstone about the weight of a talent (about 100 pounds). Men blasphemed God because of the plague of the hail, since that plague was exceedingly great. 16:18-21

And yet, for the third time in this chapter, "Men blasphemed God" (v. 21).

CLOSING THOUGHTS

Revelation 16 shows us heaven and it shows us earth. While heaven is rejoicing over God's ways, those on the earth are blaspheming them. While heaven is shouting, "He is right! He is right!" those on earth are shouting, "He is wrong! He is wrong!"

If you get nothing else from this chapter, may you glean this: The book of Revelation is the Revelation of Jesus Christ, not just His majesty, but the heart of God. He loves to bless and He hates to judge. His righteousness demands these actions because He must do what is right.

There is promised blessing for reading and heeding the book of Revelation, for making the investment to know His character better and to understand His righteousness in a deeper way. He mentioned three times in this chapter that men's response to His judgments was to blaspheme Him, to speak ill or contrary of Him. Oh, may we not even come close to accusing our loving, righteous God of ever, ever doing anything wrong.

REFLECTION QUESTIONS

(For more extensive study questions visit CathyDickinson.com)

1. Look again at the song recorded in Revelation 15:3-4. Arise (if you are able) and read these verses aloud, BOLDLY, several times. Now record how it affected your perspective.

2. Ponder the idea of God grieving alone in the temple over the wrath He must pour out on unbelieving mankind. When we choose our own way over God's, it is an act of unbelief. Ask the Lord to reveal any area or attitude of your life that grieves Him. Now ask Him what He would have you to do.

3. Zephaniah 3:17 says that God rejoices over you with singing. Believing this pleases Him. Based upon Scripture, what are some of the phrases He might be singing over you?

4. Repeatedly, unbelieving mankind blasphemed God. Consider that to blaspheme simply means to declare things about God that are contrary to His character. What are some ways we blaspheme God?

5. What did you learn about the heart of God from these chapters? (If you need more room to write, use the notes section on page 258.)

6. Draw one of the scenes as described by John in Revelation chapters 15 and 16.

Notes

Chapter Nineteen

THE DOOM OF RELIGION: REVELATION 17

Jesus is about to reign; it's almost over. Chapters 17-19 are about what He must do for that to happen. As Revelation 16 ended with the pouring out of the seventh bowl, we saw "noises and thunderings and lightnings; and there was a great earthquake … and great Babylon was remembered before God, to give her the cup of the wine of the fierceness of His wrath" (vv. 18-19). Now in Revelation 17 and 18, we pause, zoom in, and take a look at what led up to this judgment.

Revelation 17 is about the destruction of the religious system and Revelation 18 is the destruction of the political and economic systems. We see religious Babylon in chapter 17 and commercial Babylon in chapter 18. Both appear to be so powerful, yet both will meet their doom, just as God promised.

> Then one of the seven angels who had the seven bowls came and talked with me, saying to me, "Come, I will show you the judgment of the great harlot who sits on many waters, 17:1

THE GREAT HARLOT

Revelation 17 begins with an angel inviting John to show him the judgment of the harlot. We'll come to find out later that John is also invited to see the bride, "Come, I will show you the bride, the Lamb's wife" (Revelation 21:9). But before John can see the bride, he has to see the harlot dealt with. The harlot has to go before the bride (the church) can marry the Groom. No party crashers can come to the wedding!

Revelation 17:15 identifies these many waters that the harlot sits on as "peoples, multitudes, nations, and tongues." This basically means that she rules over the world. Verse 18 identifies the harlot—she is "that great city which reigns over the kings of the earth."

Let's look at this false religious system called the harlot.

> with whom the kings of the earth committed fornication, and the inhabitants of the earth were made drunk with the wine of her fornication." 17:2

The Bible speaks of those who claim to have a way to God, yet live contrary to God's ways as harlots. She is called a harlot because she "committed fornication." She joined herself to things or people other than God. Note that it doesn't say that she committed adultery. She couldn't have. That would indicate that she belonged to God, which she never did. Thus her sin is not adultery, violating a relationship, but fornication, never having the relationship but running to others instead.

THE FALSE RELIGIOUS SYSTEM

We are told that the kings and the inhabitants of the earth (the earth dwellers, the unsaved) followed her, and "were made drunk with the wine of her fornication." When a person is drunk, they are controlled by its influences and deceptions. Their thinking is distorted.

There has always been religion. God made us with a longing for something outside of ourselves and He purposed to be the One to fill that longing. Man still longs, but that longing has become twisted, leading man to long for a god that accommodates his desire to sin, a god that fits his agenda and criteria.

Paul describes this in his letter to the Romans. "For since the creation of the world His invisible attributes are clearly seen, being understood by the things that are made, even His eternal power and Godhead, so that they are without excuse, because, although they knew God, they did not glorify Him as God, nor were thankful, but became futile in their thoughts, and their foolish hearts were darkened" (Romans 1:20-21).

Revelation 17 reveals to us just how dark man's foolish heart can get. There are many systems or religions that attempt to meet man's quest for God through ceremonies, rituals, rites, self-achievements, and the like. In the last days, they will all come together under a one-world religion.

> So he carried me away in the Spirit into the wilderness. And I saw a woman sitting on a scarlet beast which was full of names of blasphemy, having seven heads and ten horns. 17:3

THE HARLOT AND THE BEAST

John saw this beast before. "Then I stood on the sand of the sea. And I saw a beast rising up out of the sea, having seven heads and ten horns, and on his horns ten crowns, and on his heads a blasphemous name" (Revelation 13:1). As we have already established, this beast is the Antichrist. The harlot sits on the Antichrist. They co-exist for a while. She rides on his power and he holds her up.

Notice the scarlet beast "was full of names of blasphemy." This beast is going to take all the names that belong to God and wear them himself. Look again at how Jesus introduced Himself to John in Revelation 1: "I am the Living One; I was dead, and behold I am alive for ever and ever!" (v. 18 NIV). Is that how the Antichrist will present himself after he is mortally wounded and comes back to life? Will that be one of his blasphemous names?

> The woman was arrayed in purple and scarlet, and adorned with gold and precious stones and pearls, 17:4

THE HARLOT'S PRICE

Her adornments are ornate, indicating wealth. She has prostituted herself to gain wealth, position, and political power.

I heard a story about a man who offered a woman a million dollars to have sex with him. She agreed. Then later he offered her $100. She responded indignantly, "What do you think I am, a harlot? He said, "Well, we've already established that. Now we're just negotiating."

A harlot is someone who will sell out for a price. It seems Satan uses a reverse tactic with us by offering something with little payoff. We are indignant that he would think we'd be so foolish. Then he offers something bigger and better and we find ourselves wavering, because we, like this woman in the story, are willing to sell ourselves for the right price.

YOUR PRICE

You had a price and you were very expensive, but you have been bought by the precious blood of Jesus Christ. If you have received Jesus as your Savior, You now belong to Him. Just as you have no right to sell your neighbor's home because it doesn't belong to you, neither do you belong to yourself. Therefore you no longer have a price because you no longer are for sale. Paul makes this clear in 1 Corinthians 6.

> "Or do you not know that your body is the temple of the Holy Spirit who is in you, whom you have from God, and you are not your own? For you were bought at a price; therefore glorify God in your body and in your spirit, which are God's." (1 Corinthians 6:19-20)

How can we, who are His, sell out to the ways of the world for such a small price? Satan knows your price. He doesn't come along like this man did and offer the woman one hundred bucks. You would probably be insulted as she was. But just as the man offered the woman a million dollars first, Satan puts bait in front of you that is tempting. Do you have a price?

You and I choose sin because there is a payoff to it. What's the payoff that you sell out for? Pleasure, attention, safety, money, security? What do you choose over Jesus? It doesn't make you a harlot, but it does cause you to fit the description of her beginnings—selling out for a price.

If you and I don't remember how precious we are, that we are not harlots, but brides of the King, we will sell out for the million dollars discovering it to be pretty worthless. You see, it isn't the price we should be concerned about—there should be no price on us at all. We've already been bought.

> having in her hand a golden cup full of abominations and the filthiness of her fornication. 17:4

The harlot is shown having a cup in her hand. Apparently, many of the ancient religions had pagan rites pertaining to drinking of certain cups, and it's full of abomination and filthiness to God. Thus far, we see what she is wearing, what she holds in her hand; next we learn her name.

And on her forehead a name was written:

> MYSTERY, BABYLON THE GREAT, THE MOTHER OF HARLOTS AND OF THE ABOMINATIONS OF THE EARTH. 17:5

History shows it was customary for prostitutes to wear a band on their forehead with their name on it. False religion has its foundation in Babylon back in Genesis 11 with the attempt to build the tower of Babel. It's amazing how many times Babylon is associated with false religion in both biblical and secular history. It's not really talking about a city here as much as it is referring to the false religion that will govern the world. It's identifying with the ways of the city of Babylon. The city of Babylon will have its religion that will permeate the entire world.

When it says she is "the mother of harlots," that's a good description of the Babylonian system; it has given birth to false religions. She has seduced men into opposing God and persecuting His people.

I read a quote yesterday that said, "The Bible is about two cities, Babylon and Jerusalem; the city against God and the city that belonged to God." [41]

> I saw the woman, drunk with the blood of the saints and with the blood of the martyrs of Jesus. And when I saw her, I marveled with great amazement. 17:6

She appears to get some sort of warped satisfaction out of persecuting God's people, which reveals to us her source of power. Recall from Revelation 12:17, that Satan is enraged against God's people during this time and we see that this false religious system will be a part of the saints' persecution.

> But the angel said to me, "Why did you marvel? I will tell you the mystery of the woman and of the beast that carries her, which has the seven heads and the ten horns. 17:7

Why did John marvel? We'll discuss that in a moment.

As part of the angel's explanation of what John is seeing, he once again identifies the beast that the woman was sitting on as having "seven heads and ten horns" (v. 3).

> The beast that you saw was, and is not, and will ascend out of the bottomless pit and go to perdition. 17:8

It's a quick summary of the life of the beast (the Antichrist). The "is not" probably refers to the time of his mortal wound.

He "will ascend out of the bottomless pit" has two possibilities. If he really did die, his soul would not have gone to heaven, but to the bottomless pit. So when he came back to life, he would have come out of the bottomless pit. Or it is simply saying his power came from Satan. Either way, when the Antichrist comes back, he's going to come back different. He's going to come back with a new satanic power, demanding to be worshiped. Therefore, the harlot won't be needed. There won't be a need for a worldwide religion. It has accomplished its purpose.

And when all is said and done, then the Antichrist will "go to perdition." This definition of perdition punctuates his reign perfectly: "Perdition refers to the state after death wherein exclusion from salvation is a realized fact." [42] That pretty much describes his brief seven-year reign.

> And those who dwell on the earth will marvel, whose names are not written in the Book of Life from the foundation of the world, when they see the beast that was, and is not, and yet is. 17:8

In verse 6 we are told that John "marveled." Here we are told that "those who dwell on the earth will marvel." This is the same word, yet there was a different response. John marveled but certainly was not taken in by the Beast, while those who dwell on the earth will marvel and get sucked into his lies.

HOW ARE YOU INFLUENCED?

We see it today. We even see Christians and people who claim to be Christians get sucked into his lies or pulled away from God's truths, distracted from God's purposes for them. Satan uses any means he can to pull us away from our relationship with the Lord. He uses means from outside the church and he uses means from inside the church.

What would you say is the greatest influence on the earth presently? My answer would be the media. Would you agree that Satan is using the media to influence people? Do you think you are beyond being influenced? Be careful what you expose yourself to. You and I are not beyond his lies.

I found this yesterday and I want to park on it. "You don't have a soul. You are a soul. You have a body." [43] Only one thing appeals to the soul, God's Holy Spirit. The soul rejects everything else. The soul, quickened by the Holy Spirit, the saved soul, understands things the unsaved soul doesn't.

We are soul. It's our soul that God is after; it's our soul that He satisfies. Yet because we live with a mind and a body, we often try to meet our spiritual need through a means that at least temporarily gratifies the flesh.

SPIRITUAL DECEPTION

I see Christians duped by getting into things that appeal to their flesh. If you like the intellectual side of things, there are lots of churches out there that appeal to the intellect.

They love the study of God's Word. They love analyzing it, critiquing it, and talking about it like it's a college textbook, and matching it with history and cultures. They get a sense of satisfaction in doing that. I understand that. I love the study part. If you like to feed your emotional side, there are churches that emphasize the signs and wonders and the gifts of the Holy Spirit. I'm all for that too. But lately I have been grateful for Pastor Chuck Smith in a deeper way. I'm grateful for the balance that he brought to Calvary Chapel.

In my early years of Christianity, there was a church that became very popular that was started by people that came out of Calvary Chapel, essentially claiming that it overemphasized God's Word. I remember them saying, "Calvary Chapels worship the Father, Son, and the Holy Bible." Not the Holy Spirit.

Dale and I started going to the services for a short while. The worship was incredible. Then we went to a couple of their conferences on inner healing and I loved it. When I laid hands on people, my hand always shook. When I prayed over someone, I always had a word for them. Praise God it didn't last long because I realized my goal had changed. My desire was no longer to know Jesus in a deeper way. My desire became to have my hand shake and to be able to say to someone, "Thus saith the Lord."

Paul said in Philippians, "that I may know Him and the power of His resurrection, and the fellowship of His sufferings, being conformed to His death" (Philippians 3:10). Paul knew how to both reason with the Scriptures and how to tap into the power of God; he did both for the purpose of knowing Him.

When I was caught up in it, I didn't see it. I would have told you at the time that those things were of the Lord. It became all about the signs and wonders for me. Fortunately, I had enough of a love for Jesus in me that I missed Him and came back to Him. The point is—it's really, really easy to get caught up in a side of "religion" that appeals to the flesh.

There are still times when my hand will shake when I'm praying for someone, but I'm not thinking about whether it will shake or not. There are times when the Lord still gives me a word for someone, but I am not seeking a word, I am seeking Him.

R.A. Torrey said this: "The secret of effectual living is knowing the power of the Spirit through the Word. The secret of effectual service is using the Word in the power of the Spirit. There are some who seek to magnify the Spirit but neglect the Word. This will not do at all. Fanaticism, baseless enthusiasm, wildfire are the result. Others seek to magnify the Word, but largely ignore the Spirit. Neither will this do. It leads to dead orthodoxy, truth without life and power." [44]

Knowing the power of the Spirit through the study and application of God's Word is the key to effectual living, or living so you won't get duped. Be careful! It's so easy to get pulled away by what is presented as a movement of God. Your flesh may really like it and you just might get sucked up into it. As God's people, we must not settle for atmospheres that appeal to our flesh but not our soul. If it doesn't draw you closer to Jesus, if it doesn't make you more like Jesus in His humility and love and servanthood, stay away from it.

THE REMEDY

Five years or so before John received this revelation, he was very concerned about people in the church being deceived by false teachers in the church, pseudo antichrists. He had warned that the Antichrist would come. It's no wonder we read of him being amazed at the deception by the harlot in verse 6. He must have been shocked to see how bad it really will get.

The remedy he wrote of in 1 John is the same remedy people can rely on today and it is the same remedy that will keep believers from being deceived by the harlot and the Beast in those last days of the tribulation.

John wrote: "These things I have written to you concerning those who try to deceive you. But the anointing which you have received from Him abides in you, and you do not need that anyone teach you; but as the same anointing teaches you concerning all things, and is true, and is not a lie, and just as it has taught you, you will abide in Him" (1 John 2:26-27).

We have the Holy Spirit to discern for us the difference between truth and lies. Jesus said this about the tribulation years: "For false christs and false prophets will rise and show great signs and wonders to deceive, if possible, even the elect" (Matthew 24:24).

The people had to be warned. As believers we can still be duped. No believer will be duped by the Antichrist, because we won't be around at that point, but many others can dupe us today.

> "Here is the mind which has wisdom: The seven heads are seven mountains on which the woman sits. 17:9

THE FALSE RELIGION

This gives some insight into what the seven heads may represent. Rome is known as The City of Seven Hills. This says mountains. Rome was the ruling city of the world in John's time. Many believe this is referring to the city of Rome and the Catholic religion.

Without being too disparaging of the Catholic religion, let's acknowledge that there are Catholics who have a saving faith in Jesus, perhaps much of the time, in spite of the Catholic religion rather than because of it. There are things about the Catholic religion that are just wrong, but there are things that are right. No one will get saved through the religion of this harlot. But keep in mind, this false religion will not rise to power until the Christians are raptured and that includes all Catholic Christians, leaving behind a people who missed the gospel—the good part of what the Catholic Church taught.

This false religion is not just the Catholic Church. It will be comprised of all the different religions that are not true to the gospel, including a lot of liberal Protestant churches and churches that teach the religion of good works or positive thinking.

The seven heads or seven mountains is possibly Rome, or seven nations, or seven seats of power, as a mountain often represents a seat of power in the Bible. They could also represent the entire world since seven is the number of completion. If it is Rome, her influence is worldwide. What we know for certain is that she has great authority and influence. The people who are alive at the time will understand this well.

> There are also seven kings. Five have fallen, one is, and the other has not yet come. And when he comes, he must continue a short time. 17:10

WORLD DOMINATION

At the time John saw the revelation, there had been five world-dominating powers to date: Egypt, Assyria, Babylon, Medo-Persia, and Greece; these are the five that "have fallen." Rome is the "one that is" (the world-dominating power in John's time). "The other" (the seventh) is yet to come and will "continue a short time." The word translated a short time literally means "a little space."

> The beast that was, and is not, is himself also the eighth, and is of the seven, and is going to perdition. 17:11

Because the seventh one is yet to come, we don't know for sure what nation it is. Many feel it will be the revival of the Roman Empire. Whatever it is, the Antichrist will come out of it, will take it, and rule over it. We already learned that his time will also be short and we are reminded again at the end of this that he "is going to perdition."

> The ten horns which you saw are ten kings who have received no kingdom as yet, but they receive authority for one hour as kings with the beast. 17:12

This is not a literal hour, as we will see in chapters 18 and 19. It just means that they will enjoy their authority for a very brief time. We don't know who these ten kings are. There have been many guesses. It seems that these ten kings will represent the entire world.

> These are of one mind, and they will give their power and authority to the beast. These will make war with the Lamb, and the Lamb will overcome them, for He is Lord of lords and King of kings; and those who are with Him are called, chosen, and faithful." 17:13-14

WE WILL WATCH THE LAMB OVERCOME

"Those who are with Him"exposes the heart of God toward His own. This phrase goes beyond expressing how He views us; it reveals how Jesus likes you and me to be with Him.

He wanted the disciples to be with Him in His toughest of times. He expressed His desire to be with us when He prayed, "Father, I desire that they also whom You gave Me may be with Me where I am, that they may behold My glory which You have given Me" (John 17:24).

And here, Jesus takes us with Him so we can, in a sense, behold His glory and watch Him demonstrate His power to conquer any and all who would come against Him.

It's kind of a male thing more than female. You that are married women (and I'm sure the married men would nod in agreement), if you pay attention, you will notice your husband just likes you to be with him. He wants you to watch him do what he does. He loves it when you are his cheerleader. When I teach on the role of the wife, I often use the example of a statement a man shared. "We men never grow out of some desires; like the desire I had in high school when I was on the football field and I could hear my girlfriend cry out, 'Yea, Andy. You're the best!'" God tells us over and over again in the Bible that He loves our praises. One day He's going to invite us to go with Him to this great battle. He's going to say, "Come ride with Me!" We will get to see the One who is King of kings and Lord of lords take over. We won't have to do a thing—just ride alongside Him, watch, and exclaim His praises.

CALLED, CHOSEN, AND FAITHFUL

Those who are "called, chosen, and faithful" will make up the army that rides with Jesus when He overcomes the Beast. These are words that describe the believer. Angels aren't referred to as "called, chosen, and faithful." The twenty-four elders are not referred to as "called, chosen, and faithful." The four living creatures aren't described as this either. But you and I, believers, are described as "called, chosen, and faithful." Just as His names should help us to know who He is, the names He calls us as believers help us to know how He views us.

Names are important to Him.

Jesus means: "He will save His people from their sins" (Matthew 1:21).

John means: Jehovah is a gracious Giver.

CALLED

We are "called" indicating we are both "invited ones" and "welcomed ones" because we have received and accepted the invitation.

Have you ever received an invitation in the church bulletin? "All are invited!" At least you haven't been told you can't come, but it isn't particularly personal. It is in the welcoming that you feel special. When someone takes the time to walk over to you, give you a hug, and let you know they are glad you are there, that makes you feel loved. They called you out.

CHOSEN

We are also the chosen ones, cherished and beloved of God, selected to accomplish a work. Ephesians 2:8-10 confirms,

> "For by grace you have been saved through faith, and that not of yourselves; it is the gift of God, not of works, lest anyone should boast. For we are His workmanship, created in Christ Jesus for good works, which God prepared beforehand that we should walk in them."

We are "saved through faith." Once we are saved, we become chosen for a work, set aside for God's purposes, set aside for Him.

FAITHFUL

We are called "faithful." God is faithful. It's hard to comprehend how we can be called faithful. But if we are truly called, if we have truly said yes to His invitation to salvation, we will be faithful to Him overall. We won't be one hundred percent faithful while we are in these bodies of flesh, but people should be able to look at our lives and our choices and say of us that we are faithful to live what we say we believe.

In the sense of the action described here in Revelation 17, I like to think of it as the Lord saying to us, "Welcome to the kingdom. Now get on the horse and let's take it back!" One day we'll get to climb up on a horse and ride with Jesus. Now we know very well that Jesus doesn't need us, in these bodies or in our glorified bodies, to defeat an army that comes against Him, He just wants our company.

> Then he said to me, "The waters which you saw, where the harlot sits, are peoples, multitudes, nations, and tongues. And the ten horns which you saw on the beast, these will hate the harlot, make her desolate and naked, eat her flesh and burn her with fire. 17:15-16

THE HARLOT IS JUDGED

Before this war takes place, the harlot will be judged. She will be made "desolate and naked." Her flesh will be eaten and she will be burned with fire. To put it simply, this harlot is going down. What goes around comes around, or as John wrote in Revelation 13:10, "He who leads into captivity shall go into captivity; he who kills with the sword must be killed with the sword."

People and movements can be significant and influential one day and forgotten the next. They are deceived into thinking they are on top but the next moment they are plummeting to the bottom because God has purposed it to be so.

The harlot's influence will be over one day, probably at that three-and-a-half-year mark of the tribulation, when the Antichrist walks into the temple and declares himself to be the object of worship.

> For God has put it into their hearts to fulfill His purpose, to be of one mind, and to give their kingdom to the beast, until the words of God are fulfilled. And the woman whom you saw is that great city which reigns over the kings of the earth." 17:17-18

These kings who committed fornication with the harlot will turn and give their kingdom to the Beast, for a short time, "until the words of God are fulfilled." Then the time of the Beast and those who worship him will come to a devastating end, but for the believer it's all going to end well.

CLOSING THOUGHTS

As we learned from Revelation 15:3, we will one day sing, "Great and marvelous are Your works, Lord God Almighty! Just and true are Your ways, O King of the saints!"

Let us live like the victors we will one day be because THE LAMB HAS OVERCOME. Until then, there will be deceivers out there to get you and me. They can't get our souls, but they sure can try to get our attention. Then one glorious day, the King of kings and Lord of lords will say to you and me, "Come, ride with Me!"

REFLECTION QUESTIONS

(For more extensive study questions visit CathyDickinson.com)

1. Describe how the false religion (the harlot) in chapter 17 has committed fornication.

False religion joins with things or people other than God... Those who follow false religion are controlled by its influences or deceptions. Their thinking is distorted. Man's quest → ceremonies, rituals, rites, self-achievements...

2. When we compromise and choose sin over our relationship with the Lord, what is the payoff you tend to sell out for—pleasure, attention, security, money, or something else?

Sin - pleasure and rest, security and intellectual superiority draw me into sinful activity comfort.

3. In your own words, what are we encouraged to remember to keep us from selling out?

I am a body and soul. I need to nourish my soul by seeking God's word and appeal of the Holy Spirit which requires ignoring media and lusts

4. Reflect on each of these descriptions the Lord declares of you: called, chosen, and faithful. Which one encourages you the most and why? Everyone wants to be chosen. It means that you belong and you are selected "for a purpose." To be chosen is to belong with a purpose since someone wanted you.

5. Draw one of the scenes as described by John in Revelation chapter 17.

Chapter Twenty

COME OUT OF BABYLON, MY PEOPLE: REVELATION 18

The main thrust of evangelism at this point is focused toward the Jews. We see times in the Bible where portions of the Old Testament are quoted that are meant to take the Jewish people back to other portions of scripture that describe what is happening in a fuller context.

The most familiar to us is probably when Jesus hung on the cross and cried out, "My God, My God, why have You forsaken Me?" (Matthew 27:46, Mark 15:34). We believe that should have triggered the memory of the Jews back to Psalm 22, which begins with those words and then continues to describe the suffering of the Messiah. If the people had read Psalm 22 with open hearts, they would have seen how the suffering of the Messiah, as predicted in that psalm, lined up with the suffering of Jesus the day of His crucifixion.

A CAUSE TO REMEMBER

In the same way, the scripture references to Babylon in Revelation 18 should cause God's people to remember the plethora of verses about the destruction of Babylon written in the Old Testament and God's cry to His people to "come out" before His judgment is poured out.

There are at least six chapters in the Old Testament that speak of a final destruction of Babylon. Some scriptures speak of a partial destruction, but a final destruction, as described in some of the scriptures referenced in this chapter, is yet to occur.

Here is one example found in Isaiah 13 titled, "Proclamation Against Babylon." It begins with these words: "The burden against Babylon which Isaiah the son of Amoz saw." Verse 9 continues,

> "Behold, the day of the Lord comes, cruel, with both wrath and fierce anger, to lay the land desolate; and He will destroy its sinners from it. For the stars of heaven and their constellations will not give their light; the sun will be darkened in its going forth, and the moon will not cause its light to shine. I will punish the world for its evil, and the wicked for their iniquity; I will halt the arrogance of the proud, and will lay low the haughtiness of the terrible. I will make a mortal more rare than fine gold, a man more than the golden wedge of Ophir. Therefore I will shake the heavens, and the earth will move out of her place, in the wrath of the Lord of hosts and in the day of His fierce anger." (Isaiah 13:9-13)

If God made certain prophecies that were to come to pass in Babylon and they haven't come to pass, then they must be yet to come as it is written in Matthew 5:18, "For assuredly, I say to you, till heaven and earth pass away, one jot or one tittle will by no means pass from the law till all is fulfilled."

> After these things I saw another angel coming down from heaven, having great authority, and the earth was illuminated with his glory. 18:1

Revelation chapter 18 begins with the words, "After these things." After John saw the destruction of religious Babylon, he saw the destruction of commercial Babylon. This is most likely a literal city. Chronologically, the destruction of commercial Babylon takes place after, but not necessarily immediately. The events of this chapter will probably occur toward the very end of the tribulation.

> And he cried mightily with a loud voice, 18:2

As revealed in verse 1, the light from this angel lit up the earth. It does not appear that this declaration goes out to the whole earth, as we saw in Revelation 14:6 when the angels declared the gospel and warnings "to every nation, tribe, tongue, and people." It seems this illumination and this announcement might have been only for those in the city of Babylon itself.

> saying, "Babylon the great is fallen, is fallen and has become a dwelling place of demons, 18:2

"Babylon is fallen, is fallen!" is a quote from Isaiah 21:9.

Look at what Babylon has fallen into, "a dwelling place of demons."

A DWELLING FOR DEMONS

Satan and his demons were thrown out of heaven and unleash all the power they have. We may think of that power as physical might, but throughout history Satan's most powerful tactics have been through lies and deception. Satan and his demons will dwell in Babylon, deceiving and lying to the people, distracting them from the true and living God.

I don't know if you have ever been in a room or even a city that has been given over to satanic powers, but the sense of their presence is just awful.

> a prison for every foul spirit, and a cage for every unclean and hated bird! 18:2

A HAUNTED PRISON

The word *cage* used here is the same Greek word translated "prison" as it described the place for the foul spirit, more of a haunting place for demons.

Unclean birds are used in the parables to represent the enemy, or it could literally refer to unclean birds that inhabit an uninhabitable place. Put all three of these descriptions together and we can see it's a place ruled by evil.

For all the nations have drunk of the wine of the wrath of her fornication, the kings of the earth have committed fornication with her, and the merchants of the earth have become rich through the abundance of her luxury." 18:3

ABUNDANCE OF LUXURY

Notice that although the earth is experiencing incredible calamities during this time, somehow the Antichrist is able to keep things going and keep them going well. Luxuries and wealth abound; all nations have participated in Babylon's economy and her ways to secure riches.

And I heard another voice from heaven saying, "Come out of her, my people, 18:4

GET OUT!

Before Babylon goes down, God has a warning for His people: "Come out of her, my people, lest you share in her sins, and lest you receive of her plagues."

Such has been the cry of our God to His people throughout the ages.

He called Noah out (Genesis 6:17-18).

He called Abraham out (Genesis 12:1).

He called Lot out before He destroyed Sodom and Gomorrah (Genesis 19:17).

He called the people out before He punished Korah for his rebellion (Numbers 16:2, 24).

And Jeremiah delivered God's warning to God's people to get out of Babylon.

"Flee from the midst of Babylon, and every one save his life! Do not be cut off in her iniquity, for this is the time of the LORD's vengeance; He shall recompense her." (Jeremiah 51:6)

"My people, go out of the midst of her! And let everyone deliver himself from the fierce anger of the LORD." (Jeremiah 51:45)

Over and over again God's cry to His people is, "Get out! I am about to judge." God's heart is to keep His people from suffering in the coming judgment and a two-fold warning follows His plea.

God warns that there would be consequences if His people remained in Babylon.

lest you share in her sins, 18:4

1. LEST YOU PARTICIPATE IN SIN

That's such a warning to us today. Babylon was full of evil. This is commercial Babylon we are talking about, where evil reigns because of an insatiable desire for luxuries.

Do you know that your desire for material things and comforts is insatiable—not satisfiable? Do you resist that statement? They probably would have too. Yes, the world is more drawn to those things than believers are, but we are still drawn to them too.

The world buys into this lie, to a greater extent than many of us do, but it's the same lie. It is the same lie you are tempted by when you see the television commercial promoting a product that you want, that you think, *If I just had that, life would be better.* We may find ourselves having a similar response when we see someone that has something we don't have. It's that discontentment in us that Satan goes after.

SINS OF COMMERCIAL BABYLON

Babylon was full of people who had compromised. Some had compromised spiritually by taking the mark of the beast and worshiping his image. But notice that God did not call His people to come out of religious Babylon in Revelation 17, because religious Babylon denied Jesus. Religious Babylon rejected Jesus; a believer just can't do that. Therefore God did not call His people to come out of religious Babylon. Religious Babylon was void of God's people.

On the other hand, God's people were still in commercial Babylon. Had they compromised to its values or lack thereof? We can assume so when we look at the warning. *Come out lest you share or partake in their sins.* Come out lest you fall into the same sins.

TO BENEFIT SELF

Look at the United States of America. Spiritually, we are probably as good as it gets as far as Christian countries right now. Yet how many Americans, including Christian Americans, vote according to what will benefit them financially rather than voting biblically or even in accord with their own convictions?

Don't you know that if the government wanted to take away housing benefits for pastors that just about every pastor and his wife would vote against it? Not because of the rightness or wrongness of it, but because it would affect them financially. If you are union, you tend to vote union. If you are unemployed, you would probably vote for extended unemployment. We often don't consider the rightness or wrongness or how it would affect others. Sadly, we tend to vote and live according to what we think would benefit us the most.

If we aren't satisfied with Jesus and on a daily basis thankful for His benefits, Satan will constantly put before us other means to satisfaction, which not only do not satisfy, but when we choose them, will have consequences. When we play with fire, we will get burned. When we live among sin, we will end up sharing or participating in it. Why do believers so often think they are beyond temptation?

What about you? Are you dabbling? Are you just a little too close to something you shouldn't be? How can you know? It's what you are thinking of right now. If it's okay, why does it bother you? Why did it just pop up? What are you exposing yourself to that you shouldn't? A person? Some people? Some thing? God would say to you the very same thing He will say to His people in Babylon and for the very same reason, "Come out lest you share in their sins." A voice from heaven said that. Imagine the conviction of hearing that voice.

and lest you receive of her plagues. 18:4

2. AND RECEIVE PUNISHMENT

The other part of this warning is that God's people would receive Babylon's plagues. The word *plague* here is a strike or blow inflicted by God. The sense is come out of her lest you get caught up in her sins and you experience God's affliction upon her, or her punishment—the consequences of her sin.

May we not be so foolish as to think that because we have His grace, our sins don't reach up to heaven every bit as much as the sins of those who do not belong to Him. He is clear about this in His Word. Here are just a few examples:

> "For the time has come for judgment to begin at the house of God; and if it begins with us first, what will be the end of those who do not obey the gospel of God?" (1 Peter 4:17)
>
> "Do not be deceived, God is not mocked; for whatever a man sows, that he will also reap." (Galatians 6:7)
>
> "And you have forgotten the exhortation which speaks to you as to sons: 'My son, do not despise the chastening of the Lord, nor be discouraged when you are rebuked by Him; for whom the Lord loves He chastens, and scourges every son whom He receives.'" (Hebrews 12:5-6)
>
> "Your iniquities have turned these things away, and your sins have withheld good from you." (Jeremiah 5:25)
>
> "But your iniquities have separated you from your God; and your sins have hidden His face from you, so that He will not hear." (Isaiah 59:2)

GRACE FOR REPENTANCE

Yes, there is grace. But we should not count on grace unless we have repented. Repentance is agreeing with God about the sin you have committed or are committing. It is saying, "If I had to do it over again, I wouldn't do it." Repentance is coming out of the situation in which you are sinning. God is calling His people out so that they will not experience the punishment He has for those who refuse to come out.

This is serious stuff. We deceive ourselves if we subscribe to the belief that God does not take the sin of a believer just as seriously, or perhaps even more so, than that of an unbeliever. We are to come out of the ways and the thinking of the world, the Babylonian system.

For her sins have reached to heaven, and God has remembered her iniquities. 18:5

GOD REMEMBERS

We find the same phrase about God remembering her sins back in Revelation 16:19, "Now the great city was divided into three parts, and the cities of the nations fell. And great Babylon was remembered before God, to give her the cup of the wine of the fierceness of His wrath."

God is about to punish Babylon for her sins. As forgiveness of sin is signified by a non-remembrance of it, so is punishment of sin by a remembrance of it and of the persons that commit it. Whether God will remember our sins or not is up to us. His non-remembrance of our sin is dependent upon our decision to repent of them. This is not specifically talking about salvation, but rather the chastisement for sin that we choose to not repent of.

Throughout Revelation, God's heart is unveiled to us. He must judge the evil, but He doesn't want His people to suffer that judgment.

> Render to her just as she rendered to you, and repay her double according to her works; in the cup which she has mixed, mix double for her. 18:6

DOUBLE JUDGMENT

The word *double* is mentioned two times as it refers to God's judgment upon Babylon. God uses statements such as "repay double" and "mix double."

The word *double* in verse 6 refers more to a mirrored image or a duplicate of something. A twin is a double of the other, a matching. Therefore, God in His righteous and fair judgment repays in a way that matches the sin. And when all is said and done, no one will say His judgment was unjust. No one will blame Him.

If we reap what we sow, if God pays back double, that could scare us a little or cause us to think that God is harsh or unfair. When we look at what this word *double* actually means, we see how truly just God is.

> In the measure that she glorified herself and lived luxuriously, 18:7

What are Babylon's sins? Glorifying herself and living in luxury, pride, and materialism.

God hates both—that shouldn't be news to us. This pride and materialism of Babylon certainly exceeds what you and I have done; nonetheless, even if ours is to a lesser degree, He still hates it. Does that bother you? It should. The psalmist hated what God hated. Shouldn't our lives reflect God's heart as well?

> in the same measure give her torment and sorrow; for she says in her heart, 'I sit as queen, and am no widow, and will not see sorrow.' 18:7

THE PRIDE OF BABYLON

Verse 7 begins, "In the same measure" and goes on to reveal her attitude. "She says in her heart, 'I sit as queen and am no widow.'"

Isaiah 47 speaks of a final destruction of Babylon. Notice the similarities.

> "Therefore hear this now, you who are given to pleasures, who dwell securely, who say in your heart, 'I am, and there is no one else besides me; I shall not sit as a widow, nor shall I know the loss of children.'" (Isaiah 47:8)

It's like Babylon's saying, "You can't take me down, God. I've endured the sun turning dark, the moon turning red, the stars falling, the sea turning to blood, earthquakes, famines, and wars and I'm still here!"

> Therefore her plagues will come in one day—death and mourning and famine. 18:8

THE HUMILIATION OF BABYLON

God's judgments will come upon her in "one day." These are the judgments or plagues that will come upon Babylon: "death, mourning, and famine."

Continuing on in Isaiah 47, look at God's response to Babylon,

> "But these two things shall come to you in a moment, in one day: the loss of children, and widowhood. They shall come upon you in their fullness because of the multitude of your sorceries, for the great abundance of your enchantments. For you have trusted in your wickedness; you have said, 'No one sees me'; your wisdom and your knowledge have warped you; and you have said in your heart, 'I am, and there is no one else besides me.'
>
> "Therefore evil shall come upon you; you shall not know from where it arises. And trouble shall fall upon you; you will not be able to put it off. And desolation shall come upon you suddenly, which you shall not know.
>
> "Stand now with your enchantments and the multitude of your sorceries, in which you have labored from your youth—perhaps you will be able to profit, perhaps you will prevail.
>
> "You are wearied in the multitude of your counsels; let now the astrologers, the stargazers, and the monthly prognosticators stand up and save you from what shall come upon you.
>
> "Behold, they shall be as stubble, the fire shall burn them; they shall not deliver themselves from the power of the flame; it shall not be a coal to be warmed by, nor a fire to sit before!
>
> "Thus shall they be to you with whom you have labored, your merchants from your youth; they shall wander each one to his quarter. No one shall save you." (Isaiah 47:9-15)

Did you notice the similarities? "I am no widow, and will not see sorrow" (v. 7); "her plagues will come in one day" (v. 8). God said Babylon is going down—it will go down just as He said.

> And she will be utterly burned with fire for strong is the Lord God who judges her. 18:8

STRONG IS THE LORD GOD

Babylon will be utterly (completely) burned with fire, for strong is the Lord who judges her.

This word *strong* means "mighty and powerful." A little deeper definition is "valiant in war; able to overcome." As it relates to God, we get that. As I looked at the definition I remembered something I wrote in my devotions as I was studying 1 John. Look at this verse:

> "I have written to you, fathers, because you have known Him who is from the beginning. I have written to you, young men, because you are strong, and the word of God abides in you, and you have overcome the wicked one." (1 John 2:14)

The word *strong* used to describe God in Revelation 18:8 is the same word used to describe you and me as believers in 1 John 2:14. And I remembered the definition of *strong* in *Thayer's Greek Dictionary*: "strength of soul to sustain the attacks of Satan." [45]

God is stronger than any enemy that can come against Him. We know that, and because we are His, He gives us His strength as promised in Philippians 4:13: "I can do all things through Christ who strengthens me."

GOD GIVES HIS OWN STRENGTH TO US

The Lord does not take your strength and my strength and multiply it to make us stronger. John 15:5 tells us "for without Me (Jesus) you can do nothing." Multiplying our own strength would still leave us with nothing and therefore utterly inadequate to stand. Instead, He gives us His own strength. And with His strength, we can stand and sustain satanic attacks. That's powerful!

Do you believe that? Do your actions reveal that you believe it when it feels like the forces of hell are set against you? Do you cave in or do you stand?

> "The kings of the earth who committed fornication and lived luxuriously with her will weep and lament for her, when they see the smoke of her burning, standing at a distance for fear of her torment, saying, 'Alas, alas, that great city Babylon, that mighty city! For in one hour your judgment has come.'
>
> "And the merchants of the earth will weep and mourn over her, for no one buys their merchandise anymore: 18:9-11

Babylon went down and the kings of the world wept and the merchants of the world wept. They lamented because their source of income was burning up because no one bought their merchandise anymore.

> merchandise of gold and silver, precious stones and pearls, fine linen and purple, silk and scarlet, every kind of citron wood, every kind of object of ivory, every kind of object of most precious wood, bronze, iron, and marble; and cinnamon and

> incense, fragrant oil and frankincense, wine and oil, fine flour and wheat, cattle and sheep, horses and chariots, and bodies and souls of men. The fruit that your soul longed for has gone from you, and all the things which are rich and splendid have gone from you, and you shall find them no more at all. 18:12-14

This city, whether it is literal Babylon or a city with satanic influences like that of historical Babylon, had influenced the entire world. It controlled the economy and commerce of the entire world. All the kings and all the merchants were affected by its business. Therefore, when the city falls, the economy of the entire world will collapse along with it, never to recover.

That which they lived for was gone forever. That which brought them pleasure would bring them pleasure no more. It's over—only hell awaits them now.

> The merchants of these things, who became rich by her, will stand at a distance for fear of her torment, weeping and wailing, and saying, 'Alas, alas, that great city that was clothed in fine linen, purple, and scarlet, and adorned with gold and precious stones and pearls! For in one hour such great riches came to nothing.' Every shipmaster, all who travel by ship, sailors, and as many as trade on the sea, stood at a distance and cried out when they saw the smoke of her burning, saying, 'What is like this great city?' 18:15-18

The shipmasters and sailors wept. Everybody and anybody who benefited from the evil ways of Babylon wept as they stood at a distance and cried out, "What is like this great city?"

> "They threw dust on their heads and cried out, weeping and wailing, and saying, 'Alas, alas, that great city, in which all who had ships on the sea became rich by her wealth! For in one hour she is made desolate.' 18:19

Babylon is fallen! If Babylon can't stand, what can? Nothing—nothing can stand against our strong God.

> "Rejoice over her, O heaven, and you holy apostles and prophets, for God has avenged you on her!" 18:20

REJOICE! GOD HAS DEALT WITH EVIL

John's attention is turned again to heaven. Rejoice heaven! God has dealt with evil! You see, Jesus can't reign until all that is wrong is gone. He is fully able to take what is wrong and make it right. Look in the mirror. You and I are great examples of that. But for those who don't want to be made right, He must judge them. He has to rid the world of evil because such cannot inherit the kingdom of God. There is no place for them in His kingdom, because they do not want a place in His kingdom.

> Then a mighty angel took up a stone like a great millstone and threw it into the sea, saying, "Thus with violence the great city Babylon shall be thrown down, and shall not be found anymore. 18:21

THE FINAL DESTRUCTION

John got to see this final destruction, and it may have caused him to remember what the prophet Jeremiah wrote so long ago of this final destruction of the great city of Babylon.

> "So Jeremiah wrote in a book all the evil that would come upon Babylon, all these words that are written against Babylon. And Jeremiah said to Seraiah, 'When you arrive in Babylon and see it, and read all these words, then you shall say, "O LORD, You have spoken against this place to cut it off, so that none shall remain in it, neither man nor beast, but it shall be desolate forever." Now it shall be, when you have finished reading this book, that you shall tie a stone to it and throw it out into the Euphrates. Then you shall say, "Thus Babylon shall sink and not rise from the catastrophe that I will bring upon her. And they shall be weary."' (Jeremiah 51:60-64)

The concept of *weary* used to describe those in fallen Babylon is the same word that is found in the promise of Isaiah 40:31. "But those who wait on the LORD shall renew their strength; they shall mount up with wings like eagles, they shall run and not be *weary*, they shall walk and not faint." The believer, who waits on the LORD, is promised he or she will NOT experience this weariness; while for the fallen, it is declared that they certainly will.

> The sound of harpists, musicians, flutists, and trumpeters shall not be heard in you anymore. No craftsman of any craft shall be found in you anymore, and the sound of a millstone shall not be heard in you anymore. The light of a lamp shall not shine in you anymore, and the voice of bridegroom and bride shall not be heard in you anymore. For your merchants were the great men of the earth, for by your sorcery all the nations were deceived. And in her was found the blood of prophets and saints, and of all who were slain on the earth." 18:22-24

These final verses continue to describe what was no more because the city was gone; music, creativity, building, and happy times like marriage. For us, as believers, it will be just the opposite. There will be plenty of music, plenty of chances to express ourselves, and we will be a part of the greatest wedding feast ever.

CLOSING THOUGHTS

A few years ago, some devastating news was announced to a church on a Sunday morning. I knew about it though before it was announced. I remember visiting the church website the following Saturday night before the announcement was made and I watched a little of the service. As I viewed the shots of the people there, I was mindful that they had no clue how their lives were going to be changed the next day. In a way, I knew the future. I knew what was going to happen and they didn't. They were caught unaware. No one had warned them. They didn't see it coming.

But as we read Revelation, we see that doesn't need to happen. God is letting us know, and He's letting those who will go through the tribulation know, what to expect and He is warning His people to get out before it's too late.

May heaven not look upon us and see us living our lives in pride and materialism like we don't believe heaven awaits us. May the angels not say, "Don't they know? Don't they realize if they partake of Babylon's sins, punishment awaits them? Lord, you've told them the future. Why do they live like they don't know?"

Just like that, the great Babylon is gone.

God's cry to some of us is, "Come out! Come out lest you get caught up in the sins of the world and lest you suffer her punishments."

And remember, you can do all things through Christ who strengthens you. You are strong when you are in Him. You have overcome the satanic devises meant to take you down.

REFLECTION QUESTIONS

(For more extensive study questions visit CathyDickinson.com)

1. What does God calling His people out of Babylon reveal about His heart?

2. Consider God's plea, "Come out of her, my people." Is there any place, activity, relationship or thing that God is calling you out of? (This may include any attitude that the world condones but God would have you come out of.)

3. What two "lest you" statements does God make when He implores His people to come out? (See Revelation 18:4.)

4. Explain what you understand the statement "lest you share in her sins" to mean?

5. Describe what you understand the statement "lest you receive of her plagues" to mean?

6. How have you experienced the truth of God's two "lest you" warnings?

7. Draw one of the scenes as described by John in Revelation chapter 18.

Chapter Twenty-One

IT'S ALL ABOUT THE BRIDEGROOM: REVELATION 19

There was a command toward the end of Revelation 18. "Rejoice over her, O heaven, and you holy apostles and prophets, for God has avenged you on her!" (Revelation 18:20). Revelation 19 opens with heaven's response to that command. One day, if you are a believer, you will be a part of this rejoicing.

> After these things I heard a loud voice of a great multitude in heaven, saying, "Alleluia! 19:1

PRAISE THE LORD

This praise in heaven begins with the word, "Alleluia!" We will say it four times during this time of rejoicing. This same word is translated *Hallelujah* in the Old Testament. In breaking the word down, its meaning is clear. *Allel* or *hallel* means "praise;" *yah* means "Yahweh or Jehovah." Put them together—"praise the Lord!" This is the only time the word is used in the New Testament. There is a lot of praise in the New Testament, but not like we will see woven throughout Revelation 19. There seems to be a sense of celebration and relief.

As a pastor's wife and counselor, I often get to come alongside others, and consequently I am exposed to a lot of pain. And like everyone, I have my own personal pains in life too. I see so much pain. I hate what the world system is doing to people. I hate how the media is deceiving people into buying its lies, tempting people to choose sin. I hate what it's doing to women, tempting us to usurp our husband's authority or lying to us saying we can do it all. Pushing the belief that "I am woman. Hear me roar;" [46] when the cry of a woman's heart is truly, "I'm so weary of trying to do it all." I hate how the world tempts us to want what we don't have both emotionally and materially. I hate how it tries to convince us that our goal in life should be happiness rather than holiness. I hate what the world is doing to men. I hate the visual stuff they are exposed to and can't avoid because it's on billboards and store windows—everywhere. I'm sickened by the effects of abuse and neglect of precious, precious children. I hate it! And I'm going to shout "Alleluia!" when it all goes down. And I'm not going to be alone.

> Salvation and glory and honor and power belong to the Lord our God! 19:1

These attributes have always belonged to the Lord, but the unbelieving world has never gotten that. Now they will. They will see that it's all about Jesus and it always has been. And heaven declares,

For true and righteous are His judgments because He has judged the great harlot who corrupted the earth with her fornication; and He has avenged on her the blood of His servants shed by her." 19:2

TRUE AND RIGHTEOUS

In Revelation 16:7, when the bowls were being poured out upon the earth, the same declaration is heard in heaven "Even so, Lord God Almighty, true and righteous are Your judgments." We can know that when the events of Revelation 18 have unfolded, when Babylon goes down, we are going to declare it's the right thing to judge Babylon. She has corrupted the earth and shed the blood of God's servants. She's got to go down. Left to herself, she will continue in her corruption.

God is the same yesterday, today, and forever, which means true and righteous are His judgments in sending or allowing the trials in our lives. Because He is true and righteous, He does everything right. Perhaps this is written here as a reminder to us when we might doubt His ways. We certainly need reminding.

Again they said, "Alleluia! Her smoke rises up forever and ever!" And the twenty-four elders and the four living creatures fell down and worshiped God who sat on the throne, saying, "Amen! Alleluia!" Then a voice came from the throne, saying, "Praise our God, all you His servants and those who fear Him, both small and great!" 19:3-5

The events of Revelation 18 will provoke the response of "woe" from the earth dwellers. These same events will produce a very different response from us. Our response to this awesome manifestation of His power will be shouts of "Alleluia!" But for now we identify with the saints in heaven, as seen in chapter 6, who cry out, "How long, O Lord?" (Revelation 6:10)

And I heard, as it were, the voice of a great multitude, as the sound of many waters and as the sound of mighty thunderings, saying, "Alleluia! 19:6

In Revelation 5:11, we are reminded that John heard "ten thousand times ten thousand, and thousands of thousands." It's going to be an incredible shout of glorious exclamation.

For the Lord God Omnipotent reigns! 19:6

JESUS OMNIPOTENT

Jesus has always been the Lord God Omnipotent; all-powerful, most powerful, but here He is going to use His power to take His rightful place. God is all-powerful. God is most powerful. There is absolutely nothing God cannot do that He wills to do—nothing.

Man bought the deception that he could be the one in charge, in power. But it is God, and only God, who can claim the title Omnipotent.

Let us be glad and rejoice and give Him glory, for the marriage of the Lamb has come, 19:7

FIVE REASONS TO REJOICE

The first seven verses of Revelation 19 reveal five reasons heaven rejoices:

1. JESUS REIGNS

> "Say among the nations, 'The LORD reigns; the world also is firmly established, it shall not be moved; He shall judge the peoples righteously.'" (Psalm 96:10)

"Salvation and glory and honor and power belong to the Lord our God!" (v. 1). That which the prophets only dreamed of will finally happen.

2. JESUS HAS EXECUTED JUDGMENT

"He has judged the great harlot" (v. 2).

3. JESUS HAS ENDED CORRUPTION

"He has judged the great harlot who corrupted the earth with her fornication" (v. 2). He has ended the rebellion and He has rid the earth of that which corrupted it.

4. JESUS SITS ON THE THRONE

They "worshiped God who sat on the throne" (v. 4). Jesus is in control. God has been reigning on the throne in heaven, but He is about to conquer the thrones of the earth. Now is the time for God's will to be done on earth as it is in heaven; and so the twenty-four elders and the four living creatures are celebrating and they have been praising Jesus throughout the book of Revelation as we have been reading it. We would be wise to do the same.

That makes me think of the song in *The Wizard of Oz* at the death of the wicked witch. "Ding dong the witch is dead. Which old witch? The wicked witch." [47] Why did they celebrate? Because the wicked witch had caused great havoc in their lives and provoked much fear. The wicked witch liked being evil. So did Babylon.

5. THE MARRIAGE OF THE LAMB

This is the culmination of human history—the judgment of the wicked and the wedding of the Lamb and His wife, the church. To fully grasp the significance of this beautiful picture, it is helpful to understand how marriages occurred at the time John was writing this.

THE BETROTHAL

First there was the betrothal or the time when the couple was promised to each other. The prospective groom traveled from his father's house to the home of the prospective bride, paying the purchase price, and thus establishing the marriage covenant. At that point they were engaged.

In the same way, Jesus left His Father's house in heaven and came to the earth, the home of the bride. Acts 20:28 and 1 Corinthians 11:20 tell us Jesus purchased us with His own blood, and we were bought at a price.

When we trust in Jesus to save us, it is in a sense our betrothal to Him. We have said yes to His proposal. We receive the Holy Spirit as our engagement ring, God's guarantee that one day Jesus is going to take us to heaven to be with Him forever. Ephesians 1:13-14 confirms,

> "In Him you also trusted, after you heard the word of truth, the gospel of your salvation; in whom also, having believed, you were sealed with the Holy Spirit of promise, who is the guarantee of our inheritance until the redemption of the purchased possession, to the praise of His glory." (Ephesians 1:13-14)

This is the stage that we who have trusted Him are in right now. We are engaged and the Bridegroom has gone home to His Father's house to prepare a home for us.

JESUS PREPARES THE BRIDE'S HOUSE

After the betrothal, the son returns to his father's house and prepares the living accommodations for his bride-to-be.

Jesus said, "In My Father's house are many mansions; if it were not so, I would have told you. I go to prepare a place for you" (John 14:2). Although the details are unknown to us, Jesus has promised that He is preparing a place for us to spend all of eternity together with Him.

The mansion could be that glorious new body that He has gone to prepare for you, "a building of God, not made with hands, eternal in the heavens" (2 Corinthians 5:1).

JESUS COMES FOR THE BRIDE

At a time determined by the father, the groom fetches the bride to bring her to his father's house. Although the bride was expecting her groom to return for her, she did not know the time of his coming. As a result, the groom's arrival was preceded by a shout, which forewarned the bride to be prepared for his coming. [48]

Jesus said, "But of that day and hour no one knows, not even the angels of heaven, but My Father only. And if I go and prepare a place for you, I will come again and receive you to Myself; that where I am, there you may be also" (Matthew 24:36; John 14:2-3).

We have been guaranteed that Jesus will come back for us. Just as it was for the Hebrew brides in John's day, the Bridegroom (Jesus) will come for His bride (us) at a time the bride does not know and take her back to His home. For us, this is the rapture.

THE BRIDAL CLEANSING

> and His wife has made herself ready." 19:7

Once the bride was aware of her groom's coming, the bride underwent a ritual cleansing prior to the wedding ceremony. [49]

Have you made yourself ready? Have you done that? You who are married, do you remember how you didn't want even a smudge on anything? You examined yourself very thoroughly.

> And to her it was granted to be arrayed in fine linen, clean and bright, for the fine linen is the righteous acts of the saints. 19:8

The word *granted* speaks of something someone does for another. Jesus is going to come up to you and to me and wrap some sort of linen garment around us. He will put "fine linen, clean and white" around you and me. We are told this "fine linen is the righteous acts of the saints." The good works we have done that are righteous are the ones inspired by God and empowered by Him.

Zodhiates says regarding the word *granted*, "The product or result of being justified by God. The rights or claims which one has before God when he becomes His child by faith through Christ." [50]

For me, it's just too holy to imagine. However, I know with certainty that it is going to be the most beautiful bridal gown ever and Jesus is going to wrap it around me and He's going to wrap it around you too.

It must be an amazing sight because the angel once again reminds John not only to take in what he sees but also to write it down. Throughout this revelation, John has to be reminded to write. Picture John standing there in amazement and the angel saying, "John! John! Write!"

THE WEDDING FEAST

> Then he said to me, "Write: 'Blessed are those who are called to the marriage supper of the Lamb!'" 19:9

After the bride and groom had a private wedding ceremony, then there would be a wedding feast lasting about a week with the best supper saved until last. After the marriage supper or the feasting, the groom returns to the guests with his bride and presents her to them. It is at this time that we have come to, in Revelation 19, the time for our Bridegroom to return to the earth with His bride.

I'm not sure about the chronology as it appears here. It is believed this supper, this wedding feast, lasts the whole seven years of the tribulation and that this is the culmination of it, as it leads up to His second coming in a few verses. As much as you can, get into Jesus' heart here in these verses. Heaven says, "Let us be glad and rejoice and give Him glory" (v. 7). Oh, He has so looked forward to this time of celebrating with you and with me. Are you looking forward to that time with Him—the time when you look into your

S.MayFie
6/8/20

Beloved's eyes and realize you will be with Him forever? Are you looking forward to that time when all that He has promised will actually happen?

Consider Jesus' words at the last supper. "Then He said to them, 'With fervent desire I have desired to eat this Passover with you before I suffer'"(Luke 22:15). I've always been taken aback by those words. Jesus desired *fervently*. That Passover meal was so very important to Him. I believe every communion is important to Him as we remember the price He paid so we could be His. Jesus added in verse 16, "I will no longer eat of it until it is fulfilled in the kingdom of God." We are at that time—this supper, here in Revelation 19.

Again, for you who are married, do you remember the anticipation of your wedding day? Everything you did was about that day and then the day finally came. This is it—this is the day. And for many, your wedding day was the best day ever. This wedding day, yet to come as described in Revelation 19, will be your best day that will go on forever and ever.

Someone said to me, "Revelation is one of the greatest love stories ever!" I hope you have discovered that. It's all about our Bridegroom, Jesus, His majesty, and handsomeness, if you will. It's about His love for His bride. It is awe-inspiring that He would even call us His bride. It's about how He removes all obstacles so that we can be together with Him forever. He loves being with us and having us with Him. He loves for us to watch Him do what He does and praise Him for it. Since He loves that, may we do it now.

> And he said to me, "These are the true sayings of God." And I fell at his feet to worship him. But he said to me, "See that you do not do that! I am your fellow servant, and of your brethren who have the testimony of Jesus. Worship God! 19:9-10

Yes, it was wrong and the angel corrected him. But let's give John some grace. We probably cannot fathom how overwhelmed we would be with the praise from heaven and the sight of Jesus wrapping His bride with the wedding garment. Perhaps John even saw himself being arrayed for the marriage supper. Surely he would have been undone! Not surprisingly, John fell on his face to worship the angel, the closest thing there was to Jesus at the time.

> For the testimony of Jesus is the spirit of prophecy." 19:10

PROPHECY IS ABOUT JESUS

All prophecy is about Jesus. It's all about Jesus. John had written earlier about Jesus, "You search the Scriptures, for in them you think you have eternal life; and these are they which testify of Me" (John 5:39). And David had declared of Jesus long before. "Then I said, 'Behold, I come; in the scroll of the book it is written of me'" (Psalm 40:7).

The marriage supper has come. John saw heaven opened.

> Now I saw heaven opened, and behold, a white horse. And He who sat on him was called Faithful and True, 19:11

When the first seal was opened in Revelation 6, we saw someone coming on a white horse. He brought a false peace. He was the Antichrist, the fake Christ. Now heaven opens "and behold, a white horse" and the rider is the real Christ bringing real peace.

He who sat on this horse is called "Faithful and True," faithful to execute all He promised, true to His word, and true to His character. He is the antithesis of the Antichrist who was faithful and true to nothing.

> and in righteousness He judges and makes war. 19:11

Remember the questions in Revelation 13:4? "So they worshiped the dragon who gave authority to the beast; and they worshiped the beast, saying, 'Who is like the beast? Who is able to make war with him?'" Revelation 19:11 is the answer to that question. Jesus is able, so very able to make war with the Beast. Christ's judgments are always executed in righteousness. That's just who He is.

> His eyes were like a flame of fire, 19:12

Meaning Jesus sees through everything; He is blind to nothing, He misses nothing.

> and on His head were many crowns. 19:12

Jesus did not have just one crown; He had many, indicating He is the ultimate ruler.

> He had a name written that no one knew except Himself. 19:12

There is no guessing it. John saw something, but he didn't understand it. It is likely something we will understand about Him one day. It's exciting to think that one day we will realize something new about Him that we have no idea about now.

> He was clothed with a robe dipped in blood, 19:13

It could be the blood of those Jesus was about to conquer. There are scriptures in both the Psalms and the book of Isaiah to support this.

"The righteous shall rejoice when he sees the vengeance; he shall wash his feet in the blood of the wicked" (Psalm 58:10).

"Who is this who comes from Edom, with dyed garments from Bozrah, this One who is glorious in His apparel, traveling in the greatness of His strength?—'I who speak in righteousness, mighty to save.' Why is Your apparel red, and Your garments like one who treads in the winepress? 'I have trodden the winepress alone, and from the peoples no one was with Me. For I have trodden them in My anger, and trampled them in My fury; their blood is sprinkled upon My garments, and I have stained all My robes. For the day of vengeance is in My heart, and the year of My redeemed has come" (Isaiah 63:1-4).

> and His name is called The Word of God. 19:13

Up to this point, John has been overwhelmed with intense images of things to come—some of them horrifying and many of them beautiful. It's likely he would have found a comforting familiarity in the name for Jesus. The Holy Spirit had inspired him to refer to Jesus as "the Word" in his gospel account.

> "In the beginning was the Word, and the Word was with God, and the Word was God." (John 1:1)
>
> "And the Word became flesh and dwelt among us, and we beheld His glory, the glory as of the only begotten of the Father, full of grace and truth." (John 1:14)

Heaven opened and here He comes on a white horse—the very One John proclaimed to be the Word of God. John sees Him. Although He looks so very different than the One whom the world rejected and crucified, John knows the One on the white horse is the very Word of God.

> And the armies in heaven, clothed in fine linen, white and clean, followed Him on white horses. 19:14

COME RIDE WITH JESUS

Jesus is about to make war with the Beast and his armies and we will be with Him when He does.

We saw in Revelation 17:14 that we will be with Him when He conquers. There we are referred to as "called, chosen, and faithful." This bears repeating. Although Jesus will do the conquering, He will invite us to come with Him and witness His victory. He wants us to be with Him when He sets things right. He wants us to watch Him in His power over the world that caused so much harm in our lives. One day He's going to say to you and to me, "Come! Come ride with Me!"

Your horsemanship will be perfect. You'll fearlessly and excitedly hop upon that white horse as it takes off following its Creator. You will be wearing your wedding garment, that fine linen, white and clean. And it will be so nice not to have to think about taking care of our clothes anymore.

> Now out of His mouth goes a sharp sword, that with it He should strike the nations. 19:15

JESUS IS THE (S)WORD

This is the mighty weapon that the enemies of the Lord cannot fight against—His Word. Jesus is the Word of God. He spoke and the worlds came into being. And He can speak and wipe out all those who came to war against Him. He can take a sword and with one swift swipe take them all out.

S. Mayfiel
10/15

Isaiah prophesied about this when he said, "He shall strike the earth with the rod of His mouth, and with the breath of His lips He shall slay the wicked" (Isaiah 11:4).

When He touches the ground, something will happen. Zechariah 14 begins with the words, "Behold, the day of the LORD is coming." Verse 3 continues, "Then the LORD will go forth and fight against those nations, as He fights in the day of battle. And in that day His feet will stand on the Mount of Olives, which faces Jerusalem on the east. And the Mount of Olives shall be split in two, from east to west, making a very large valley; half of the mountain shall move toward the north and half of it toward the south" (Zechariah 14:3-4).

Verse 5 of Zechariah ends with the words, "Thus the LORD my God will come, and all the saints with You."

> And He Himself will rule them with a rod of iron. He Himself treads the winepress of the fierceness and wrath of Almighty God. 19:15

Jesus will tread or trample upon His enemies. Picture the grapes gathering in a winepress to be crushed. Here the nations have gathered together. Chapter 17 tells us demons actually brought them together, but it was all for God's purpose. It was all a setup for Jesus to trample them. Satan gathered his own people together for God to destroy. We saw this in Revelation 14 when we got a preview of this moment. The result was blood spreading for miles and miles.

> "So the angel thrust his sickle into the earth and gathered the vine of the earth, and threw it into the great winepress of the wrath of God. And the winepress was trampled outside the city, and blood came out of the winepress, up to the horses' bridles, for one thousand six hundred furlongs" [180 miles]. (Revelation 14:19-20)

> And He has on His robe and on His thigh a name written: KING OF KINGS AND LORD OF LORDS. 19:16

John saw it. I bet all those on earth saw it too. The kings of the earth had gathered to battle. The lords of the earth, the Antichrist, his False Prophet, and Satan himself had gathered to join the fight. But the KING OF KINGS AND LORD OF LORDS was about to take them down. To those who see themselves as kings, He identifies Himself as "the King of kings." To those who see themselves as lords, He identifies Himself as "the Lord of lords." And in stark and beautiful contrast, He reveals Himself to us as our Bridegroom.

> Then I saw an angel standing in the sun; 19:17

Maybe it was when the sun was darkened and the angel stood there in His magnificent light that John looked and saw. We don't know.

> and he cried with a loud voice, saying to all the birds that fly in the midst of heaven, "Come and gather together for the supper of the great God, that you may eat the flesh of

> kings, the flesh of captains, the flesh of mighty men, the flesh of horses and of those who sit on them, and the flesh of all people, free and slave, both small and great." 19:17-18

THE COMING OF THE SON OF MAN

Revelation 19 contrasts two suppers: the wedding feast of those who belong to Jesus and the great supper of birds of prey as they consume the flesh of those who reject Jesus.

When the angel cried with a loud voice to all the birds, we see the fulfillment of Jesus' words of prophecy. "For as the lightning comes from the east and flashes to the west, so also will the coming of the Son of Man be (stop and picture that for a moment). For wherever the carcass is, there the eagles (or really vultures; birds that prey on dead bodies) will be gathered together" (Matthew 24:27-28).

This is the end of their bodies, but their souls will see no end. God will deal with them in Revelation 20. These words are faithful and true. It's going to happen. We don't know the exact date and we don't know the exact time, but we know it is going to happen just as He said.

> And I saw the beast, the kings of the earth, and their armies, gathered together to make war against Him who sat on the horse and against His army. Then the beast was captured, and with him the false prophet who worked signs in his presence, by which he deceived those who received the mark of the beast and those who worshiped his image. These two were cast alive into the lake of fire burning with brimstone. 19:19-20

HELL'S FIRST RESIDENTS

The Beast (the Antichrist) and the False Prophet were among those who "gathered together to make war against Him who sat on the horse and against His army." They were captured and "cast alive into the lake of fire burning with brimstone." Everyone else who rejected Christ will stand before the throne of God for judgment, but not these two. They have already been judged. They will be the first residents of the lake of fire, or what is probably better known as hell. They will be done—forever doomed. They will have a three-and-a-half-year reign and then it will all be over because Jesus said so.

One point of clarification—all those who die without Jesus are now in what we call hades (or *Sheol*)—a place of suffering, but not like hell. We will see hades emptied and all those who have been in it facing their final judgment in chapter 20 of Revelation.

> And the rest were killed with the sword which proceeded from the mouth of Him who sat on the horse. And all the birds were filled with their flesh. 19:20

Jesus is coming to the earth. One day, He will pull us up from the earth in the rapture. In the second coming, He will take us back to the earth with Him. He will take down the false religious system. He will take down the false commercial system that has corrupted the world. And we will respond with a cry of "Alleluia! For the Lord God Omnipotent reigns! Let us be glad and rejoice and give Him glory, for the marriage of the Lamb has come, and His wife has made herself ready" (vv. 6-7).

CLOSING THOUGHTS

Dale and I have been hit hard with some stuff lately. I found myself texting a friend this morning, saying, "I've got to go. I'm working on Revelation 19. It's about the King of kings and the Lord of lords coming to put an end to this messed up world. I think I'm in an especially good place to rejoice in that right now." As soon as I hit send, I was so very convicted.

Is that why I will rejoice when Jesus comes—just because the hard times will be over? Is that all He is to me—a Savior who is better than a hurting, painful world? Is that all He is to you—a God who is better than the bad parts of life? Is that the only time you really look forward to His coming—to get you out of this life when it's painful?

As fast as I could, I texted back, "But there's never ever a time when I wouldn't want Him to come, because He's better than the best in this life."

And the most amazing thing happened. The weight I was feeling from being hammered with trials was lifted—immediately lifted.

I followed up with a text that said, "I'm smiling right now. I can feel His strength."

She wrote back, "That's pretty special."

"You're 3,000 miles away," I replied, "yet you just got to watch God work. There's power in the choice to praise. The minute I said 'He is better than the best,' the heaviness lifted."

COME AWAY

I was recently listening to a song of Sherri Youngward's titled, "Come Away," and there's a line in the song that goes, "Come in from the cold; leave the war outside." [51] I found myself asking, "How do I do that? How do I leave the war outside?" The answer is praise. God inhabits the praises of His people. It's all about our love for Jesus. It's all about the Bridegroom.

The great harlot who has corrupted the world will be defeated. There is a glorious wedding day awaiting you and me. We get to ride with the King of kings and Lord of lords as He establishes His kingdom. The command to us is, "Rejoice! Shout alleluia! Praise the Lord!" Whatever you and I have faced, are facing, or will face while we sojourn on this earth, one day, it's all going to be best—not better. It won't be just better than what it is now, even when it's all good. But it is going to be best. It's going to be exceedingly abundantly above all that you and I could ask or imagine.

We didn't get to witness firsthand the fulfillment of the first 300 or so prophecies about Jesus' first coming. We are just a product of them. But all the rest of the prophecies that were not fulfilled in the first coming, we get to be a part of in His second coming. We get to be there when they are fulfilled. We *are* the bride of the Bridegroom.

How do you view the events exposed in chapter 19? God says they are faithful and true. They are going to happen. You and I are going to respond by saying, "Alleluia!" at least four times. So let's plan on saying it a lot now—let's plan on saying it forever.

Most people would say they can endure just about anything if they know there will be an end to it. God promises an end to all tears and pain. AND He promises a glorious, best of best forever and ever.

REFLECTION QUESTIONS

(For more extensive study questions visit CathyDickinson.com)

1. Verses 1-7 reveal five reasons heaven has to rejoice. What are they?

a. Salvation, glory, honor and power belong to the Lord

b. True and righteous are His judgments

c. God is omnipotent

d The marriage of the Lamb has come

e. ① He reigns ② He has executed judgment ③ He ends corruption ④ He sits on the throne ⑤ the marriage of the Lamb

2. Consider the thought that Revelation is one of the greatest love stories ever written. How have you personally discovered this to be true? Only Jesus would take me as a sinner, die for me and prepare a place for me eternally. He provides his Holy Spirit and His word to guide me and He speaks to me and listens in prayer

3. Revelation 19:7 says, "His wife has made herself ready." How would you describe this in practical and applicable terms? We must know Him - His word and prayer. Show obedience through living life and doing what his word says.

4. How does this challenge you in your current state of readiness?

He > me. Am I living for the Lord and reflecting who He is? Am I a good light??

5. Jesus Himself is going to wrap you in your bridal garment of fine linen, clean and white. The sight of this was so overwhelming to John that he fell on his face and worshiped the angel (an error, but an understandable one). Take some time to imagine this and allow the Lord to overwhelm you. Write a declaration of praise and thanksgiving.

Thank you Lord for cleansing me and bringing me home. I am so weary of our distracting world. I long to rest in your presence and be still before your perfection

6. Verse 15 says that Jesus will strike the nations with a sharp sword out of His mouth. What does this mean? The sword is Jesus, it is the Word of God. He speaks things into existence and he can also remove them by speaking. Demons brought them (worldly) together for God's purposes - God will wipe away enemies

7. How does this minister to you regarding the power that we have in God's Word to prevail against the enemy or our own flesh?

The Lord preserves and protects through His Word if I choose to listen, obey, and follow Him. He does the work, I must obey and submit to His perfect leading.

8. What comes predominately to mind when you think about Jesus coming again—relief or rejoicing? How has this chapter affected your perspective of His return?

Both - relief because this world is so oppressive and dark and evil - it upsets me. Rejoicing because we will be free of darkness and will enter light and beauty

9. When Jesus returns, you will be riding with the King of kings and Lord of lords to establish His kingdom. Take some time to rejoice, shout alleluia, and praise the Lord (out loud if possible).

Peace, perfect protection, no worries or fears - surrounded by love, warmth and goodness forever - pastoral peace not fast paced destruction and pain

10. Draw one of the scenes as described by John in Revelation chapter 19.

Chapter Twenty-Two

THE THOUSAND-YEAR ERA: REVELATION 20

Whereas Revelation 19 covered a very short span of time, chapter 20 covers one thousand years; but that's relatively brief compared to chapters 21 and 22, since there will be no end. The events of chapter 20, when compared to eternity, are merely seconds.

If given the choice, we would probably choose to skip this part of history and move right into eternity in heaven. But God has other plans; throughout Scripture He is excited about those plans. If He's excited, we should be excited too.

Chapter 19 concluded with two of the most evil villains being defeated and thrown into the lake of fire, hell. They are the only ones who will be thrown in alive. It seems like there should be some significance in that, but I don't know what it is. Apparently their lives aren't worth judgment.

> Then I saw an angel coming down from heaven, having the key to the bottomless pit and a great chain in his hand. 20:1

THE BOTTOMLESS PIT

We've seen the bottomless pit mentioned other times in Revelation. Chapter 9:1-3 told us that an angel was given the key to open the bottomless pit and smoke and locusts (probably demons) came out. We saw in Revelation 11:7 that the Beast ascended out of the bottomless pit.

Peter wrote, "God did not spare the angels who sinned, but cast them down to hell (not hell like their final destination, but some sort of holding place) and delivered them into chains of darkness, to be reserved for judgment" (2 Peter 2:4).

The angel in Revelation 20 not only had a key, but he had a great chain in his hand.

> He laid hold of the dragon, that serpent of old, who is the Devil and Satan, and bound him for a thousand years; 20:2

BOUND FOR 1,000 YEARS

It is noteworthy that there's no account of a battle here in Revelation 20. It doesn't even take God's direct power to cast him into the bottomless pit; instead God delegated it to an angel. It's important to remember that Satan is not God's counterpart. Satan is a created being. He's simply a fallen angel. Therefore one of God's angels has the power to pick him up and cast him into the bottomless pit to join the Antichrist and the False Prophet.

In Mark 5 we read about the man who was possessed by a number of demons and no one could bind him, not even with shackles and chains. He pulled the chains apart and broke the shackles into pieces. This man, empowered by demons, could not be bound by mere man with chains and shackles, yet this angel was able to bind Satan and keep him bound until God was ready to let him go. That made me think of movies where someone is tied up and they eventually figure out how to get untied. Satan will have a thousand years and he still won't be able to figure out how to get loose from God's great chain.

We would be wise to remember that Satan is "seeking whom he may devour" (1 Peter 5:8). In our own strength, we are no match for him. But when we lean on the power of God, Satan is a defeated foe.

and he cast him into the bottomless pit, and shut him up, and set a seal on him, 20:3

SATAN SHUT UP AND SEALED

Consider God's power to maintain that seal over the bottomless pit. I thought of another seal that Satan is powerless to break and it made me smile—and rejoice. We talked about the seal of the Holy Spirit that God places on us when we believe in Jesus. That seal cannot be broken either. Satan may be able to break through into a lot of places in our lives (because we let him), but he can't break the seal of the Holy Spirit that God places on the believer—it is God's guarantee to get us to heaven. Alleluia!

so that he should deceive the nations no more till the 1,000 years were finished. 20:3

DECEIVED NO MORE

The word most often used to describe Satan's actions is that he *deceives*. When he is bound he will no longer be able to deceive the nations. The world has to be rid of Satan for Jesus to establish His kingdom. Then righteousness shall reign, not the prince of the power of the air. Things will be different. When Satan is bound he won't be around to tempt, lie, deceive, blind minds, give thorns in the flesh, work disobedience, hinder, or devour.

Remember the promise in Revelation 1:3 of blessing for those who read and heed the words of this book? Just imagine what it would be like if we didn't have God's Word.

Imagine not knowing upfront that Satan loses. What if God didn't promise that? What if you didn't know that for sure? But we can shout, "Alleluia!" now because we know that Satan is a defeated foe. Imagine having peace and joy even in the hardest times; that God can take our trials and turn them for good, that God can keep us from falling while we are in them, that we can learn patience and character in them because we won't be deceived any more.

When we return with Jesus to set up this kingdom, we are coming in our wedding gowns that cover brand new bodies—bodies free from sin and free from being deceived.

> But after these things he must be released for a little while. 20:3

Satan is not quite done, but he's done as far as we are concerned. Alleluia! Yet some people who believe we are already in the millennial kingdom today, believe that Satan was bound when Jesus died on the cross. If he is bound, he is bound with a very, very long chain.

> And I saw thrones, and they sat on them, and judgment was committed to them. 20:4

KINGS AND PRIESTS

We saw earlier in Revelation that the saints will sit with Jesus on His throne. "To him who overcomes I will grant to sit with Me on My throne, as I also overcame and sat down with My Father on His throne" (Revelation 3:21).

As I studied this it got more exciting. In Revelation 5, we have the account of Jesus taking the scroll and then the four living creatures and the twenty-four elders falling down before the Lamb and "they sang a new song" (vv. 8-9). Part of what they praised Him for is in verse 10. "And have made us kings and priests to our God; and we shall reign on the earth."

Does this mean only the four living creatures and twenty-four elders? We can go back to the very beginning of Revelation. "... and from Jesus Christ, the faithful witness, the first-born from the dead, and the ruler over the kings of the earth. To Him who loved us and washed us from our sins in His own blood, and has made us kings and priests to His God and Father, to Him be glory and dominion forever and ever. Amen" (Revelation 1:5-6).

The priest was the mediator between God and the people. The priests brought people to God. That's going to be the good part, being the perfect witness and bringing people to Jesus. But even though we will witness perfectly, always remember it's the Holy Spirit who does the convincing, not our perfect words. We won't have to make decisions. We will just be carrying out the Lord's decisions. Have you been washed from your sins by the blood of Jesus? Then He has made you a king and a priest.

> Then I saw the souls of those who had been beheaded for their witness to Jesus and for the word of God, who had not worshiped the beast or his image, and had not received his mark on their foreheads or on their hands. And they lived and reigned with Christ for a thousand years. 20:4

TRIBULATION SAINTS REIGN TOO

John sees those who had been martyred during the tribulation reigning with Christ. All believers who have died before the time of the second coming of Jesus will rule and reign with Him.

> "To him who overcomes I will grant to sit with Me on My throne, as I also overcame and sat down with My Father on His throne. And have made us kings and priests to our God; and we shall reign on the earth." (Revelation 3:21; 5:10).

Who will we rule and reign over? Believers who survived the great tribulation. They will move into the kingdom in their mortal bodies in the same physical condition you and I are in now.

THE THOUSAND-YEAR REIGN

We can't help but notice that Revelation 20 tells us nothing about these thousand years except that Christ and the saints will rule and reign. However, the Bible is full of references to this time. From these references we can piece together what this time will be like.

> "The wolf also shall dwell with the lamb, the leopard shall lie down with the young goat, the calf and the young lion and the fatling together; and a little child shall lead them. The cow and the bear shall graze; their young ones shall lie down together; and the lion shall eat straw like the ox. The nursing child shall play by the cobra's hole, and the weaned child shall put his hand in the viper's den." (Isaiah 11:6-8)

> "No more shall an infant from there live but a few days, nor an old man who has not fulfilled his days; for the child shall die one hundred years old, but the sinner being one hundred years old shall be accursed. They shall build houses and inhabit them; they shall plant vineyards and eat their fruit. They shall not build and another inhabit; they shall not plant and another eat; for as the days of a tree, so shall be the days of My people, and My elect shall long enjoy the work of their hands. They shall not labor in vain, nor bring forth children for trouble; for they shall be the descendants of the blessed of the LORD, and their offspring with them." (Isaiah 65:20-23)

A PERFECT EARTH

From these scriptures we can ascertain that there will be complete safety, no sickness; death will be a rarity. There will be fairness and peace. There will be no punishment for crime, because there will be no crime. It will be a perfect earth, ruled perfectly by our perfect Lord and His perfected people, but we will not be ruling over perfect people. We will be ruling over people like you and I are now—believers, but still in the flesh. They will have children who have the same free choice as our children do—to give their lives to Jesus or not.

EVERYONE WILL KNOW JESUS

Another thing that will be different is this: "They shall not hurt nor destroy in all My holy mountain, for the earth shall be full of the knowledge of the LORD as the waters cover the sea" (Isaiah 11:9).

People will know all about Jesus' holiness and His goodness. They will know Him as King, but not all will know Him as Savior. I'm guessing they won't know His mercy and grace like we do since people will not be allowed to harm others, so in a way, the evil intents of their hearts will be controlled. That makes me think of the little boy who was misbehaving in church and was told to sit down. He sat down and said to his mother, "I may be sitting down on the outside, but I'm standing up on the inside!" That's a pretty good description of what it will be like for some of the people.

Most Christians who come out of the tribulation will be Jews. Their dream wasn't to be with Jesus, it was to live in a restored Israel. That was their dream. That's what they thought would make them happy. Remember, the disciples continually wondered when Jesus was going to set up the kingdom. Even after Jesus rose from the dead, one of the very last questions the disciples asked Him was, "Lord, will You at this time restore the kingdom to Israel?" (Acts 1:6). This millennium is God's answer to Israel's desire. The millennial kingdom will be centered on Israel's dream city, the city of Jerusalem.

NOT EVERYONE WILL LOVE JESUS

The Jehovah's Witnesses have picked up on man's desire for the perfect kingdom. If you have read one of their booklets then you know that they present a new world where peace and righteousness reign; a world where there is no strife and everything is right. But there's no Jesus in their world. He's in heaven. And sadly, they are okay with that.

I tell them, "I don't want your perfect world. I want to be with Jesus." I want to be with Jesus more than I want a perfect world because I love Jesus more.

There will be many people living in the millennial kingdom who will be serving Jesus, but who won't love Him. They will be in it for the benefits. That's a challenge to us. Do you love Jesus more than the benefits that come with living a Christian life?

Or maybe you think that happiness is a perfect kingdom. If certain things would change, then you would be happy. The millennium is God's answer to that lie. God is going to give man a chance to see that living with that kind of thinking is a lie. The millennial kingdom will be perfect, yet those who do not love Jesus will find a perfect world does nothing to heal a longing soul. A perfect world does nothing to change the core of who you are. Only a life surrendered to Jesus can make wrongs right. Only being in love with Him satisfies the longings of our soul. We must be born again and we must abide in Him. We've got to love Him!

Are you in love with Jesus? Or did you ask Him into your life only for the benefits? Sure, no more tears and sorrows is going to be really nice, but if you're longing for those things more than you are for Jesus, may you be challenged not to settle for anything else but a love relationship with Him, because anything short of that makes this life very unsatisfying.

During the millennial reign, you and I we will be beyond Satan's temptations. Our eternity has been settled. We won't have to move into the millennium wondering whether we will choose Jesus or not. We already have. As Paul wrote to the Thessalonians, "Therefore comfort one another with these words" (1 Thessalonians 4:18). What a comfort to know that one day we will be totally and completely free from Satan's deception.

> But the rest of the dead did not live again until the thousand years were finished. This is the first resurrection. 20:5

Those who live and reign with Christ are part of the first resurrection. The first resurrection includes all those who have been raptured or died in Christ up to the last minute of the tribulation, while "the rest of the dead did not live again until the thousand years were finished." This would include those who die during the thousand-year reign.

> Blessed and holy is he who has part in the first resurrection. Over such the second death has no power, but they shall be priests of God and of Christ, and shall reign with Him a thousand years. 20:6

Those who are part of the first resurrection are "blessed and holy." That's for sure. And it gives us three reasons why:

1. THE SECOND DEATH HAS NO POWER OVER US.

What is the second death? Hebrews 9:27 gives us the answer. "And as it is appointed for men to die once, but after this the judgment." The death of the body is the first death. Every person that ever lived (except Enoch and Elijah as far as we know) will experience the first death. Those who face the judgment are all those not found in the Book of Life. They will experience the second death—eternal death. As the saying goes, "Born once, die twice. Born twice, die once." In John 3:5 Jesus said that to inherit eternal life we must be "born of water" (normal birth) "and of the Spirit" (born again by receiving Jesus as Savior)—hence "born twice, die once." Blessed are those who are born twice and have died their first and only death prior to Jesus' second coming—they have their part in the first resurrection.

2. THEY SHALL BE PRIESTS OF GOD AND OF CHRIST.

First Peter 2:9 tells us, "You are a chosen generation, a royal priesthood, a holy nation, His own special people, that you may proclaim the praises of Him who called you out of darkness into His marvelous light."

> "The saints of the Most High shall receive the kingdom, and possess the kingdom forever, even forever and ever. The kingdom and dominion, and the greatness of the kingdoms under the whole heaven, shall be given to the people, the saints of the Most High. His kingdom is an everlasting kingdom, and all dominions shall serve and obey Him. (Daniel 7:18, 27)

3. THEY SHALL REIGN WITH JESUS A THOUSAND YEARS.

"There shall be no night there: They need no lamp nor light of the sun, for the Lord God gives them light. And they shall reign forever and ever" (Revelation 22:5).

This should clear up any doubt that you, as a believer, will rule and reign with Jesus during the millennium.

> Now when the thousand years have expired, Satan will be released from his prison and will go out to deceive the nations which are in the four corners of the earth, Gog and Magog, to gather them together to battle, whose number is as the sand of the sea. 20:7-8

ONE LAST LIE

This is a real shift in focus from the believer to Satan, the one we thought we were done with, as he comes back on the scene, but only for one more time. People all over the earth will be involved in this deception—not those who have come to a saving faith in Jesus Christ, but all those who have not.

ONE LAST BATTLE

> They went up on the breadth of the earth and surrounded the camp of the saints and the beloved city. 20:9

This beloved city is Jerusalem. We saw how Satan gathered the kings of the earth and deceived them in coming together for the battle of Armageddon in Revelation chapters 16 and 19. God used Satan to gather people for destruction then, and God does it again after the thousand-year reign. Satan will gather together people who do not love Jesus to war against the saints. And once again God destroys them.

MAN'S SIN NATURE

Satan had been bound for a thousand years, yet there were still people who did not receive Jesus as their Savior, people who were not born twice. We blame so much on Satan, but here we can see that man can reject Jesus all by himself because man has a sin nature. During the millennium, man will still be born a sinner.

I love the saying, "We are not sinners because we sin. We sin because we are sinners." No one has to teach a child to sin. You who have children, did you sit down with them when they were two and have this conversation? "Okay, Mommy is going to take you to a crowded store. We are going to walk by the candy counter. When you see the candy, I want you to ask for some. Mommy is going to tell you no. When I do, I want you to throw yourself down on the ground and start screaming and kicking your feet. Now, let's practice that." Of course not! It's just their nature. They were born that way. Don't you just hate it when you see one of your bad traits in your children and you know you passed it down to them? Well, you passed sin down too. It's not a perfect environment that keeps man from wanting to sin. Sin is hereditary. It goes all the way back to our parents, Adam and Eve, and it has not skipped one of us.

> And fire came down from God out of heaven and devoured them. 20:9

What happens when Satan comes at God's people with everything he's got? Will a world war ensue? Will there be a great battle? Nope. Satan and his army didn't even have a chance to put up a fight because God's fire came out of heaven and devoured them.

> The devil, who deceived them, was cast into the lake of fire and brimstone where the beast and the false prophet are. And they will be tormented day and night forever and ever. 20:10

FOREVER HELL

Finally. These words translated as *forever and ever* mean for "all eternity," "never ending," always—always—always, no stopping. This is the same word that describes God who lives *forever and ever* and it's the same word that describes the life God has promised to those who believe in His Son—*forever* with Him.

The lake of fire is what we know as hell. It is, as described here, a place of forever torment, which means "afflicted with pain, harassed, tortured." For the inhabitants of the lake of fire, this torment will go on forever and ever.

Jesus made it possible for those who believe in Him to experience heaven forever and ever. And Jesus, more than anyone else in the Bible, warned and warned and warned that those who did not believe in Him would experience hell forever and ever.

Five times Jesus used the phrase "weeping and gnashing of teeth" to describe hell. Weeping is beating the chest wailing. Gnashing of teeth is a grinding of teeth because of pain or anger. Some people grind their teeth at night from stress. There will be endless chest beating, endless wailing, endless stress and endless teeth gnashing in hell.

Satan is thrown into the lake of fire "where the Beast and the False Prophet are." They are still there and have been there since they were thrown in a thousand years before. This verse reminds us that even though they've been there a thousand years, their torment has only just begun. They will be tormented day and night forever and ever.

FOREVER GONE

John saw Satan thrown into the bottomless pit. He saw thrones and those who will reign on them. He saw Satan released and men deceived by him again. He saw God save His people and His beloved city. He saw Satan finally exiled to the lake of fire forever, though not destroyed. He will never ever be destroyed. He will be tormented forever. But as far as you, I, and all other believers are concerned, Satan will be gone, out of the picture, out of our lives.

> Then I saw a great white throne and Him who sat on it, from whose face the earth and the heaven fled away. And there was found no place for them. 20:11

JUDGMENT

Who is on the throne doing the judging? It's Jesus. He certainly has earned the right. We saw that He has the right to open the scrolls of judgment in Revelation 5 and He has the right to judge all who have rejected Him.

Seeing this wouldn't have come as a surprise to John because he had the privilege of declaring, "For the Father judges no one, but has committed all judgment to the Son, that all should honor the Son just as they honor the Father. He who does not honor the Son does not honor the Father who sent Him" (John 5:22-23).

Paul wrote about two very different judgments. One for the believer and one for the unbeliever.

"For we must all appear before the judgment seat of Christ, that each one may receive the things done in the body, according to what he has done, whether good or bad" (2 Corinthians 5:10). The believer will stand before Him and have his or her good works judged, whether they are of value to the Lord or not. We stand to be judged not for the purpose of punishment, but for the purpose of reward. We will be judged for the good done in our bodies while we lived on this earth.

The other judgment is for the unbeliever for the bad they have done. Our bad, all of it, has been forgiven. So here it is—the time when all who did not honor the Son will stand before Him and be judged.

> And I saw the dead, small and great, standing before God, 20:12

PERFECTLY FAIR

We in the United States have a relatively good sense of fairness, because for the most part, the rich face the same judgment for a crime as the poor. Though even in America, we see a lot of inequities. This judgment that the dead will face will be perfectly equitable. The great will have no advantage over the poor.

We saw this in the story Jesus told about Lazarus and the rich man in Luke 16:19-27. Lazarus went to paradise; the rich man went to torment. Everyone will be judged fairly, equally, and according to the very same standard—God's holiness.

They are "standing before God." Isn't that an absolutely terrifying statement? I wonder if any of them will still have excuses or dare to even try to explain why they did what they did.

> and books were opened. And another book was opened, which is the Book of Life. And the dead were judged according to their works, by the things which were written in the books. 20:12

The "books" were opened—books—plural. One could be the book of the law, putting before these great and small people what their consciences already know—God's law—if you violate one, you have violated them all.

The Book of Life contains all of the names of those who are saved. If you have trusted in Jesus for your salvation, then your name is written in the Book of Life, simply and only because you belong to Jesus.

> The sea gave up the dead who were in it, and Death and Hades delivered up the dead who were in them. 20:13

THE SECOND RESURRECTION

Verse 5 tells us the rest of the dead who still remained in their graves until after the thousand years have ended will be resurrected. All of these who are resurrected after the millennium are unbelievers.

The dead were pulled up from wherever they were buried, even the sea. God has no problem finding us or putting us back together, cremated or not. These souls have been dead at least a thousand years, so there's not much left of any of them, no matter where or how they were buried. Just recently, all the super forces and highest government intelligence couldn't locate Malaysia Flight 370, let alone the bodies of those who were in the airplane. But God knows their precise location and God will pull each and every one of them up one day—either in the rapture to be rewarded or in the second resurrection to be judged.

> And they were judged, each one according to his works. 20:13

Just think about that day and having to stand before Holy God and to have one's sins revealed before Him and before everyone else who will be there. It's impossible to imagine how horrible that would be. We won't have to worry about that—no one who belongs to Jesus will. The video of your life won't be shown. You can have confidence in this absolutely wonderful fact, because God says that all of your trespasses have been wiped out.

> "And you, being dead in your trespasses and the uncircumcision of your flesh, He has made alive together with Him, having forgiven you all trespasses, having wiped out the handwriting of requirements that was against us, which was contrary to us. And He has taken it out of the way, having nailed it to the cross" (Colossians 2:13-14).

PAID IN FULL

Before merchants could electronically keep track of charges made by customers, especially in the days of small towns, people would charge their purchases at the general store. The clerk would record the customer's purchases on a sheet and keep track of the debt owed. Sometimes when a debt was unusually large, the debt sheet would be nailed to the outside of the store. But once it was paid, it would be stamped "Paid in Full," acknowledging that the debt was cleared and the debtor free.

You who have been born twice had one of those debt sheets. It's been stamped "Paid in Full." There will be no standing before the Judge for payment. That's a glorious thing. Do you appreciate the enormity of it? Have you thanked God for it lately?

> Then Death and Hades were cast into the lake of fire. This is the second death. 20:14

SECOND DEATH

For these dead souls, their debts are not paid. They will stand before the Judge and be judged according to what they have done. This is the second death because they rejected Jesus as Savior. This judgment is to determine the punishment for their sins. All unbelievers will not experience the same degree of punishment. The Bible says that those who harm little children or widows are in for greater punishment (Luke 17:2, Mark 12:40).

Here are other examples of unbelievers who will suffer a greater degree of punishment:

> "Then He (Jesus) said to them in His teaching, 'Beware of the scribes, who desire to go around in long robes, love greetings in the marketplaces, the best seats in the synagogues, and the best places at feasts, who devour widows' houses, and for a pretense make long prayers. These will receive greater condemnation.'" (Mark 12:38-40)

> "Of how much worse punishment, do you suppose, will he be thought worthy who has trampled the Son of God underfoot, counted the blood of the covenant by which he was sanctified a common thing, and insulted the Spirit of grace?" (Hebrews 10:29)

> And anyone not found written in the Book of Life was cast into the lake of fire. 20:15

Neither judgment—the judgment for the believer nor the judgment for the unbeliever—is for the purpose of deciding their destination for eternity. For the believer, it is for the purpose of determining rewards; for the unbeliever it is for the purpose of determining punishments. The only criteria for deciding our eternal destination is putting your faith in Jesus or not, and this John knew very well.

> "And this is the testimony: that God has given us eternal life, and this life is in His Son. He who has the Son has life; he who does not have the Son of God does not have life." (1 John 5:11-12)

CLOSING THOUGHTS

God measures sin and He punishes accordingly. When we get to chapter 22 of Revelation, we will see that God also measures good works and He rewards accordingly. Nothing gets by Him. Nothing goes unpunished that is bad and nothing goes unrewarded that is good.

Bask in these words of Daniel:

> "I watched till thrones were put in place, and the Ancient of Days was seated; His garment was white as snow, and the hair of His head was like pure wool. His throne was a fiery flame, its wheels a burning fire; a fiery stream issued and came forth from before Him. A thousand thousands ministered to Him; ten thousand times

ten thousand stood before Him. The court was seated, and the books were opened. I watched then because of the sound of the pompous words which the horn was speaking; I watched till the beast was slain, and its body destroyed and given to the burning flame. As for the rest of the beasts, they had their dominion taken away, yet their lives were prolonged for a season and a time. I was watching in the night visions, and behold, One like the Son of Man, coming with the clouds of heaven! He came to the Ancient of Days, and they brought Him near before Him. Then to Him was given dominion and glory and a kingdom, that all peoples, nations, and languages should serve Him. His dominion is an everlasting dominion, which shall not pass away, and His kingdom the one which shall not be destroyed." (Daniel 7:9-14)

REFLECTION QUESTIONS

(For more extensive study questions visit CathyDickinson.com)

1. This chapter accounts Satan's absolute defeat. How does knowing this minister to you?

I am grateful that my perfect father takes care of all the wrongs and will remove evil from the earth

2. Explain this statement: Jesus has "made us kings and priests to our God."

Our true purpose can be completed, ruling and serving Jesus, without distractions All will serve and obey Him.

3. List what it will be like during the one-thousand-year reign? Harmony

No tears, All will obey Jesus and know him as King, but not all will know Him as Savior. There will be no crime, yet not everyone will love Jesus, Peace, unity

4. Briefly explain the great white throne judgment.

Jesus will judge those who rejected Him. The great white throne is for those who are not believers/Believers whose good works will be judged for the purpose of a reward, our bad deeds are forgiven in Christ. - bema seat.

5. How has this study of Revelation chapter 20 affected your heart for unbelievers?

I pray for my lost family, friends, and students who are not saved. I love my son in action and point my students to the Lord at school

6. All unbelievers will one day be cast into the lake of fire. Ask the Lord to put someone on your heart that needs a saving relationship with Jesus; then ask Him how He wants to use you in their life. (If you need more room to write, use the notes section on page 312.)

John - unconditional patience and love

Sister, nephews, and niece - glorify the Lord whenever possible.

Websters' kids, brother, his girlfriend

7. Draw one of the scenes as described by John in Revelation chapter 20.

Notes

Chapter Twenty-Three

JESUS MAKES ALL THINGS NEW: REVELATION 21

Revelation 20 described the culmination of what God, in His holiness, must do with sinful man who refuses to admit his need for cleansing and never turns to Jesus.

In Revelation 21 we begin to see the culmination of what God promises to do with believers, those whom God calls overcomers. The last two chapters of Revelation are just a sampling of what life will be like from this point on. God tells us about heaven—who will be there, who won't be there, and what it will be like.

> Now I saw a new heaven and a new earth, for the first heaven and the first earth had passed away. 21:1

Chapter 20 ends with the words, "anyone not found written in the Book of Life was cast into the lake of fire." Revelation 21 begins with the word "Now." Now sin has been judged. Now it's family time, just the King and His bride forever and ever.

A NEW HEAVEN AND EARTH

There are three parts to the heavens. The first heaven is the atmosphere above us, which includes the sky and the clouds. The second heaven includes the stars, the sun, and the moon. The third heaven is our eternal dwelling place with Jesus. The first two will be gone, leaving the third heaven which is our eternal dwelling place with Jesus.

Jesus not only created the heavens and the earth, but we are told in Hebrews 1:3 that He upholds "all things by the word of His power." Jesus is not only the Creator; He is the Sustainer. He holds it all together.

I'm not a scientist, but my understanding is that everything is made up of atoms, which have positively-charged protons inside that repel each other like the positive ends of magnets when you try to put them together. Scientists can't figure out what holds atoms together, so they have given it the name "atomic glue." God's Word tells us, "He is before all things, and in him all things hold together" (Colossians 1:17 NIV). The word *hold* used here not only means that Jesus is holding it all together, but there is also a sense of "carrying it along." Jesus created the atom and is Himself the glue that keeps it intact. Jesus holds heaven and earth together as He is carrying it all along to His purposed end. Perhaps the "passing away" of the current heavens and earth will be the result of Jesus simply letting go.

Isaiah prophesied, "All the host of heaven shall be dissolved, and the heavens shall be rolled up like a scroll" (Isaiah 34:4).

Also there was no more sea. 20:1

The first thing John didn't see is probably the thing I have the most trouble with when I think of what heaven will be like. I love the ocean. My husband says I have salt water in my veins. So when I read, "there was no sea," I've got to admit that I lose a little of my excitement. Maybe John did too, just a little, as that was the first thing he noticed was missing—being a fisherman and all.

As I read about the ocean, commentators reminded me that its purpose is to provide salt, fish, sea life and more. Today, we need those things. Additionally, the sea represented torrential storms, untamable waves, and unpredictable tsunamis. But what about the way it just seems to calm me? Right away I get excited thinking, *There will be something else to calm me—or better yet, I won't need to be calmed anymore!* We have the tendency to think heaven is going to be like earth, only better. But it is not going to be a refurbished heaven and earth. It's going to be all new.

Then I, John, saw the holy city, New Jerusalem, coming down out of heaven from God, prepared as a bride adorned for her husband. 2:2

As we think about what Jerusalem looks like today, what better way to describe the care spent in making this new holy city than to compare it to a bride adorned for her husband. Most of us would agree we can't think of an event where more time and more care is spent in preparation and adorning. There is a particular beauty about a bride as there must have been a particular beauty about what John saw with the New Jerusalem for him to choose such a comparison.

And I heard a loud voice from heaven saying, "Behold, the tabernacle of God is with men, and He will dwell with them, and they shall be His people. God Himself will be with them and be their God. 21:3

This "New Jerusalem" was prepared by the Creator Himself, paying perfect attention to every detail—making the city beautiful not only for us, but for Himself—He Himself will dwell there. It's no wonder the city shone with such splendor! We will get to be in the physical presence of God. God will be right there with you and with me. That has been God's desire from the very beginning—to be with you. He's excited about this. Are you? Then Revelation 21:4 lists four things that won't be in heaven.

And God will wipe away every tear from their eyes; 21:4

1. NO MORE TEARS

I have a Precious Moments figurine titled, "No Tears Past the Gate." The Precious Moments character is separated from an angel by a gate labeled "Heaven." In front of the gate is a bucket labeled "Old Hankies." The idea is indeed precious. On this side of the gate there will be tears. Yet as we enter heaven, we can throw our hankies in the bucket. We will never need them again. On this side of the gate, we can expect to shed tears. But on the other side of the gate, we can just as certainly expect that there will be no more tears.

there shall be no more death, 21:4

2. NO DEATH

We are further encouraged by these words: "So when this corruptible has put on incorruption, and this mortal has put on immortality, then shall be brought to pass the saying that is written: 'Death is swallowed up in victory. O Death, where is your sting? O Hades, where is your victory?" (1 Corinthians 15:54-55).

Death will be swallowed up. Our bodies will be incorruptible, so there won't be any hint of "perishableness." Each of us are experiencing how corruptible, how perishable our bodies are—those of us who are getting older are experiencing it more. My body is decaying but my spiritual mind is getting better! Isn't it sad that we typically don't long for new bodies until the ones we have start wearing out? We imagine that we'll be happy with a human body like a thirty-year-old in heaven. So if you are twenty now, you don't long for a new body. Our heavenly bodies are going to far excel that of an earthly thirty-year-old.

nor sorrow, nor crying. 21:4

3. NO SORROW

No sorrow, no grief, no regrets, no bad moods, no anger, no heartache, no depression, no stress, no worries, no burdens, no pressures—none of these things. People ask about heaven hoping the things they love and love to do will be there. We don't know specifics, but we know this: if in your new glorified body and perfect heart you still want it, it will be there because there will be no sorrow and no disappointment. You won't cry about it.

When you were a child, maybe your parents said to you, "There will be no crying in this house!" God gives us tears to express our pain. There will be no need to express pain in heaven, because there won't be any! As the song says, "No more crying there...." [52]

When our two grandsons, Gabe and Dylan, were about five years old, I was playing the song with the lyrics "No more crying there." Dylan said to me, "Wait! Grandma, what does that mean?" I said, "There will be no more crying in heaven."

Dylan was quiet for a while and then asked with disappointment, "You mean when I hit Gabe in heaven, he won't cry?" Which means in heaven Dylan can't do anything to make Gabe cry. Not only that, Dylan will be changed so much that he won't want to make Gabe cry. Everyone in heaven will be perfect.

There shall be no more pain, 21:4

4. NO PAIN

No pain of any kind—not emotional, physical, mental—none whatsoever. Nothing will hurt and no one will hurt you. You will live knowing there is no pain waiting for you around the corner because the concept of pain will be totally gone. Maybe you're thinking, *That's all good, but what about now? I'm hurting now. I'm struggling now. I need help now. I need something that is going to get me through what I am going through now.* God sees your need and has answered it. Keep reading. When you get to verse 7, you'll be revived and refreshed.

> for the former things have passed away." 21:4

The ways of earth life will be gone—totally gone.

> Then He who sat on the throne said, "Behold, I make all things new." 21:5

JESUS MAKES ALL THINGS NEW

The word translated *make* is the same word used to describe God creating in Genesis. The book of Genesis begins with, "In the beginning God created the heavens and the earth" (Genesis 1:1). The Genesis account not only tells us of God making heaven and earth, it tells us of God making man. But man messed up and brought corruption into this world. Because of man's sin, God cursed the earth. No longer would earth be paradise; no longer would man be perfect. Instead, man and his world became very defiled. The rest of the Bible tells us of God's dealings with sinful man.

But He who sat on the throne and rules over all declares, "I make all things new." This is the solution to sinful man. Some politicians today make a similar claim promising, "*I* will make all things new." They can promise but they can't make it happen. Only God can make all things new AND perfect, including you and me.

> And He said to me, "Write, for these words are true and faithful." 21:5

Jesus' next word to John is, "Write." "Look, John! I make all things new! Write this down, John." Can't you just see it? John standing there—"Whoa, this is all absolutely incredible!"—probably stunned, extremely stunned and in awe. And the Lord says, "Write." If I were John, I'd probably say, "Write? Oh yeah." It's no wonder that John needed to be reminded of the instruction he received in the beginning of this whole revelation, "Write" (Revelation 1:11, 19).

These words are true and faithful, backed up by the Almighty Creator Holy God. You can stake your life on it, because He has given His.

> And He said to me, "It is done! I am the Alpha and the Omega, the Beginning and the End. 21:6

IT IS DONE!

All evil has been judged and eliminated. Jesus makes an awesome three-word declaration, "It is done!" Heaven probably sighs a big "Phew!"

We can hardly look at these words without being reminded of Jesus' final declaration on the cross, "It is finished!" (John 19:30). At first glance, these two statements appear to mean the same thing but, in fact, they have quite opposite meanings. The words, *It is finished!* translate as "bring to a close," "the last act that completes a process," "an ending." Jesus is declaring an end to the penalty for the sin of the believer, our price had been paid, slavery to sin is ended.

In contrast, *It is done!* translates as "to become," "begin," "arise." Jesus is declaring not an end to sin, but the beginning of sinless existence, the beginning of no tears or sorrows, the beginning of eternity living in the light of His glory. How very like our Jesus, "the Alpha and the Omega," to cover both our beginnings and endings with His goodness. It is sweet to note that both of these declarations are punctuated with an exclamation point. Jesus is excited; therefore, we should be too. When we take communion, we are called to remember what He finished for us on the cross. How much richer our gratitude becomes when we also choose to remember, "It is done!"

> I will give of the fountain of the water of life freely to him who thirsts. He who overcomes shall inherit all things, and I will be his God and he shall be My son. 21:6-7

"Therefore be patient, brethren, until the coming of the Lord" (James 5:7). What's the reason we are to be patient and establish our hearts and remain steadfast? "The coming of the Lord is at hand." Jesus is coming and when He does, He will revive and refresh us with the fountain of the water of life.

James continues, "You also be patient. Establish your hearts, for the coming of the Lord is at hand. Do not grumble against one another, brethren, lest you be condemned. Behold, the Judge is standing at the door!" (James 5:8-9).

PARADISE AWAITS

A few years ago, Dale and I led a couples' retreat to Kauai. One day, a group of us kayaked the Wailua River and hiked to Uluwehi Falls, known to the locals as Secret Falls. After paddling as far as we could toward the falls, we tied our kayaks to nearby branches and headed up the trail. The trail was not marked and it was muddy and slippery. Dale and I, along with twenty other couples, treaded through the mud and slipped on the rocks, not really knowing when we might, or even if we might, reach the falls. Not too long into the hike, the complaining began as we became tired, wounded from slipping, and hungry. I don't know how long we hiked before we suddenly heard the sound of crashing water. We made a turn through the bushes and suddenly we were confronted with one of the most beautiful, picturesque scenes I have ever experienced. In a moment, it all changed. The comments from those in our group went from grumbling to awe as we took in the beauty of the falls, the pool catching the water, and the smell of the flowers blooming all around. The words echoed from one couple to another, "Wow. Oh, wow. I never knew. This is absolutely incredible." In a moment of time, we had forgotten the mud, the pain, and the hunger. It didn't matter. We were in paradise.

> But the cowardly, unbelieving, abominable, murderers, sexually immoral, sorcerers, idolaters, and all liars 21:8

Sadly, we have all been guilty *of* at least some of these sins, but this addresses those whose lives can be described *by* these kinds of sins because they never surrendered their lives to the saving power of Jesus. Jesus warned them during His ministry,

> "Not everyone who says to Me, 'Lord, Lord,' shall enter the kingdom of heaven, but he who does the will of My Father in heaven. Many will say to Me in that day, 'Lord, Lord, have we not prophesied in Your name, cast out demons in Your name, and done many wonders in Your name?' And then I will declare to them, 'I never knew you; depart from Me, you who practice lawlessness!'" (Matthew 7:21-23).

Paul warned us several times in his letters that those who practice these sins would not inherit the kingdom of God. "Do you not know that the unrighteous will not inherit the kingdom of God? Do not be deceived. Neither fornicators, nor idolaters, nor adulterers, nor homosexuals, nor sodomites, nor thieves, nor covetous, nor drunkards, nor revilers, nor extortioners will inherit the kingdom of God" (1 Corinthians 6:9-10).

> shall have their part in the lake which burns with fire and brimstone, which is the second death." 21:8

This is the sad truth.

> Then one of the seven angels who had the seven bowls filled with the seven last plagues came to me and talked with me, saying, "Come, I will show you the bride, the Lamb's wife." 21:9

THE JOYFUL WIFE

There's a story about a bride whose wedding day was a disaster. If anything could go wrong, it did. It began when she dropped her dress in the gutter on the way to the church. Her maid of honor showed up an hour late. Her hair looked terrible. She tripped on her way down the aisle. And the cake top fell off. Ten years later the family got together to watch the video of the wedding. Along with the rest of the family, the bride laughed hysterically. Why? None of the disasters mattered because she got the groom. Revelation promises that we too will get the Groom. When we do, when we see Him face to face, life's disasters will dim in the light of His glory. I wonder what the Lamb's wife looked like to John.

> And he carried me away in the Spirit to a great and high mountain, and showed me the great city, the holy Jerusalem, descending out of heaven from God, having the glory of God. Her light was like a most precious stone, like a jasper stone, clear as crystal. Also she had a great and high wall with twelve gates, and twelve angels at the gates, and names written on them, which are the names of the twelve tribes of the children of Israel: three gates on the east, three gates on the north, three gates on the south, and three gates on the west. Now the wall of the city had twelve foundations, and on them were the names of the twelve apostles of the Lamb. 21:10-14

THE NEW JERUSALEM

Hebrews 11:10 says of Abraham, "he waited for the city which has foundations, whose builder and maker is God." Hebrews 11 is often referred to as the Hall of Faith. We are told of the patience and suffering of the Old Testaments saints. Each of their lives was different, they each suffered differently, but they all had something in common.

> "These all died in faith, not having received the promises, but having seen them afar off were assured of them, embraced them and confessed that they were strangers and pilgrims on the earth. For those who say such things declare plainly that they seek a homeland. But now they desire a better, that is, a heavenly country. Therefore God is not ashamed to be called their God, for He has prepared a city for them" (Hebrews 11:13, 14, 16).

In paraphrasing, these saints would say to us, "Be patient in the suffering! It's worth it!" Jesus Himself used the fact of heaven as an incentive for patience and endurance. When Jesus told His disciples that He was leaving them, they were very sorrowful. They didn't know how they could make it without Him. He told them not to sorrow because He would send them the Holy Spirit. And they were to be comforted by this promise: "In My Father's house are many mansions; if it were not so, I would have told you … that where I am, there you may be also" (John 14:2-3). As far as we know, Jesus told them nothing more at that time about the place He would prepare. Now Jesus pulls back the veil and shows John this place He prepared, a city that had twelve foundations with the names of the twelve apostles of the Lamb. Maybe John saw his own name.

> And he who talked with me had a gold reed to measure the city, its gates, and its wall. The city is laid out as a square; its length is as great as its breadth. And he measured the city with the reed: twelve thousand furlongs. Its length, breadth, and height are equal. Then he measured its wall: one hundred and forty-four cubits, according to the measure of a man, that is, of an angel. 21:15-17

S. May
6/16/1

The beautiful construction of the New Jerusalem is going to surpass anything and everything we've ever seen or imagined. It will be like a cube, 1,400 miles high, wide, and deep, about the size of the moon.

> The construction of its wall was of jasper; and the city was pure gold, like clear glass. The foundations of the wall of the city were adorned with all kinds of precious stones: the first foundation was jasper, the second sapphire, the third chalcedony, the fourth emerald, the fifth sardonyx, the sixth sardius, the seventh chrysolite, the eighth beryl, the ninth topaz, the tenth chrysoprase, the eleventh jacinth, and the twelfth amethyst. The twelve gates were twelve pearls: each individual gate was of one pearl. And the street of the city was pure gold, like transparent glass. 21:18-21

Put yourself in John's sandals. Certainly it was nothing like he had imagined. I bet His jaw dropped as he saw the jewels and the golden streets and the light, all the light—yet no sun, no stars, no light bulbs. The Lamb was the light, his Jesus was on the throne making all things new!

We are told in Ecclesiastes 3:11, "He has made everything beautiful in its time. Also He has put eternity in their hearts…." This is just a taste of the beauty that is meant to keep us going, to encourage our patience and endurance, and to cause us to look for and excitedly wait for His coming. It is the anticipation of heaven that is meant to give our lives meaning, not life itself. Too often, our attitudes reveal a heart belief that if just a few things were different we could find utopia right here on earth. Jesus didn't promise a utopia in this world, He promised tribulation. But He did promise a utopia in heaven.

However, there are some interesting things to be discovered when we focus in again on what John tells us was NOT seen in the New Jerusalem.

> But I saw no temple in it, for the Lord God Almighty and the Lamb are its temple. 21:22

1. NO TEMPLE

Now that would perk up the attention of a Jew. Where do you go to worship God if there's no temple? When we go to Israel, I love to just watch the people at the Western Wall. I'm moved by the seriousness and sincerity of their prayers, yet saddened that people believe there is something holy about that wall. They believe God will answer their prayers because they prayed at that wall. But at the same time, it stirs gratitude and such joy knowing, as a believer, that I can pray anytime and anywhere. There's no need for a temple, because as this verse concludes, "the Lord God Almighty and the Lamb are its temple."

> The city had no need of the sun or of the moon to shine in it, for the glory of God illuminated it. The Lamb is its light. And the nations of those who are saved shall walk in its light, and the kings of the earth bring their glory and honor into it.

> Its gates shall not be shut at all by day (there shall be no night there). And they shall bring the glory and the honor of the nations into it. 21:23-26

2. NO SUN OR MOON

This was foretold in Isaiah 60: "The sun shall no longer be your light by day, nor for brightness shall the moon give light to you; but the LORD will be to you an everlasting light, and your God your glory. Your sun shall no longer go down, nor shall your moon withdraw itself; for the LORD will be your everlasting light, and the days of your mourning shall be ended" (Isaiah 60:19-20).

> But there shall by no means enter it anything that defiles, or causes an abomination or a lie, but only those who are written in the Lamb's Book of Life. 21:27

3. NO DEFILEMENT, ABOMINATION, OR A LIE

No more will Satan deceive us and there will be no one who walks in Satan's ways.

> "Now the serpent was more cunning than any beast of the field which the LORD God had made. And he said to the woman, 'Has God indeed said, "You shall not eat of every tree of the garden?"'" (Genesis 3:1)

There will be no more battle with our own flesh.

> "For the flesh lusts against the Spirit, and the Spirit against the flesh; and these are contrary to one another, so that you do not do the things that you wish." (Galatians 5:17)

Sin will not exist in heaven. Of all the things that are going to be different about our lives in heaven, that's one of the most exciting. No more sorrow and no more pain is definitely something to look forward to, but it's glorious beyond imagination that our selfish, sinful hearts are not going with us.

This knowledge should cause us to look forward with excited anticipation to being totally loving and totally unselfish with one hundred percent pure motives and actions all of the time.

CLOSING THOUGHTS

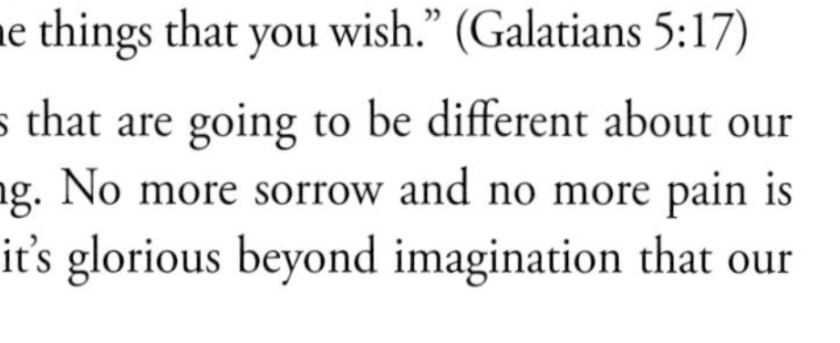

A few years ago, we had a memorial service at our church for a young man, twenty-nine years old, who died of a drug overdose. His girlfriend, a very new believer, shared a little of his life and then spoke of heaven. She concluded by saying, "In heaven, sin can't do to us what it does to us here, because there aren't any of those temptations in heaven." She said she couldn't wait to get to heaven. She was tired of the relentless pull of sin in her life. Yes, as she walks with the Lord she will learn to have victory, but the battle will always be there. Oh, for the day that the battle will be over and we can put down our armor and rest.

REFLECTION QUESTIONS

(For more extensive study questions visit CathyDickinson.com)

1. How does contemplating the truth of the Lord's words, "Behold, I make all things new" minister to you when you are struggling? Breathtaking

To be free of pain, poor choices and suffering. New is clean and fresh and gives us a feeling of hope and promise.

2. How does the promise of a new heaven and a new earth serve as an incentive for patience and endurance in tribulation?

What we go through and experience is not without a rest and beauty in the end of the struggle - There will be freedom.

3. Knowing certain things will NOT be in heaven is as encouraging as the wonderful things that will be there. What will not be in heaven?

No tears, death, mourning, crying or pain.

4. In verse 6 Jesus declares, "It is done!" Your eternal home has already been prepared for you, a place illuminated by the glory of God and the Lamb, a place where you will be new. What aspect of being new excites you the most? Why?

Not being tired. Life and bad choices are exhausting, Seeing the suffering associated with sin is deeply saddening.

5. Read the physical description of the New Jerusalem (Revelation 21:10-21). What features make an impression on you? Pure, colorful, majestic and good.

6. How has this study of Revelation chapter 21 enhanced your perception of heaven?

Neverending beauty and peace and rest. Life seems so exhausting right now.

7. Draw a scene as described by John in Revelation chapter 21.

Chapter Twenty-Four

BEHOLD, JESUS IS COMING QUICKLY: REVELATION 22

There is a lot of important stuff in Revelation. Jesus Christ has been revealed in His glory. God's judgment has been promised. We have been reminded that the One who began it all is the One who will bring it all to an end—at least as far as earthly life is concerned. But Jesus didn't stop there. He opened a window to heaven and gave us a glimpse. He told us He is coming again to bring us to His home and give us all that is good, and that it's all going to happen suddenly. God is a Giver and givers love watching people receive from them.

As we come to the last chapter in Revelation, God has told us what He wants us to know—all that we need to know—so that we who are His will be blessed and those who are not His will be sufficiently warned. For those who have chosen Jesus, Revelation is a wonderful book. It is a love story.

> And he showed me a pure river of water of life, clear as crystal, proceeding from the throne of God and of the Lamb. 22:1

THE CITY OF MY GOD

Revelation 22 begins as a continuation of chapter 21, with the angel giving John a tour of the New Jerusalem. We can only speculate what this will be like, but we gain some insight from Psalm 46.

> "There is a river whose streams shall make glad the city of God, the holy place of the tabernacle of the Most High." (Psalm 46:4)

We know it is pure, it gives life abundantly, it makes glad, and its source is God and the Lamb—therefore, it is absolutely perfect. Here on earth we accept, by faith, that God is the source of life. In heaven we will see this river proceed from His throne, flowing with living water that will never cease.

> In the middle of its street, and on either side of the river, was the tree of life, which bore twelve fruits, each tree yielding its fruit every month. The leaves of the tree were for the healing of the nations. 22:2

There was a tree of life in the midst of the garden of Eden. Adam and Eve were told they could eat freely of it but then they sinned. Consequently, they were banned from the tree of life and a flaming sword was set to keep all away from it, lest man live forever in his sinful condition. The tree was once in the midst of Paradise and now we read of it again, yielding fruit, and giving healing.

We learned earlier in Revelation that overcomers will eat of the tree of life. "He who has an ear, let him hear what the Spirit says to the churches. To him who overcomes I will give to eat from the tree of life, which is in the midst of the Paradise of God" (Revelation 2:7).

> And there shall be no more curse, 22:3

In paradise "there shall be no more curse." We will suffer no condemnation for what we have done. No curse will result because of what we have done, no punishment, no chastisement, and no correction. God promised that to us. That's why Jesus came—to save us from the power of sin and the curse of death.

> but the throne of God and of the Lamb shall be in it, and His servants shall serve Him. 22:3

Eternity will be far from boring or without purpose. The angel told John overcomers will be God's servants and serve Him. Will we be slaves? Hardly!

If we look ahead to the end of verse 5, along with serving comes reigning "forever and ever." We are heirs, not slaves. "He who overcomes shall inherit all things, and I will be his God and he shall be My son" (Revelation 21:7). Son! That's the same term of endearment the Father calls Jesus! All that is in heaven is ours.

> They shall see His face, and His name shall be on their foreheads. 22:4

David kept his perspective in difficult times by reminding himself of this truth: "As for me, I will see Your face in righteousness; I shall be satisfied when I awake in Your likeness" (Psalm 17:15). Not only will we see His face, but "His name shall be on their (our) foreheads." We saw this promise earlier in Revelation when Jesus addressed the church in Philadelphia.

> "He who overcomes, I will make him a pillar in the temple of My God, and he shall go out no more. I will write on him the name of My God and the name of the city of My God, the New Jerusalem, which comes down out of heaven from My God" (Revelation 3:12).

> There shall be no night there: They need no lamp nor light of the sun, for the Lord God gives them light. And they shall reign forever and ever. 22:5

This wraps up our tour of the New Jerusalem reiterating a concept we can scarcely understand. There will be no need for night, as there will be no need for rest. We will never become weary as we reign forever and ever and ever.

LIVING WITH A HOLY GOD

Of all the glorious things we have learned about heaven through John's tour, the most important is that God indwells heaven. We are going to see the face of God and live with

God. Consider Isaiah's account when he saw the Lord on His throne, high and lifted up in all of His glory.

> "I saw the Lord sitting on a throne, high and lifted up, and the train of His robe filled the temple. Above it stood seraphim; each one had six wings: with two he covered his face, with two he covered his feet, and with two he flew. And one cried to another and said: 'Holy, holy, holy is the Lord of hosts; the whole earth is full of His glory!' And the posts of the door were shaken by the voice of him who cried out, and the house was filled with smoke." And Isaiah's response was, "Woe is me, for I am undone!" (Isaiah 6:1-5)

Contemplate John's story. He had seen Jesus' earthly body. John even experienced a glimpse of Jesus' glory on the Mount of Transfiguration when "His face shone like the sun, and His clothes became as white as the light" (Matthew 17:2). In Revelation 1, when John saw Jesus in ALL of His glory, he "fell at His feet as dead" (v. 17). Holiness makes us so aware of how unholy we are, but in heaven we will be able to dwell in holiness, comfortably in the presence of Holiness. Amazing, just amazing.

> "Blessed be the God and Father of our Lord Jesus Christ, who according to His abundant mercy has begotten us again to a living hope through the resurrection of Jesus Christ from the dead, to an inheritance incorruptible and undefiled and that does not fade away, reserved in heaven for you." (1 Peter 1:3-4)

> Then he said to me, "These words are faithful and true." 22:6

As we move forward in this chapter, it can be challenging to discern who is speaking—the angel or Jesus—as John shifts from one to the other as he writes. That's the way it should be. The servant's message should be no different than his Master's. A servant's message should be his Master's message. One of the definitions of the word *angel* is "messenger." While the angel could never have the same description as Jesus, he can and should have the same message.

FAITHFUL AND TRUE

The angel uses the same words Jesus did in Revelation 21:5, "these words are true and faithful." God is so wonderful. He knew John. John, just like the rest of us, could have begun to doubt this whole vision, thinking maybe it was a dream or sunstroke, or maybe he shouldn't take it all literally. So the angel, like Jesus, reminded John "these words are faithful and true."

The words spoken to John are "faithful and true" because they are from the One who is faithful and true. Essentially God is saying to John, "I have presented this to you just how I want you to write it. Don't speculate and don't add your own interpretation, but only, "Write the things which you have seen, and the things which are, and the things which will take place after this" (Revelation 1:19).

And the Lord God of the holy prophets sent His angel to show His servants the things which must shortly take place. 22:6

MUST SHORTLY TAKE PLACE

Revelation began with these words: "The Revelation of Jesus Christ, which God gave Him to show His servants—things which must shortly take place. And He sent and signified it by His angel to His servant John" (Revelation 1:1). And now John starts to wrap up the revelation with essentially the same words here. The same God who spoke all of those incredibly, impossible prophecies to the Old Testament prophets and fulfilled them all, has spoken the prophecies contained in Revelation.

Notice the word *must*. How do we know these things "must shortly take place?" God said they would, therefore, they "must." What about that little qualifying word *shortly*? It's been over 2,000 years—that's not shortly by our definition of the word. A vital thing to remember is that whenever we don't understand something in the Bible, it's always due to our lack of insight, not God's lack of faithfulness to His Word. Most of the time, digging a little deeper will yield a better awareness on our part. Such is the case here when we dig into the meaning of the word translated as *shortly*.

Shortly does not mean "soon" as in "when," rather it has more the sense of it's all going to happen in a short period of time and once it starts happening, it's all going to happen quickly. You may have experienced something like that in your own life when you pray and pray and pray, saying, "How much longer, Lord?" or "When, Lord, when?" And all of a sudden He begins working and you can hardly keep up with Him. In fact, "all of a sudden" may be a good way to grasp what is being said here. Matthew described it this way:

"But as the days of Noah were, so also will the coming of the Son of Man be. For as in the days before the flood, they were eating and drinking, marrying and giving in marriage, until the day that Noah entered the ark" (Matthew 24:37-38). Once Noah entered the ark, the flood *shortly* took place.

"Behold, I am coming quickly! 22:7

Three of the four times Jesus says this in chapter 22. *Behold* means "Be sure to see!" "Don't miss this!" I am coming quickly. *Quickly* is almost the same Greek word as the one translated "shortly." The only difference is how they are used in a sentence. This word *quickly* is actually translated as *shortly* in other verses of the Bible.

Robert Mounce has an interesting way of putting it: "We are not rushing towards a distant brink of the consummation of all things; we are running parallel along the edge of that brink, and have been since the time of the apostles." [53]

SUDDENLY

It's like comparing life as we know it to running along a cliff. We don't know where the edge is that will cause believers to be taken up—and unbelievers to slip into the tribulation. Just like earthquakes happen *suddenly*, yet the rift that finally causes the earth to split had been developing for a very long time. Consider the warning to those Peter called scoffers who would say,

> "Where is the promise of His coming? For since the fathers fell asleep, all things continue as they were from the beginning of creation. For this they willfully forget: that by the word of God the heavens were of old, and the earth standing out of water and in the water, by which the world that then existed perished, being flooded with water. But the heavens and the earth which are now preserved by the same word, are reserved for fire until the day of judgment and perdition of ungodly men. But, beloved, do not forget this one thing, that with the Lord one day is as a thousand years, and a thousand years as one day. The Lord is not slack concerning His promise, as some count slackness, but is longsuffering toward us, not willing that any should perish but that all should come to repentance." (2 Peter 3:4-9)

Peter was reminding the scoffers that God's word is sure; therefore, Jesus is coming again. We would be wise to remember that the same God who created the heavens and the earth—the same God who promised the flood and sent the flood is the same God who is showing us the things recorded in Revelation. There are scoffers who don't think it's going to happen, just like in Noah's day. Sadly, there are believers who live as if it's not going to happen or at least as if it's not imminent. They run along as if the brink of the cliff is not alongside them, but way off in the distance. Jesus' message to John two thousand years ago is the same as His message to us. "Behold, I am coming quickly!" Since John's time, man has been standing on the brink and God has been chipping away at the cliff. We don't know when the cliff is going to fall away, but when it does, it's going to happen quickly.

AN ANCHOR OF OUR SOUL

> "This hope we have as an anchor of the soul, both sure and steadfast, and which enters the Presence behind the veil, where the forerunner has entered for us, even Jesus, having become High Priest forever according to the order of Melchizedek" (Hebrews 6:19-20).

The Holy Spirit is our guarantee of salvation. When you made Jesus your Savior, it's as if He tied a rope around you (the Holy Spirit). Jesus has gone before us, entering heaven and securing an anchor at the other end of your rope. You and I may flail around down here, but we are always anchored to heaven. When the time comes and the cliff falls away, whoosh! He will pull that rope up. This is going to happen shortly, or quickly. There will be no time to reevaluate your life or your choices. It will all be over as far as your life on this earth is concerned. It's all going to happen suddenly; we don't know when, but Jesus wants us to know this for a reason.

> Blessed is he who keeps the words of the prophecy of this book." 22:7

BLESSED BY OBEYING IT

This is the reason: blessing. Blessed is he who **keeps** it. Again, Revelation begins with the same sort of promise: "Blessed is he who reads and those who hear the words of this prophecy, and **keep** those things which are written in it; for the time is near" (Revelation 1:3).

This word translated as *keep* is the same word used when Jesus spoke of "obeying" or "keeping" His commandments. Outside of the instructions to the churches, there really aren't any commandments in the book of Revelation to keep. The blessing is found in living in the imminence of Jesus' return, living like it might be today, keeping these visions of the glory and majesty of Jesus Christ foremost in our minds and hearts.

Over the weekend, I had the privilege of soaking in this chapter of Revelation and I was flying high just basking in Jesus and heaven and me being changed. But with Monday came the phone calls, the need to go grocery shopping and wash clothes. All of this necessary stuff to do had the tendency to cause me to forget the glories I had been soaking in. Before I knew it, I found my mind leaving the heavenly places and coming down to earth—changing my perspective and my mood considerably.

We all want to live the blessed life. Jesus is revealing to us the way to have it. Keep the words of this prophecy and you will build on, rather than lose, what God has been teaching you through Revelation.

> Now I, John, saw and heard these things. And when I heard and saw, I fell down to worship before the feet of the angel who showed me these things. 22:8

Once again, understandably, we see John overwhelmed by the awe of seeing Jesus in His majesty, splendor, and power, but the angel corrected John.

> Then he said to me, "See that you do not do that. For I am your fellow servant, and of your brethren the prophets, and of those who keep the words of this book. Worship God." 22:9

That's the second correction for the same thing. The angel corrected John the same way in Revelation 19:10. This angel was presenting an incredible message to John, falling down in worship was likely a hard thing to resist, but we are to worship the Source—not anything or anyone else. The Lamb is Jesus and Jesus is God. He is to be worshiped and we will get to worship Him forever—get to—not have to.

As it was John's response to worship the angel after being overwhelmed with the wonders of God, so it will be ours as we see Jesus face to face and we will never, ever lose that wonder!

> And he said to me, "Do not seal the words of the prophecy of this book, for the time is at hand. 22:10

The angel gave John an instruction. Daniel was instructed to "shut up the words" he had received and to "seal the book" (Daniel 12:4). When Paul had a glimpse of paradise, he couldn't utter what he had seen (2 Corinthians 12:1-4). But the angel tells John, "Do not seal the words." The time had come for people to know these things.

> He who is unjust, let him be unjust still; he who is filthy, let him be filthy still; he who is righteous, let him be righteous still; he who is holy, let him be holy still." 22:11

IT'S ENOUGH

This is a bit confusing. Here is the gist of it: God's word affects people; therefore, the words of this prophecy should be enough. If these words don't change someone, nothing will and they will stay like they are.

Daniel confirms, "Many shall be purified, made white, and refined, but the wicked shall do wickedly; and none of the wicked shall understand, but the wise shall understand" (Daniel 12:10). This also punctuates the warning, "Behold, I am coming quickly!" Jesus is going to come suddenly. Whatever condition you are in when Jesus comes, is the condition you will remain in. Now is the time to receive the Lamb of God who came to take away your sins. One day it will be too late.

I am reminded of a story about a meeting in hell. Satan called his four leading demons together and commanded them to think up a new lie that would trap more souls. "I have it!" one demon said. "I'll go to earth and tell people there is no God."

"It will never work," said Satan. "People can look around them and see that there is a God."

"I'll go and tell them there is no heaven!" suggested a second demon, but Satan rejected that idea. "Everybody knows there is life after death and they all want to go to heaven."

"Let's tell them there is no hell!" said a third demon.

"No, conscience tells them their sins will be judged," said the devil. "We need a better lie than that."

Subtly, the fourth demon spoke. "I think I've solved your problem," he said. "I'll go to earth and tell everybody **there is no hurry**." To that they all agreed and left the meeting to begin their mission. [54]

So much of this book is about the judgment of those who are unjust, filthy, and refuse to be counted among those who will be blessed by the prophecies of this book. They are destined to everlastingly horrible stuff. Just in case you think the words *unjust* and *filthy* are words saved for murderers and really evil people, please remember, all of us are unjust. The only One who is just is God, but He declares the believer to be just. He justifies those who come to Jesus, but everyone needs to hurry and come!

> And behold, I am coming quickly, and My reward is with Me, to give to every one according to his work. 22:12

REWARDS

Jesus speaks the same message of encouragement He did in verse 7, but He adds something wonderful, "My reward is with Me."

When we think of people being rewarded, we tend to think of the missionaries in Africa or anyone in full-time service for Jesus. Yes, there will be rewards for that kind of thing. But lest you think yourself disqualified for rewards, be encouraged by these words: "Beloved, do not think it strange concerning the fiery trial which is to try you, as though some strange thing happened to you; but rejoice to the extent that you partake of Christ's sufferings, that when His glory is revealed, you may also be glad with exceeding joy" (1 Peter 4:12-13).

If you are in a rough marriage, Jesus sees. Or maybe you are struggling with the loneliness and pain of being single or a gamut of other situations this life directs at us. Jesus sees. And if you react as God would have you, one day He's going to say to you, "Well done!" Well done when you kept loving. Well done when you stayed when you wanted to run. You will be rewarded, and as Peter said, you will "be glad with exceeding joy." You will be so very glad you didn't do it your way. The promise of rewards is meant to keep us going when life is hard. Behold, He's coming quickly and it's all going to be worth it; it's going to be glorious.

THE MOTIVE

One of the definitions of *reward* is "pay for service." Jesus Himself amplifies on the words as He adds, "to give to everyone according to his work." Paul wrote of these rewards.

"For we must all appear before the judgment seat of Christ, that each one may receive the things done in the body, according to what he has done, whether good or bad. Knowing, therefore, the terror of the Lord, we persuade men; but we are well known to God, and I also trust are well known in your consciences." (2 Corinthians 5:10-11)

Writing to believers, Paul wrote that "we must all appear before the judgment seat of Christ," but not to receive punishment—since that is why Jesus died—so that we would not be punished or judged for our sins. This judgment is for the purpose of rewarding us for what we have done, to determine or reveal whether it was good or bad. The seemingly good things will be tested. Believers do a lot of good things, but you and I can't see the heart or the motivation behind those good things. Were they done for the praise of man, for attention, to get something, to look spiritual? We don't know, but God does. One day all of those things are going to be revealed for what they are. Paul also wrote,

> "For no other foundation can anyone lay than that which is laid, which is Jesus Christ. Now if anyone builds on this foundation with gold, silver, precious stones,

wood, hay, straw, each one's work will become clear; for the Day will declare it, because it will be revealed by fire; and the fire will test each one's work, of what sort it is. If anyone's work which he has built on it endures, he will receive a reward. If anyone's work is burned, he will suffer loss; but he himself will be saved, yet so as through fire." (1 Corinthians 3:11-15)

"The Day will declare" what sort of work we have done—some will be revealed as "gold, silver, precious stones, wood, hay, straw." The wood, hay, and straw will be burned away as meaningless. Jesus will not be impressed. Paul wrote that our works must be founded on Jesus. He must be the source and the reason for them. He must be why we do what we do.

I am the Alpha and the Omega, the Beginning and the End, the First and the Last." 22:13

JESUS IS THE FIRST AND THE LAST

In case the reader of this prophecy is wondering by whose authority all of this is promised, Jesus makes it crystal clear. This is the fourth time He used this name for Himself in this prophecy of Revelation, although it's not the first time we see this title in the Bible. The Father used it three times to describe Himself in Isaiah.

"Who has performed and done it, calling the generations from the beginning? 'I, the LORD, am the first; and with the last I am He.'" (Isaiah 41:4)

"Thus says the LORD, the King of Israel, and his Redeemer, the LORD of hosts: 'I am the First and I am the Last; besides Me there is no God.'" (Isaiah 44:6)

"Listen to Me, O Jacob, and Israel, My called: I am He, I am the First, I am also the Last." (Isaiah 48:12)

Jesus Christ is God. He claims the same titles and He claims the same right to be worshiped. He is the source of all things, the Creator. He began this earth and He is going to end it, in His timing, according to His plan, exactly as He said He would do it.

Blessed are those who do His commandments, that they may have the right to the tree of life, and may enter through the gates into the city. 22:14

The angel speaks now.

But outside are dogs and sorcerers and sexually immoral and murderers and idolaters, and whoever loves and practices a lie. 22:15

Paul said to the Corinthian church, "Do you not know that the unrighteous will not inherit the kingdom of God? Do not be deceived. Neither fornicators, nor idolaters, nor adulterers, nor homosexuals, nor sodomites, nor thieves, nor covetous, nor drunkards, nor revilers, nor extortioners will inherit the kingdom of God. And such were some of you. But you were washed, but you were sanctified, but you were justified in the name of the Lord Jesus and by the Spirit of our God" (1 Corinthians 6:9-11).

> "And I will come near you for judgment; I will be a swift witness against sorcerers, against adulterers, against perjurers, against those who exploit wage earners and widows and orphans, and against those who turn away an alien—because they do not fear Me," says the Lord of hosts. "For I am the Lord, I do not change." (Malachi 3:5-6)

> "I, Jesus, have sent My angel to testify to you these things in the churches. I am the Root and the Offspring of David, the Bright and Morning Star." 22:16

THE ROOT AND OFFSPRING OF DAVID

There are so many titles and characteristics that are true of Jesus—so we have to pay attention, when He chooses particular ones to describe Himself.

He is "the Root and Offspring of David." He is the source of David. He came before him, way before him—yet He is David's offspring. David came from Jesus and Jesus came from David. The prophets of the Old Testament prophesied that the Messiah would come from David's line. Jesus baffled the religious leaders with the question, "If David then calls Him 'Lord,' how is He his Son?" (Matthew 22:45). How could one be both the root (source) and offspring? This could only happen by the Source, the Creator, becoming man, by coming from man. Only Jesus qualifies.

John saw Jesus and heard the words in Revelation 5, "Behold, the Lion of the tribe of Judah, the Root of David, has prevailed to open the scroll and to loose its seven seals" (v. 5). Jesus had John write the same title here as the Revelation is coming to a close, as a reminder that He is the Root of David. He has prevailed.

THE BRIGHT AND MORNING STAR

Jesus also refers to Himself as "the Bright and Morning Star." He promised the morning star to overcomers in the church of Thyatira. What was He promising? He was promising Himself. Both the Old and New Testaments speak of this Star that is God. Baalam prophesied, "I see Him, but not now; I behold Him, but not near; a Star shall come out of Jacob; a Scepter shall rise out of Israel" (Numbers 24:17).

Peter said, "And so we have the prophetic word confirmed, which you do well to heed as a light that shines in a dark place, until the day dawns and the morning star rises in your hearts" (2 Peter 1:19).

The morning star is the brightest star, the first star of the day announcing the new dawn. Our Lord Jesus appears right before the dawning of the new Day—the new kingdom.

> And the Spirit and the bride say, "Come!" And let him who hears say, "Come!" And let him who thirsts come. 22:17

Do you want the inheritance of the overcomers? Then come. That's the invitation. Come! Let him who thirsts come.

ALL ARE INVITED

Two of my grandchildren celebrate their birthdays in February. At the close of Christmas day, they started planning their parties and who they wanted to invite. My grandson wanted a slumber party, so his mom told him he could limit his list to four. I was so blessed when he turned to me and said, "Grandma, do you want to come to my slumber party?"

I said, "Gabe, you really want me to come and hang out with you and your friends?" My question provoked some second thoughts in my grandson.

To that he said, "Well, we are going to play football."

I said, "Okay, I can do that."

"Tackle," he said.

I said, "Okay."

"Grandma, do you really think you can tackle me?" to which I responded, "Do you think you can tackle me?"

I think the thought of his grandma playing football with his friends made him reconsider his invitation, because after a little thought, he looked at me and said, "Well, maybe you should just come for the presents part."

God isn't like that. He doesn't reconsider and change His mind. We have been conditioned to think that there's got to be something about us that is of value for Him to want us to be at His party. He's not inviting you because of what you can give Him. We have nothing to give except our hearts. He's looking for thirsty people, not those who are satisfied with their lives and think they have no need for Him. Those are the people who can't get into heaven. But for overcomers, there are no limits. Revelation 21:7 reminds us that those who overcome "shall inherit **all** things."

> Whoever desires, let him take the water of life freely. 22:17

ARE YOU THIRSTY?

We need to hear it again—we need to hear it a lot. Jesus has an invitation to the thirsty. He extended it during His ministry here on earth—He extends it still. "On the last day, that great day of the feast, Jesus stood and cried out, saying, 'If anyone thirsts, let him come to Me and drink'" (John 7:37).

Jesus says, "Come to Me." Many of us have lived a lifetime of people saying to us, "Go away!" Jesus says to you, "Come!" What will He do if you come? Rebuke you, lecture you, condemn you, punish you? He told us what He will do. Jesus said, "I will give of the fountain of the water of life freely to him who thirsts" (Revelation 21:6).

Come and take the water of life freely. It's not an invitation to the good, beautiful, successful, or those who have done it right, but to whoever desires.

> For I testify to everyone who hears the words of the prophecy of this book: If anyone adds to these things, God will add to him the plagues that are written in this book; and if anyone takes away from the words of the book of this prophecy, God shall take away his part from the Book of Life, from the holy city, and from the things which are written in this book. 22:18-19

This is another warning. As I shared at the beginning of this book, don't mess with what God has written. There are severe consequences for those who do. God is not referring to those who tweak it or misinterpret (although I'm sure there are consequences for that too), but the consequences here are for those who have rejected Jesus. If you belong to Him, you won't deny His deity as revealed in Revelation. If you belong to Him, you won't deny the reality of either heaven or hell.

> He who testifies to these things says, "Surely I am coming quickly." 22:20

Clearly Jesus REALLY desires for us to live in this expectation as this is the third time in this chapter that He has said, "I am coming quickly."

> Amen. Even so, come, Lord Jesus! 22:20

Finally, the Revelation of Jesus Christ concludes with John's response and the response Jesus longs for from all who are His, "Amen (So be it!). Even so, come, Lord Jesus!"

JESUS IS COMING

He is coming as a thief comes—unexpectedly. This is a warning to unbelievers and believers. For believers, He is giving us inside information. He's giving us the heads up to bless us. The church is much more productive and much more joyful when it is doing what it is called to do—we have been called to live in this expectancy that Jesus is coming at any time.

We look at the early church and wonder, why isn't the church today like that? What happened? The doctrine that Jesus is coming, and that He is coming at any moment, was the predominant teaching of their time, therefore, they lived with an excited expectancy and a readiness. Consequently, the world and its difficulties didn't bog them down like it does us.

MARANATHA

In the early church, there was a common proclamation, "Maranatha! O Lord, come!"

Although it was an Aramaic word coined by the Jews, Paul wrote it to the Gentiles in Corinth. They often said, "Maranatha!" meaning, "Our Lord is coming!" because they lived with a Maranatha perspective. Today we often say, "Hallelujah!" or "Praise the Lord!"

A while ago, some of us were talking about how prevalent this word was during the Jesus Movement of the 70s. The downside was that some were so expectant that they stopped paying their bills, thinking, *"Why bother? Jesus is coming any minute."* Someone shared that her teenage son said something like, "Of course you want Jesus to come, Mom. That's fine for you. You already have your driver's license, you're married, and have children." It's as if he was saying, "Sure you want Jesus to come. You've got nothing left to live for!"

I am way on the other side of getting my driver's license. Dale and I have celebrated close to fifty years of marriage. We have children and grandchildren. We've done all the "fun stuff." As wonderful as all of that has been, Jesus is better.

In the first years of our marriage, Dale was stationed in Phoenix, Arizona, with the Air Force. Frequently, he would get a three-day pass and we would head home to California. As we drew nearer to home, I could sense the excitement in both of us. Phoenix was definitely our temporary assignment. We lived for going home. Who can mind the journey when the road leads home?

Once in heaven, no believer will feel like they missed out because Jesus came too soon. Do you believe that? Do you believe that God, who designed relationships, can give you something even better in heaven?

LIVE LIKE TODAY IS IMPORTANT

Given this truth—Jesus is coming back—how are we supposed to live? Like there's no tomorrow? No, rather we are to live like today is important. The Scriptures tell us how.

> "Therefore, since all these things will be dissolved, what manner of persons ought you to be in holy conduct and godliness, looking for and hastening the coming of the day of God, because of which the heavens will be dissolved, being on fire, and the elements will melt with fervent heat?" (2 Peter 3:11-12)

> "Behold what manner of love the Father has bestowed on us, that we should be called children of God! Therefore the world does not know us, because it did not know Him. Beloved, now we are children of God; and it has not yet been revealed what we shall be, but we know that when He is revealed, we shall be like Him, for we shall see Him as He is. And everyone who has this hope in Him purifies himself, just as He is pure." (1 John 3:1-3)

CLOSING THOUGHTS

Consider the words of Jesus' prayer the night He was betrayed. "Father, I desire that they also whom You gave Me may be with Me where I am, that they may behold My glory which You have given Me; for You loved Me before the foundation of the world" (John 17:24).

Do you see what Jesus said He desires? He desires that those the Father gave Him be with Him—forever! He is praying, asking the Father regarding you and me, "Father, can I keep her or him?" Bask in this one truth and then respond by giving Him praise.

Finally, the Old Testament ends with the words, "Lest I come and strike the earth with a curse" (Malachi 4:6). The New Testament ends with these words:

> "The grace of our Lord Jesus Christ be with you all. Amen. 22:21

So be it!

These promises will give you hope, because these words are faithful and true. Blessed is the one who keeps the words of this prophecy.

REFLECTION QUESTIONS

(For more extensive study questions visit CathyDickinson.com)

1. In addition to worship and enjoying the New Jerusalem, what else can we expect to be doing in paradise? (See vv. 3, 5.)

2. Revelation 22:4 says, "They shall see His face." How will reminding yourself of this promise help you to have a proper perspective?

3. John was told to, "Write, for these words are true and faithful." In what ways have you personally discovered His Word to be true and faithful?

4. Revelation promises that those who keep the words of this prophecy will be blessed. In practical terms, how is this done?

5. How do you plan to build on, rather than lose, what you have learned through studying Revelation?

Live as though each day is important. Pray and love others. Be obedient to God's word

6. Describe the meaning of Jesus' declaration, "I am coming quickly!"

We are to be ready since we don't know the timing. We need to be ready for the world to literally "fall away" like the edge of a cliff

7. "Amen. Even so, come, Lord Jesus!" What response does this exclamation produce in you—elated agreement or a deep down hope that He won't come just yet? Take your honest response before the Lord in prayer or praise.

Elated agreement but sorrow for those who are "not in a hurry" or for those who have rejected Jesus

8. What impact has studying Revelation had on your heart for the lost?

I want to reach them and sorrow for the obstinate scoffers.

9. After studying Revelation, how has it changed the way you face your daily life?

I need to pray more

10. Draw a scene as described by John in Revelation chapter 22.

Footnotes

OVERVIEW:

[1] H.A. Ironside, *Ironside, H. A. Lectures on the Book of Revelation* (Neptune, NJ: Loizeaux Brothers, 1960).

[2] Amy Carmichael, *God's Missionary* (CLC Publications, 1939).

CHAPTER 1:

[3] Toni Scott, *Seven Churches of Revelation*, typologiepaperco.etsy.com.

[4] Max Lucado, *The Great House of God* (Thomas Nelson, 2011) pp. 77-79.

[5] Jehovah's Witnesses, 2013 New World Translation of the Holy Scriptures, (https://www.jw.org/en/publications/bible/nwt/books/revelation/1/#fn7966023).

CHAPTER 2

[6] Twila Paris, "The Warrior Is a Child" (Benson Music Group, 1980).

[7] *Wordsearch Bible Study Software*, Spiros Zodhiates, The Complete Word Study Dictionary, Strong's Greek Word G 2556 (Lifeway, August 1, 1992).

[8] Keith and Kristyn Getty, "Don't Let Me Lose My Wonder" (Kingsway's ThankYou Music, 2005).

[9] Eugene Peterson, *The Message*. Copyright © 1993, 1994, 1995, 1996, 2000, 2001, 2002. Used by permission of NavPress Publishing Group.

[10] R.A. Torrey, *How to Obtain Fullness of Power in Christian Life and Service*, (Fleming H. Revell Company, 1897).

CHAPTER 3

[11] http://homemadegospel.org/?p=5679.

CHAPTER 4

[12] http://www.pergamon.secondpage.de/index_en.html.

[13] https://en.wikipedia.org/wiki/Pergamon_Altar.

[14] https://en.wikipedia.org/wiki/Rod_of_Asclepius, Catherin Munro derivative work.

[15] Warren Baker and Eugene Carpenter, *The Complete Word Study Dictionary Old Testament,* (AMG Publishers, 2003).

[16] *Wordsearch Bible Study Software*, Spiros Zodhiates, The Complete Word Study Dictionary, Strong's Greek Word H 2719, (Lifeway, August 1, 1992).

[17] https://en.wikipedia.org/wiki/Brazen_bull, by Pierre Woeiriot, Unknown, Public Domain.

[18] Beth Moore, *Jesus, the One and Only,* (B&H Publishing Group), p. 235.

CHAPTER 5

[19] GotQuestions.org/who-Baal.html.

CHAPTER 6

[20] http://www.sardisexpedition.org/en/essays/about-sardis.

[21] Ibid.

[22] http://biblehub.com/commentaries/poole/revelation/3.htm.

CHAPTER 7

[23] http://catholicbiblestudent.com/2012/11/philadelphia.html.

[24] Kenneth Wuest Commentaries, (Wm B. Eerdman Publishing Co. 1961).

CHAPTER 8

[25] https://www.gty.org/library/sermons-library/66-14/laodicea%E2%80%93the-lukewarm-church-part-1.

[26] *Wordsearch Bible Study Software*, Spiros Zodhiates, The Complete Word Study Dictionary, Strong's Greek Word G5593, (Lifeway, August 1, 1992).

[27] Ibid.

[28] Anonymous.

CHAPTER 9

[29] JRCF.com Message Library 1 Thessalonians 4:13-18 Words of Comfort http://media.jrcf7.com/jrcf/messages/20130403-1830-WN0402.mp3.

CHAPTER 10

[30] https://www.goodreads.com/author/quotes/802465.Eric_Liddel.

CHAPTER 11

[31] Chuck Smith, *The Word For Today Bible* (The Word For Today, 2012) p. 1637.

[32] The Spurgeon Series 1857 & 1858: *Unabridged Sermons In Modern Language*, By Charles H. Spurgeon KJV language here http://www.spurgeon.org/sermons/0125.php.

CHAPTER 12

[33] 10,000 Reasons, Songwriters: Jonas Myrin / Matt Redman 10,000 Reasons lyrics © Capitol Christian Music Group February 2012.

CHAPTER 13

[34] Max Lucado, *The Great House of God*, (Thomas Nelson, 2011), p. 80.

[35] Ibid, p. 82.

CHAPTER 14

[36] Author unknown http://www.beliefnet.com/quotes/evangelical/u/unknown/men-do-not-reject-the-bible-because-it-contradicts.aspx.

CHAPTER 16

[37] Randy Alcorn, *Heaven*, (Tyndale House, 2004), *http://www.goodreads.com/quotes/search?utf8=%E2%9C%93&q=for+unbelievers+is+is+the+closest&commit=Search.*

CHAPTER 17

[38] Jamieson-Faussett-Brown Bible Commentary, biblehub.com/commentaries/revelation/14-3.htm.

[39] John F. Walvord, *The Victory of the Lamb and His Followers*, https://bible.org/seriespage/14-victory-lamb-and-his-followers.

[40] Battle Hymn of the Republic https://en.wikipedia.org/wiki/The_Battle_Hymn_of_the_Republic.

CHAPTER 19

[41] https://www.theologyofwork.org/new-testament/revelation/a-tale-of-two-cities-revelation-17-22.

[42] *Wordsearch Bible Study Software,* Spiros Zodhiates, The Complete Word Study Dictionary, Strong's Greek Word G684, (Lifeway, August 1, 1992).

[43] http://peoplegetready.org/christian-apologetics/soul-body/.

[44] R.A. Torrey, *How to Obtain Fullness of Power in Christian Life and Service,* (New York, Chicago, Fleming H. Revell Company, 1897) pp. 43-44.

CHAPTER 20

[45] Thayers Greek Dictionary
http://www.bibletools.org/index.cfm/fuseaction/Lexicon.show/ID/G2478/ischuros.htm.

CHAPTER 21

[46] Ray Burton and Helen Reddy, "I Am Woman," Jay Center (1972).

[47] E. Harburg, E.Y. Harburg, and Harold Arlen, "Ding-Dong! The Witch Is Dead," Sony/ATV Music Publishing LLC (1939).

[48] http://www.biblestudytools.com/commentaries/revelation/related-topics/the-jewish-wedding-analogy.html#98515E.

[49] Ibid.

[50] *Wordsearch Bible Study Software*, Spiros Zodhiates, The Complete Word Study Dictionary, Strong's Greek Word G 1345 (Lifeway, August 1, 1992).

[51] Sherri Youngward, "Come Away," Danny Donnelly (2014).

CHAPTER 23

[52] Andrae Crouch, "Soon and Very Soon," Bud John Songs, INC/Crouch Music/ASCAP (1976).

CHAPTER 24

[53] Robert Mounce, quoted by David Guzik.

https://enduringword.com/bible-commentary/revelation-22/.

[54] Warren W. Weirsbe, The Weirsbe Bible Commentary: New Testament, (Colorado Springs, CO: David C. Cook Publishing, 2007), 401

Do you struggle with overwhelming emotions? Does it seem like you experience more defeat than victory in the battle against the giants you face? *Taming the Giants* will provide you with biblical tools and insights to help strip the power of the emotional giants you face, such as

Discouragement
Fear
Temptation
Guilt
Anger
Depression
Jealousy
Worry
Ingratitude

The enemy of our souls has no new tools to provoke our emotions than he did with Adam and Eve. They are still very effective tools and he will continue to use them until we get to heaven. Then and only then will the war be over. But today we can walk in victory experiencing the joy, peace, and freedom God has secured for us. This study is for both personal and small groups. It consists of nine weekly lessons, each concluding with a set of ten questions.

For product information, visit CathyDickinson.com

Notes

Notes

Notes

Notes

Notes